THE SECOND HALF

THE
SECOND
HALF

ROY
KEANE

with
RODDY DOYLE

Weidenfeld & Nicolson

LONDON

First published in Great Britain in 2014
by Weidenfeld & Nicolson

7 9 10 8 6

A CIP catalogue record for this book
is available from the British Library.

HB ISBN 978 0 297 60888 2
TPB ISBN 978 0 29760889 9

Typeset at The Spartan Press Ltd,
Lymington, Hants

Printed and bound in Great Britain by Clays Ltd,
St Ives plc

Weidenfeld & Nicolson

The Orion Publishing Group Ltd
Orion House
5 Upper Saint Martin's Lane
London, WC2H 9EA
An Hachette UK Company

The Orion Publishing Group's policy is to use papers that
are natural, renewable and recyclable products and made
from wood grown in sustainable forests. The logging and
manufacturing processes are expected to conform to the
environmental regulations of the country of origin.

www.orionbooks.co.uk

When you're physically in trouble, it plays on your mind. You don't get to a ball, and you tell yourself that you would have got it ten years ago, even though you mightn't have. There's a physical pain that you can put up with every day – but it's what it does to your head. I still look back and wonder if I could have played for another year or two.

'Did I make the right decision?'

My wife reminds me, 'Roy, do you not remember? You couldn't even get out of your car.'

I could, but it would be torture. And getting out of bed. But I'd forget, because I loved the game so much. The carrot was always in front of me. I wanted to play for another year, and earn for another year.

ONE

He told me how much he admired me. Like all the top lawyers, he was dead polite. I thought, 'He's nice, he'll go easy on me.'

The popular version of the story is that I injured myself – I tore my anterior cruciate – when I went in for a tackle on Alfie Håland. Håland told me to get up and stop faking. So the next time I saw him, I did him. And I ended his career.

But that wasn't what happened.

My book, *Keane*, came out in September 2002, just a few months after the World Cup and Saipan, and extracts from it were serialised in the *News of the World*. One of the extracts contained this passage from the book:

> Another crap performance. They're up for it. We're not. City could have been ahead when Teddy stroked the penalty home with twenty minutes to go. Howey equalized five minutes from the end. I'd waited almost 180 minutes for Alfie, three years if you looked at it another way. Now he had the ball on the far touchline. Alfie was taking the piss. I'd waited long enough. I fucking hit him hard. The ball was there (I think). Take that, you cunt. And don't ever stand over me

3

again sneering about fake injuries. And tell your pal Wetherall there's some for him as well. I didn't wait for Mr Elleray to show the card. I turned and walked to the dressing room.

That produced the headlines – it was great publicity. It was perfect in some ways, and I'm sure the publishers, Penguin, weren't too upset, or the booksellers. I understand that when you publish a book you're selling something; you're selling part of yourself. But I didn't anticipate the volume of the coverage. It was unbelievable; it was like I'd killed somebody. It was a nightmare at the time.

The book had been planned – the deadline and publication date – a year before. The idea was that it would finish after I'd played in the World Cup. It was supposed to be an upbeat book, on the back of qualification from a tough group and a good campaign in Japan. I think it was quite an upbeat book, but I didn't play in the World Cup, and I couldn't leave my house with my poor dog without being followed. That had gone on for a month or two, and it was just beginning to settle down. But now, the Håland tackle was the latest scandal. The media were all over it; they were running the show, demanding action. And, to be fair, I'd given them something to chew on.

The pressure was on the FA to do something about it, and they did. They charged me with bringing the game into disrepute, by committing a premeditated assault on Håland, and by profiting from my description of the tackle. The charges hurt me, particularly the second one – the idea that I'd almost bragged about deliberately injuring a player, in the hope of selling some extra books.

It was physically tiring. It was affecting my sleep, and my appetite. I was still preparing for games, but I was having problems with my hip. And it was emotionally tiring, too, coming so soon after Saipan. My family, the ones closest to me, suffered. I was a footballer, but I was meeting lawyers.

The hearing took place in Bolton, at the Reebok. It wasn't a court but it felt like a court. I think that was wrong. It was a footballing matter but it wasn't being treated like a footballing matter. It was an FA charge, but I was travelling from Manchester in a car with a lawyer and a QC. That didn't feel right. It was quiet in the car; I didn't really know them. There was no positive energy, no 'We'll fight this'; it was all about damage limitation. It was a day at the office for them but it was a lot more than that for me. I knew I was going to lose. But I also knew, when I went home that night, it would be over.

Trying to get into the Reebok that day – you'd have thought I was up for murder.

I wish now I'd made my own way to the Reebok – 'Listen, I'll meet you there.' Actually, I wish I hadn't had a lawyer. I wish I'd gone in and just taken the punishment. The FA charged, and the FA delivered the verdict. Judge and jury. The pressure was on from the media. 'They've got to do what's right for the game.' I'd been in situations before where I'd been cross-examined, and I'd felt that I'd been listened to. This time, almost immediately, I felt – 'Just give me the fine.' I never felt that I was getting my point across.

The FA had a murder lawyer. A big shot up from London. Jim Sturman. He was absolutely brilliant; he had me on toast. Jesus – for a tackle. He was a big Spurs fan, he told me. In the toilets, before the hearing. I was at the urinal beside him. We were talking, as two men in a toilet do.

He said, 'I think you are a top player.'

He told me how much he admired me. Like all the top lawyers, he was dead polite.

I thought, 'He's nice, he'll go easy on me.'

He ripped me to pieces – the fucker. It was his job, to rip me to pieces. I kept thinking, 'I wish he was on my side.'

I was cross-examined for about an hour. He took out the book; he kept showing it to me.

'This is you on the cover. This is your book, isn't it?'

I said, 'Yeah.'

'This is your book, isn't it?'

And I went, 'Yeah.'

'Do you stand by everything you said in the book?'

'Yeah.'

'So, whatever you said in this book—'

'Yeah, but it was ghost-written.'

'This is your book.'

He held it in front of me.

'It's supposed to be an honest book. You said these words.'

'I didn't mean it that way – I didn't say it that way. I'm not sure I said all those words. I had a ghost writer.'

They were genuine arguments but I knew I was going to lose the fight. But you still have to fight. It's like being in a boxing ring. You might be losing, but what are you going to do? You can't drop your hands. You have to keep fighting.

He was very good. I remember thinking, 'You fucker.'

His job was to present a picture of me as a thug, a head case, a man who goes out and injures his fellow professionals. And he did it – he succeeded.

The video helped.

'Can we see the tackle?'

They had the tackle, in slow motion – my Jesus. You look at anything in slow motion, and it looks worse. Even blowing your nose looks dreadful in slow motion. The tackle in slow motion, from every angle – it looked bleak. I felt like saying, 'Stop the fuckin' video. Give me the fine and let's move on.'

Jim Sturman had an easy day. I think he enjoyed it, as a Tottenham fan. The fucker.

I remember thinking, 'I'm fucked here.'

I sat down.

It was Eamon Dunphy's turn. Eamon was my ghost writer, and had come across from Ireland for the hearing, to be a witness. He'd already said that he'd used his own words to describe the tackle. Before we went in, I'd been going to say to him, 'Eamon, if they ask you if you think I intentionally went to injure Håland, say no.'

But I decided not to; I wouldn't embarrass him by saying something as simple as that.

Sturman asked him, 'Mister Dunphy, do you think Mister Keane intentionally went to injure his fellow professional, Mister Håland?'

And Eamon's three words back to Sturman were 'Without a doubt.'

That was the case, my defence, out the window. Eamon had written the book; he was my witness. I think Eamon felt that *he* was on trial, and that it was almost a criminal court. He wanted to distance himself from it, and I could see his point of view. He'd delivered the book; he'd done his job. I'd approved it. I was on my own; it was my book, my name on it. But I think he might have thought that his account in the book was on trial; he just wanted to get it over with and get out of there. He was rushing for his flight back to Dublin.

I looked at him and thought, 'I'm definitely fucked now.'

He didn't go, 'I think so', or 'Maybe', even 'Probably', or 'I can't honestly give an answer to that.'

'Without a doubt' was what he said.

As the ghost writer, he was supposed to have been, I suppose, wrote the book. I'm not blaming Eamon – at

ᶜ help.

ᴵ doubt.'

ᴵ tell from Jim Sturman's expression, he was thinking,
'N. ᴐne.'

It was action; it was football. It was dog eat dog. I've kicked lots of players, and I know the difference between hurting somebody and injuring somebody. I didn't go to injure Håland. When you play sport, you know how to injure somebody. That's why you see people on the pitch getting upset when they see a certain type of tackle; they know what the intention behind the tackle was. I don't think any player who played against me and who I've had battles with – Patrick Vieira, the Arsenal players, the Chelsea lads – I don't think any of them would say anything too bad about me. They'd say that I was nasty, and that I liked a battle, but I don't think any of them would say that I was underhanded. I could be wrong, of course. Maybe hundreds would say, 'You fuckin' were.' I kicked people in tackles, but I never had to stand on the pitch and watch someone I'd tackled going off on a stretcher. I'm not saying that's an achievement, but they always got up and continued playing.

There was no premeditation. My simple defence was, I'd played against Håland three or four times between the game against Leeds, in 1997, when I injured my cruciate, and the game when I tackled him, in 2001, when he was playing for Manchester City. I'd played against him earlier that season, and he'd had a go at Paul Scholes. If I'd been this madman out for revenge, why would I have waited years for the opportunity to injure him? I mightn't have got that chance. Players come and go. My whole argument was, I'd played against him.

I've watched old games, where Håland is trying it on, booting me. He was an absolute prick to play against. Niggling, sneaky. The incident took place in a match against City. But I'd played against him when he was at Leeds. The rivalry was massive between United and Leeds. Was I going around for years thinking, 'I'm going to get him, I'm going to get him'?

No.

Was he at the back of my mind?

Of course, he was. Like Rob Lee was, like David Batty was, like Alan Shearer was, like Dennis Wise was, like Patrick Vieira was. All these players were at the back of my mind. 'If I get a chance, I'm going to fuckin' hit you.' Of course I am. That's the game. I played in central midfield. I wasn't a little right-back or left-back, who can coast through his career without tackling anybody. Or a tricky winger who never gets injured. I played in the middle of the park.

There's a difference between kicking somebody and injuring somebody. Any experienced player will tell you that.

Håland finished the game and played four days later, for Norway. A couple of years later he tried to claim that he'd had to retire because of the tackle. He was going to sue me. It was a bad tackle but he was still able to play four days later.

'The ball was there (I think).'

I'm convinced that there were just two words that cost me. Those two words in brackets – 'I think' – left it open to interpretation that I went in on the man, and that I didn't care if the ball was there or not, and that I'd been lying awake for years, waiting for Alfie Håland. I *knew* the ball was there. But he got there before me.

The two words in brackets cost me about four hundred grand. It was a long day.

The decision – the verdict – was given that afternoon. There was talk of an appeal, but I think my solicitor, Michael Kennedy, used the word 'closure' – 'We need closure on this, Roy'. It was a good way of describing it; I just wanted closure. I'd pay the fine, and the legal costs. They fined me £150,000, and my legal costs were over fifty. Throw the original fine in on top of that. I'd been fined two weeks' wages by United when I'd made the tackle. I'd been given a four-match ban. Now the FA imposed another ban, five games. Double jeopardy. I had to sell a lot of books. But I was glad it was over. I think it was draining me, and my family.

I should have gone to the hearing without any lawyer, and taken my punishment. They were always going to find me guilty. There was a media scrum outside the front door. I was never going to walk out and go, 'I got off.'

Do I regret what was in the book? Probably not, because I'd approved it before it was published. Did I focus on every word? Obviously not, because I don't think I would have put in '(I think)'. Did I try to injure Håland? Definitely not. But I did want to nail him and let him know what was happening. I wanted to hurt him and stand over him and go, 'Take that, you cunt.' I don't regret that. But I had no wish to injure him.

Yes, I was after him. I was after a lot of players, and players were after me. It's the game. We have the great goals, the saves, the battles. But then there are parts of the game we don't like – diving, cheating, the bad tackles. They're part of the game. People want to avoid them, to pretend they're not there. But there are players playing today who are after other players. Seamus McDonagh, the goalkeeping coach, has a great saying, advice that he gives to goalkeepers: 'When you're coming for crosses, come with violence.' Nobody says it publicly. It's not tiddlywinks we're playing.

Håland pissed me off, shooting his mouth off. He'd tried to do me a couple of times when he was at Leeds. He'd come in behind me, quite happy to leave his mark on the back of my legs. There are things I regret in my life and he's not one of them. He represents the parts of the game I don't like.

Looking back at it now, I'm disappointed in the other Manchester City players. They didn't jump in to defend their teammate. I know that if someone had done it to a United player, I'd have been right in there. They probably thought that he was a prick, too.

Everyone was telling me to move on, and I think I did move on. It had been a difficult few months. I was all about playing football. And this case had no redeeming features. Michael said, 'We need closure', and that worked for me. I believe that if you do something wrong you should take your medicine. I never felt that I was the innocent victim. I should never have spent my money on lawyers. I should have just said, 'That was what happened. I didn't mean it that way – but, obviously, it's in the book.'

I thought it was about survival, making the damage as small as possible. I wondered why I was there – a bit. I wondered why I had a lawyer. This wasn't about winning or losing, or right and wrong, innocence or guilt. It was about damage limitation. I might have come out happier if the fine had been less. But the size of the fine didn't surprise me. The pressure was there, to punish me. The legal and logical arguments were never going to work: I had a ghost writer who put his own style across; they were Eamon's words; I'd already been punished; my right to free speech.

When free speech was mentioned, Sturman just laughed.

'Does that mean I can go down the street and abuse someone? Freedom of speech!'

He said that before we were even up and running.

'If your case is based on freedom of speech, don't give me that nonsense.'

I said to myself, 'It's all we've got.'

He was brilliant. But he had a good case. And he had the video evidence. It was probably the easiest few quid he ever earned. He didn't have to break a sweat.

TWO

Footballers are intelligent. There were no rumblings in the dressing room; there was no 'The empire's crumbling.'

We'd come straight from the west coast of America – I think it was Seattle – and a few of us were left out of the team. I liked playing in every game but when the manager left me out of this one I was quite relieved because I was knackered; we all were – jet-lagged. I remembered sitting beside Ryan Giggs in the dugout, and the two of us were laughing at some of the other lads out on the pitch.

We were playing Sporting Lisbon pre-season, to celebrate the opening of their new stadium, and I saw how good Ronaldo was that day. He was playing for Sporting and he was up against John O'Shea. Sheasy ended up seeing the club doctor at half-time because he was having dizzy spells; he was being twisted inside-out.

The club had been watching Ronaldo, and I think they concluded negotiations after the game. We always joked with Sheasy that he'd sealed the deal by playing like a fuckin' clown against him. In fairness to Sheasy, he was jet-lagged, like the rest of us.

Ronaldo arrived for the start of the 2003–4 season, and I liked the lad straightaway. He had a nice presence about him, and a good attitude. What impressed me most was that he'd been given the option of staying in Lisbon for another year, on loan, but he said no; he'd come over to Manchester straightaway. I thought it was a good, brave decision – because he was only seventeen. After the first few days, watching him train, my reaction was, 'This lad is going to be one of the world's greatest players.' I didn't say it publicly, because I'd always be wary of building a player up too early – or knocking him down.

He looked like a player. You have to look the part, and he did. Zidane looked like a player – and Ronaldo looked like a player. The shape, the body language – they were there. A bit of arrogance, too. But he'd a nice way about him; he was very likeable. We forget that he was very heavily criticised when he first came on the scene. He was going down too quickly when tackled, his final product wasn't good enough. But – again – he was only seventeen, a kid. I was playing youth football for Rockmount, in Cork, at that age. He was amazing. He was immediately one of the hardest working players at United. Most of the players I knew worked hard, but Ronaldo had the talent on top of the work rate.

He was good-looking and he knew it. He was vain in that sense – at the mirror. He was a big lad, a big unit. I'd think, 'Good on yeh.' Looking at some of the other lads in front of the mirror, I'd think, 'Yeh fuckin' nugget.' But Ronaldo had an innocence to him, and a niceness. I don't think he ever slackened off, or that he was ever more worried about the mirror than his game. I always felt that football was his love. He's still criticised for going down too easily when tackled, and he was hammered for winking after Wayne Rooney was sent off in England's game against Portugal in the 2006 World Cup. But that's the game, and he plays it. It's embedded in the foreign players, in their style of play – winning a free-kick, getting an opponent sent off. It's natural to them. If they get tackled near the box, they're going to go down.

Everyone loves the Gazza stories, the tragedies, but it's great to see a player fulfil his potential. Ronaldo had a lot of critics but I think people just got tired of chipping away, and conceded that he was due a bit of credit. You could see it as unfortunate that he's been around at the same time as Messi, but Messi gave him a target – 'I want to be better than him.'

Younger players bring a different energy, a lack of fear; they'll try things. I was thirty-two at the start of the '03–'04 season, but it wasn't like I was thirty-eight. I didn't feel that I was being pushed aside. But, all the same, I knew that the club was like a machine – the Ronaldos would come in, and the Rooneys. When I was a young player myself, I'd seen Bryan Robson and Steve Bruce leaving. So when you reach the age I was now, you're always looking at the exit door. I wasn't fearful, or threatened. There was that understanding: this is the game. You reach thirty-two and you're coming to the edge of the cliff. A sports psychologist who once came to United said that the descent could be gradual, or 'Bump!' – you're over the cliff. You just hope it will be gradual.

I went downhill at United, in a nice way. I was still playing. I was doing okay; I wasn't embarrassing myself. But I wasn't dominating games like I used to. The great thing about top players coming to your football club is, you want to impress them. It's their job to impress you, but you want to impress them. That's why there's a lift when a top player arrives. 'Fuckin' hell, I don't want him to think I'm crap. I don't want him thinking, "He's on his way out".'

The dynamics of the club were changing. Huge figures had left. Peter Schmeichel went in 1999, and he was very hard to replace. We'd had Fabien Barthez, Mark Bosnich, Taibi, Roy

Carroll. Now we had Tim Howard. But it would be 2005, when Edwin van der Sar arrived, before Schmeichel was really replaced.

I had a bust-up with Peter when we were on a pre-season tour of Asia, in 1998, just after I came back from my cruciate injury. I think we were in Hong Kong. There was drink involved.

Myself and Nicky Butt had had a night out, and we bumped into Peter at the hotel reception desk. It was about two in the morning. We said a few words to one another – a bit of banter, a bit of stick. I went to Nicky's room for some room service, had a sandwich, got up to go – and Peter was waiting for me, outside the room.

There'd been a little bit of tension between us over the years, for football reasons. Peter would come out shouting at players, and I felt sometimes that he was playing up to the crowd – 'Look at me!' He was probably also doing it for his concentration levels, keeping himself on his toes. But I felt he did it too often, as if he was telling the crowd, 'Look at what I have to deal with.' I wouldn't say we disliked each other, but we weren't best buddies either.

He said, 'I've had enough of you. It's time we sorted this out.'

So I said, 'Okay.'

And we had a fight. It felt like ten minutes. There was a lot of noise – Peter's a big lad.

I woke up the next morning. I kind of vaguely remembered the fight. I was sharing with Denis Irwin, and we were a few minutes late for the bus going to the airport. We got a call from the physio: 'Where are you?' Denis was one of the best pros you could ever come across, so being late for the bus tarnished him; you'd have thought he'd been caught with drugs or something. He was having a go at me.

I remember saying to him, 'I think I was fighting last night.'

My hand was really sore and one of my fingers was bent backwards.

The manager had a go at us as we were getting on the bus, and people were going on about a fight in the hotel the night before. It started coming back to me – the fight between myself and Peter.

Throughout the flight, Peter wore his sunglasses. He never took them off, and it wasn't very sunny.

We landed – I don't remember where. When the team arrived at a new destination for a game, two of the players had to go and do a press conference. And this time, it just happened to be myself and Peter.

In the meantime, Nicky Butt had been filling me in on what had happened the night before. Butty had refereed the fight. He even got a new nickname for it – Mills Lane, after the famous boxing referee. Anyway, Peter had grabbed me, I'd head-butted him – we'd been fighting for ages.

At the press conference, Peter took his sunglasses off. He had a black eye. The questions came at him.

'Oh, Peter, what happened to your eye?'

He said, 'I just got an elbow last night, at training.'

And that was the end of it. The tour finished eight or nine days later and nobody said anything – none of the staff, nobody. My hand had recovered, and Peter's black eye had faded. But the first day back at the training ground, the manager pulled myself and Peter into his office.

He said, 'The two of you were fighting.'

He knew exactly where we'd fought – I think he mentioned the twenty-seventh floor. He told us that we were a disgrace to the club, and that we'd woken Bobby Charlton up, that Bobby had come out of his room and seen us.

'Do you have anything to say?'

Peter put his hand up.

'Gaffer, I want to apologise. It was all my fault. I was waiting for Roy in the corridor. I take responsibility.'

The manager went, 'Oh, you're a fuckin' joke', and kicked us out of his office.

Peter took responsibility for the fight, which was good. I admired him for it. But Sir Bobby could have tried to break it up.

Looking back at colossal career milestones, I remember many events very clearly, but quite often I don't know what years we won the League. But I do know we'd nicked it from Arsenal the previous season, 2002–3.

We were playing away to Tottenham on a Sunday in late April, and then at home to Charlton the following week. We were travelling on the day before the game, by bus to Stockport station, then train down to London. Arsenal were playing that afternoon at Bolton, and we needed them to slip up. I drove to the Four Seasons Hotel, in Manchester, where we were leaving the cars before getting on the bus.

That bus journey from the Four Seasons to the railway station in Stockport became one of the highlights of my career. Arsenal had been two up when we got on the bus, so they were now ahead of us in the table. Then the news came through that Bolton had pulled it back to 2–1. Djorkaeff had scored for them. And just as we arrived at the station, Bolton made it 2–2.

We still had games to play and win, but we knew on the bus – and it wasn't cockiness; we were hopping around like a load of kids, hugging one another – we knew the title was ours that day. If you'd passed us at Stockport railway station, you would have seen a load of men on a bus, jumping up and down. We were back in it and we knew we wouldn't let go.

Finishing on top was never easy. It's been said about the Liverpool team of the eighties that they had a drawer full of medals and their coach, Ronnie Moran, would say, 'Take one if you think you deserve it.' It always looked easy for Liverpool, although I'm sure it wasn't. But I watched them when I was a kid, winning all the time. When I became a player I learnt, quickly, that winning League titles is not easy. We had to fight for our success. But we were hungry. I don't think we were ever blasé about previous successes. I never thought we could live off the past and switch off for a year or two.

The top sports people aren't content with a single victory or triumph. I was surrounded by players who were like that. We were all pushing one another along. The message came from the manager and the fans: 'Don't relax just because you've won a few now.' You win something and you say, 'It's gone', and then you move on. I can be critical of myself for not enjoying the experience of winning, but – it was part of my DNA – I just wanted to go on and win more.

Arsenal were good. Arsène Wenger was reinventing the game, apparently. Sugar lumps at half-time. They were a very good counter-attacking team. The previous Arsenal teams, under George Graham and Bruce Rioch, had been a rigid 4–4–2. They would always have held their positions; you could almost predict where each player would be. Now, under Wenger, they had more pace, they had more movement; they were moving positions, interacting. They had people like Overmars, Bergkamp, Henry. They were changing not just the face of Arsenal but the face of the Premiership, too. Pace, players moving into different positions, away from the 4–4–2; brilliant on the counter-attack, and much harder to play against. They could hurt you much quicker now. I think Arsenal took counter-attacking to a new level. Not just away from home – at home, too. And they were a team of big characters, big personalities. Vieira, Keown, Campbell, Adams,

Henry. They might just have had an edge over us. But it was good for us. We had to up our game.

Myself and Vieira were at the forefront of the rivalry between the two teams. Neither of us went out of our way to become – almost – the symbols of that time. Your position in your team will, in a sense, mould you into the kind of character you become, and what part you're going to play in the club. I've worked with Lee Dixon, who was with Arsenal, and Denis Irwin, at United. You just knew they were full-backs – brilliant full-backs. But you don't see full-backs leading many teams. I think the fact that myself and Patrick were playing in the middle of the park made us the centre of things. The timing couldn't have been better. Our teams were in their prime, both of us liked to tackle, our games were very physical and – at the time – he irritated me and I'm guessing I irritated him a little bit. Maybe he loved me – I don't know. But I didn't like him. But I also knew he was doing the best for his team, like I was doing for mine. 'I don't like you, but I look forward to playing against you.' And there was always the thought: I wouldn't have minded if he'd been in my team.

The tension, the build-up to the games, made great TV.

As Arsenal were getting stronger, we were having a dip. Although it didn't show at the start of the season.

We won four of our first five games. This isn't arrogance, but that was the form we would have expected. Although we were beaten by Southampton. Tim Howard made some great saves – but that was what he was there for; he'd brought his gloves. Kevin Beattie scored their goal, a header from a Graeme Le Saux corner.

We drew 0–0 with Arsenal. Ruud Van Nistelrooy missed a penalty; he hit the crossbar. Vieira had been sent off, and there was a bit of argy-bargy afterwards, because the Arsenal players were blaming Ruud for getting Patrick sent off; they said he'd overreacted. I was holding Ruud back that day. Giggsy and Ronaldo were charged with bringing the game into disrepute, along with a couple of the Arsenal lads.

We always ended up having a laugh about the charges – the fines.

'I hope they fuckin' hit you with a big fine.'

Giggsy was fined, and we knew Giggsy liked his few bob. When I'd come back from the Håland hearing, there'd been no sympathy in the dressing room.

'Oh, you fucker – that's a heavy one. How are you going to deal with that?'

We'd slipped up against Arsenal. A 0–0 draw should have been a reasonable result, but not when you miss a penalty. Beating them would have given us that bit of momentum. I would never have expected Ruud to miss a penalty. Because Ruud Van Nistelrooy was brilliant.

There was a Champions League game last season, United played Bayern Munich, and Danny Welbeck went through, one on one with the keeper. He missed it. Ruud Van Nistelrooy wouldn't have. Ruud was the best finisher, ever, but especially in one-on-one situations, just the keeper to beat. When Ruud was going through, one on one, I never doubted him. Some players would be going, 'Fuckin' hell – hard and low? Or dink it over?', but when Ruud was through there might as well have been no goalkeeper.

Ruud had his own traits; he could be moody at times – unlike me. But he was a good guy. He missed a Cup semi-final because of an injury – I think it was the one against Arsenal, at Villa Park, in 2004. He came down the morning of the game and said, 'I can't play, my knee's sore.'

And I went, 'What's up with you?'

I had a sore hamstring myself.

He said, 'Oh, I've been feeling my knee during the night.'

21

And I was, like, 'It's the Cup semi-final, for fuck's sake.'

He said, 'Well, I've only got one body, I need to look after it.'

I was thinking he was the fool, but I think now that I probably was. I played, and my hamstring was fuckin' killing me. I think I actually had a torn hamstring. Ruud ended up playing in Spain till he was thirty-nine, and he still looks twenty-one. And I thought he was the idiot.

I got on well with Ruud. I got on well with all the foreign lads; I used to enjoy picking their brains. I wished I was a bit like some of them – a bit laid back, like Dwight Yorke, or clever like the Dutch lads when it came to looking after themselves. I wasn't jealous; I was intrigued, curious about them. Not playing when you're injured – that was pretty sensible. But I was conditioned to think that not playing if you weren't 100 per cent fit was a sign of weakness, and that you should be strong and play when you were injured. But the clever lads won't be limping around when they're forty-five, and they won't be having hip replacements. My tradition was different – 'Don't show you're hurt, just get on with it.' Don't be weak, play when you're injured. Brian Clough detested players who were injured. He'd have banned a lad on crutches from the ground. What we see as heroic, I think now is probably weakness.

'Can you go for us?'

I'd take a painkiller, and play. No one put a gun to my head, but I wish I'd had the strength of character of the foreign lads. Even in their attitude towards moving clubs. Nemanja Vidić announced that he'd be leaving United at the end of last season. He didn't torture himself with, 'Oh, what'll they think of me?' He just said he'd be going and he had a good season for United. The foreign lads are not shy about making a good living. 'I've had my two years here; I've had enough.' They end up having great experiences, in different countries.

★

I scored in our 4–1 win over Leicester.

I didn't score as many goals as I used to. My role in the team was changing. I was now more the sitting midfielder. I think the manager and Carlos Queiroz, his assistant, might have had their doubts about whether I had the discipline to do the job, because my game had been all about getting forward. But I was comfortable in the position, saving my body, using my experience. It fell into place; it suited me. I still liked the odd opportunity to get into the box. I would never have been the classic sitting midfielder like Claude Makelele; he wouldn't budge. Playing against Leicester, I didn't have to babysit the two centre-halves. I could still go forward, at the right time. If I saw a space or a gap, I'd take it. This time, the opportunity was there – a run behind the defenders; the keeper, Ian Walker, came out, I went around him, tapped it in.

At the start of the new year, 2004, we were at the top of the table. But we were used to that. We'd won fifteen, lost three – against Chelsea, Southampton and Fulham – and drawn one.

Some of the new players were taking time to settle in. Kléberson came in, but he had no luck. He picked up a bad injury. His girlfriend came to England with him. She was very young, and heavily pregnant. He found it hard to settle and get going – to get some good performances under his belt, a couple of good games, get his confidence going. Eric Djemba-Djemba – a really nice lad – struggled. He couldn't get a good run of games. David Bellion came in from Sunderland. He was another nice lad, but I think the club might have been a bit too much for him. When I was a young kid at United, Nicky Butt and Paul Scholes were coming through. Now, the likes of Beckham and Jaap Stam were leaving and I'd look at some of the new lads and think, 'No, they're not the answer.' It was just a step too far for some of them.

But we always had a good dressing room – and that's vitally

important. I remember when Diego Forlán came in, and it wasn't quite happening for him. If a player tried – and Diego did – we'd drag him with us; we'd try and help him. Plenty of praise in training, or during games; not getting on his back. Diego was honest, so in training you'd go, 'Unlucky; it'll come good tomorrow', not 'You can do fuckin' better than that.'

I wonder about the current United dressing room. When a manager like Alex Ferguson is replaced, the new man needs a helping hand along the way. Does that mean that every player should like the new manager or his coaching staff, or love his new sessions, and everything about him? No. I look at the current players, and they should have been doing a lot better. It might be argued that it was up to the manager to motivate them. But not liking a manager, for whatever reason, can never be an excuse for not going out and doing your best. Looking at what happened to David Moyes, I have to conclude that he can't have had a strong dressing room; he had a weak dressing room. If some of the players weren't 100 per cent behind the manager, then they all slackened off. You can have personality clashes, dips in form; you can have injury crises, or the club can be going through a transitional period – but you still go out and do your best. I don't think all of the United players went out and did that. They can't have – because they ended the season so far adrift of the top. I watched them play, and I always thought, 'You *can* do better.'

When Diego left, he had a chance to say goodbye to us. Often, players are just gone – another club, sometimes another country – but Diego did say goodbye.

'I'm off, Roy.'

He shook my hand.

'Where are you off to?'

'Villarreal.'

Villarreal were just starting to make noises in Spain.

I said, 'Where's Villarreal?'

And he went, 'It's twenty minutes from the beach.'

We laughed.

I went, 'You got your dream move, Diego.'

Diego went on to have a brilliant career, and I wasn't a bit surprised. But it just didn't work for him at United.

I rang him when I was managing Sunderland, after we got promoted. He was in Spain.

I said, 'Diego, would you fancy coming to Sunderland?'

He said, 'Yeah, yeah, yeah. But I've got a get-out clause in my contract.'

I went, 'Go on – tell me what it is.'

He said, 'Thirty-eight million euros', or something.

So, I said, 'I'll call you back', but I never did.

I don't remember there ever being a real bad lad – poor attitude, poor time-keeping – in the United dressing room. You might ask does being late make you a bad lad? Yes, it does, in a dressing room full of hungry players who want to keep winning trophies. If training starts at half past ten and a player is coming in at twenty past ten, I would class that as being late. Officially on time – but you're late. If you can't get in by ten o'clock, have a bit of banter, get your strappings done, your massages done, you're late. Preparation is half the training.

I'd expected more of Verón. When he arrived in 2001, I was delighted. He played in my position but the competition was good for me, and the club. It would keep me on my toes. I never resented the arrival of new players, even if they played in the same position as I did. It didn't quite happen for him – but, technically, he was a very good player. Maybe English football – the

... – just didn't suit his style of
... ar head, sometimes.

...ds – and I think I understand this a
...en I was a young player – it was the
... the environment – things that I took

...ean, the weather?'

...e conversations with Ronaldo and Mikaël
Silves... ...hey'd speak to me about the weather.

I'd go, 'Lads, when you signed, you must've known it fuckin' rains a lot in Manchester.'

They'd go, 'We knew, but we didn't know it would be this bad.'

When we know that a player is getting fifty or sixty grand a week, we don't have the patience to wait for foreign players to get used to the environment they've moved to. If they're used to going for a cappuccino at half-ten at night, sitting on a balcony somewhere, and all of a sudden it's dark at half-four and it's fuckin' freezing, that is going to change them. I know this, because they told me. Fabien Barthez and Laurent Blanc used to smoke together in the toilets, at half-time. They were French – they smoked. If it had been a couple of Irish lads, I'd have been shouting at them: 'Yeh dirty bastards – get out!'

What was good, when I first went to United, was that there were people there to help me – the staff and, in particular, the players. Even a gesture from a player, to make you feel welcome. It might have been going for a pint – not that I needed much encouragement. I don't know if that happens with the foreign players now, but you can't underestimate its importance.

We'd lost Beckham. It was sad to see him leaving, but the writing had been on the wall. It had got to the stage where I think it suited both Becks and the manager to part ways. Some moves suit everybody, and this was one of them.

There was tension between him and the manager. There'd been the incident after the FA Cup fifth-round game the previous season, when Arsenal beat us 2–0 at home. Ferguson kicked a boot on the floor in front of him and hit Becks over the eye. So, Becks going to Real Madrid – when these deals happen, you don't fall off your chair. It happens. Players leave under different circumstances. I don't even remember if Becks said goodbye. The game is horrible like that. Jaap Stam left – he was just gone! The wives are gone, the kids are gone. They haven't gone to a club down the road; they've moved to another country. At the time, you think, 'That's the game.' It only seems strange afterwards. But that's the gig – it's life.

I suppose, as a player, there's a selfish side to the way you look at it. 'I've got to look after myself a bit when players are coming and going.' Becks had been a brilliant servant to the club, but he wasn't being shoved out the door. There are certain deals that suit everyone – the player, the club he's leaving, the club he's going to. It's the machine – players in, players out. I knew: it was Becks one minute, and it could be me the next.

I was in the dressing room when Ferguson kicked the boot. I thought it was quite funny – although not at the time. We were still upset because we'd been beaten by Arsenal, at Old Trafford. They'd knocked us out of the Cup, in front of our own fans. It was claimed later that the manager aimed his kick but that was utter nonsense. He kicked the boot – managers kick boots every day of the week. But the fact that it hit Becks was a pure accident. It could have hit anybody, or nobody. But Becks – of all people. It cut him above the eye. A manager can't be hitting players, or grabbing hold of them. But the fact that it was Becks made it almost comical. And the manager didn't mean to hit him. If you tried it a million times, you wouldn't be able to do it. It was an accident.

But I didn't like it. The media attention, the sensational reporting, didn't help the club.

I remember the club doctor, Mike Stone, coming into the dressing room after training and telling Rio to go up to the medical area for the test. The drug-testing people were waiting for him there. They could turn up at any time.

He forgot, and left. It slipped his mind, and he paid the price for it. He was banned for eight months. He wasn't given the benefit of the doubt, which was a bit harsh, I thought. Why couldn't they have gone to his house that afternoon? The whole system could have been a bit more flexible. But not doing the test seemed to be regarded as the same as failing the test.

He suffered for it, and so did the team. If it had been me, and the doctor had said I had to do a drugs test, I'd have gone and done it. It wasn't something I'd have forgotten. It wouldn't have been like collecting a letter at the office, or remembering your boots. When a doctor says you've to do a drugs test, it's not an everyday thing. But, then, some people are genuinely forgetful.

This was Manchester United, so it became the big story. But I wondered at the time why they didn't just follow Rio, go to his house that afternoon. But then, from the doctor's point of view, you treat people like mature adults. You tell a man to go up for a drugs test, and you expect him to do that. In any other workplace, it would have happened. We can give footballers the benefit of the doubt – 'Ah, they're footballers, they live in a bubble, they're a bit out there.' But we also have to go, 'Fuckin' hell', sometimes. Just do the drugs test.

I don't think I was annoyed at the time, and I don't think the other players were either. But, ultimately, the team suffered. I didn't look at Rio and think that he'd been up to no good, or that there was a hidden reason for what occurred. I think he genuinely forgot. We all paid the price. He was a very good player and we missed him, especially in the second half of the season when the crunch games were coming up.

I'd been tested myself a lot of times. It happened mostly after matches and, I think, twice at the training ground. It was a pain in the arse, although I never had a hostile or negative attitude towards it. I just thought people were doing their jobs. If you won, you'd want to be celebrating with your team-mates and, if you lost, you'd be fed up. After games, you're dehydrated. At the '94 World Cup, I was tested after the Holland match, in Orlando, Florida. I was there for about three hours; and this was immediately after we'd been knocked out of the World Cup. I would imagine that if we'd won the game I'd have pissed a bit quicker.

We only drew one game in the first half of the season, but we drew a lot more in the second half – with Newcastle, Leeds, Fulham, Arsenal and Chelsea. Draws in the Premiership aren't the end of the world but too many of them, for a team like Manchester United, can have a negative impact. There are good draws – away to Chelsea, away to Arsenal – and bad draws – at home to Newcastle and away to Fulham. But too many of either won't win you titles. We beat Bolton and Southampton, and our away win against Everton was brilliant. Louis Saha scored two for us, and so did Ruud; one of the goals was his hundredth for United. We were 3–0 up at half-time, then they came back to 3–3. Ruud's second goal, a header, came very near the end. But then we went and lost to Wolves and Middlesbrough.

Scholesy was scoring regularly for us. He was a top, top player. But I still don't fall for the boy-next-door image, or that he's dead humble; he has more of an edge to him. Everyone thinks he lives in a council flat. The Class of '92 – all good players, but their role at the club has become exaggerated. 'Class of '92' seems to have grown its own legs; it has become a brand. It's as if they were a team away from the team, and they're not shy of plugging into it. But we all had the same aims; we all had the hunger.

We knew we were going through a difficult spell – not for any big reason, like Rio's ban or Beckham's departure, or the manager suing the Irish shareholders about who owned the race horse, Rock of Gibraltar. But these things, in combination, weren't helping – more negative energy around the place.

The dip isn't exactly normal, but it happens to any club. It happened at Barcelona recently and, after Real Madrid beat them in the Champions League last season, suddenly people were questioning Bayern Munich – Guardiola had got it all wrong! It's very hard to stay at the top. Players leaving, players settling in, or not settling in. The difference, when it comes to Manchester United, is that it will get a lot of attention and it will be exaggerated. We had to learn to deal with that; it was part of the package of being a United player. There really is an extra burden in playing for Manchester United. There really is – that isn't arrogance.

We were beaten at home by Liverpool – always a tough game. We lost to City, away, 4–1. This wasn't the City of today. They didn't have the same money back then, or the players. I wasn't playing in that game; I never lost to Manchester City.

A few new players arrived during the January transfer window. Louis Saha was a good player, and he'd always played particularly well against United when he was at Fulham. So the manager would have seen him at his best. He was a nice lad, but he had a lot of niggling injuries. I think there might have been a question about his willingness to play through the pain barrier. He kept the medical staff busy; they were never going to be out of work.

I never minded losing matches, as long as we had a fuckin'

go. I also had the intelligence to understand that we were going through change. It was always going to be tough going. It wasn't Norwich who were pipping us. It was Arsenal – and Chelsea were on the verge, finishing second and third, even before the money and Mourinho arrived.

We weren't sitting back, going, 'What's happening to us?' We had to step up again. There was frustration; we shared that with the fans. But we knew we weren't a million miles away. We had Ronaldo. The next year, we'd get Rooney. They were outstanding. You'd look at them, and go, 'We're fine.'

Footballers are intelligent. There were no rumblings in the dressing room; there was no 'The empire's crumbling.' The players knew: we had new lads settling in, Ronaldo was only seventeen. 'Give it time, there'll be no problem.'

Arsenal, then Chelsea, were the top dogs now. But they were up there to be shot at – like us.

In the Champions League we'd coasted through the group stage. We played Rangers, and it was brilliant. It was the first time I'd played at Ibrox. I'd been there before as a fan – a Celtic fan. We trained on the pitch at Ibrox the night before the game. It's usually a low-key event; you do a light bit of work. But as we got off the bus for training, I got a nice little welcome – 'You Fenian bastard.' I'd have expected it on the night of the game, but not the night before. I don't think it was the doorman who said it, but someone in that general area.

We won, 1–0. Phil Neville scored. That's what was memorable about the game, not that I was called a Fenian bastard but that Phil scored. He didn't score many. We hammered Rangers at Old Trafford. Diego Forlán had a great game that night.

We topped our group with fifteen points, and drew Porto in the first knock-out round. I was sent off in the first game, at

Porto. We were 1–0 up; Quinton Fortune followed up after their keeper, Baía, had fumbled a Scholesy free-kick. Then we went 2–1 down. Benni McCarthy scored two great, almost freakish, goals that night, including an unbelievable header; I think he was at the edge of the box. To go from 1–0 up away from home – job done – to 2–1 down; I just got frustrated. We were losing – that was it. I stood on the goalkeeper, Baía. He came out and I carried on. I didn't stamp on him, but I stood on his back; I used his back as leverage. He rolled around like he'd been shot. All I can say is, we were losing 2–1, and it frustrated me. I can see now that, in the Champions League, away, it's a decent score. But I had this idea that we should have been winning every match.

I was embarrassed, and upset, later in the dressing room. The manager didn't really shout at me that night. He just went, 'Fuckin' hell, Roy.' I don't remember the manager or any of the players having a go at me after I'd been sent off. They didn't have to; I'd be beating myself up. I knew I'd let people down; I'd let my team down. Excuses were no good. But it was just as well that no one did say anything to me, because I'd have gone for them if they had. I'd have accepted an attack from the manager, but not the players. I knew I'd let them down.

I had to watch the second leg up in the stand, in the directors' box. It was torture. Scholesy had a legitimate goal disallowed; he was ruled offside – dodgy linesman, the whole lot. We would have been 2–0 up. In the last minute, Phil gave away a free-kick, Tim Howard made a mistake, Mourinho was skipping down the sideline – we were out. I hated being a spectator; it was horrible. The result might have been different if I'd been playing. Every player should think that. You have to feel you can make a difference.

Porto went on to win the Champions League that year, against Monaco. Monaco had knocked Chelsea out in the semi-final. But

Monaco were very average; Chelsea should have battered them. They blew it.

Those two games gave us our first sighting of Mourinho. I didn't think he was out of order running down the sideline. It was Porto; to knock Manchester United out was a big night for him. I think he knew it was a defining moment in his career. But I'm not sure that I'd have liked playing for him. He plays *too* many games with the media. I understand the need for games. But there comes a point when you think, 'Don't play mind games today.' And poking the Barcelona coach in the eye – I wouldn't have done that. If I was still a player today, I'd like to think that I could work with Pep Guardiola. I like his style, and his presence, and the way he conducts himself.

We had a tough run to the FA Cup final. Everyone likes a cushy home draw but the tough games never bothered me. There'd be an edge to them, and if we were beaten it couldn't be written off as a 'slip-up'. We had to get past four Premiership teams, Villa, Manchester City, Fulham, and then – in the semi-final – Arsenal. There was a great atmosphere at that semi-final at Villa Park because, really, that game *was* the FA Cup final. We went into the game thinking of it as the final, and I think Arsenal did the same. The Cup final was played at Villa Park that day. We beat them, 1–0.

There are certain games you go into, when you know that if you're at your best, you'll win. It's a great way to approach a Cup final; it's a great feeling to have. We could be at our best against Arsenal and Chelsea, and still lose. But, unless we did something silly, we were going to beat Millwall.

The preparation for the game was the worst I'd ever had. I wasn't feeling well. We'd gone down to Cardiff two nights before the final. Cup finals were being played in the Millennium Stadium there while Wembley was being redeveloped. Everyone enjoyed playing in the Millennium; it was a better stadium than the old Wembley.

We ate at a fish restaurant on Thursday night. I was a bit of a health freak, and I had some scallops. I'm not sure now why I'd have been eating scallops, because I wasn't a big lover of fish. 'Well, it looks healthy – and fishy – and I'm near the sea', so I had them. I'm blaming the scallops, but I don't think I was well anyway. I was afraid I'd miss the game, so I kept it to myself. I wouldn't have jeopardised the team, but I knew that if I was in any way fit, with my experience I could stroll through the game.

I didn't eat much on Friday, and I ate nothing on the day of the game. But I remember thinking, 'It's Millwall; if I'm 10 per cent right, I should be able to get through it.'

But I felt awful.

About ten minutes before kick-off, after the warm-up – still feeling weak – I threw my guts up in the dressing-room toilet. I felt great after that. I drank a load of energy drink – it would have been Lucozade or Red Bull – and got through the game quite easily. We dominated possession, so I didn't have to use too much energy.

One of Ferguson's great strengths was that he always had a feel for the group when it came to team talks; he knew what would be needed. He'd spoken to us all week, building Millwall up. That was common sense. But in the hotel on the morning of the final, he spoke about the United players – us – where we were from, the different nationalities; he made different points about each of us. I remember thinking, 'Brilliant.' It was just what we needed, a feeling of pride – we were all together. There was no real logic to it, but it felt right. I've given team talks myself since, and I've often thought, 'I don't know where that came from', but it felt right. And I thought, that morning in Cardiff, that there was that pride. We were all playing in the Cup final. 'I'm from Mayfield, and I'm playing with Ruud Van Nistelrooy and all these other lads – Ronaldo, from Portugal. It's amazing that we're all together.' It wasn't about Millwall, and it almost had nothing to do with the Cup final. It was about us as a team. Ferguson always got it spot-on. We didn't need a tactical talk that day – 'Watch their full-back, watch their centre-half, watch Dennis Wise, he'll be grabbing your balls or pinching you' – none of that nonsense. Our attitude was – in a nice way, 'Fuck Millwall, we're Man United, we'll do what's right for us, we're all in this together, we're all from different countries – it's brilliant, our families are here, we're going to win this game.'

It was the only time I've played in a Cup final that I knew we were going to win. It was confidence, not arrogance. We had better players, *and* our attitude was right. All week, the press had been full of FA Cup shocks – Southampton against United in 1976, Sunderland beating Leeds in '73 – but I knew it wouldn't happen to us. Our group was too strong.

We won 3–0.

We wore replicas of Jimmy Davis's top – DAVIS and his squad number, '36' – when we were going up to collect the trophy and our medals. I'd suggested it. Jimmy was a good young player; he was out on loan, at Watford. He drove into the back of a parked-up truck, at about five in the morning. The team went to the funeral; it had been very, very sad.

So we finished the season with the FA Cup. Arsenal won the Premiership – and they haven't won it since. They started to lose some of their strong characters, and quite a few of them were irreplaceable. Character is just as important as skill.

THREE

The Highbury tunnel was a strange one, like a little alleyway. Very tight. It was hard to avoid contact with people, even if you were trying to.

The rivalry between ourselves and Arsenal brought energy, and passion. It was brilliant. I hated them. There was an element of jealousy there, too, because I knew they were a bloody good team. But, ultimately, they made me a better player. I had to be at my best. Petit and Vieira in the middle of the park – I couldn't have an off day against them. When we lost games to Arsenal I was the first man to shake their hands.

Chelsea were bringing a new challenge. But Arsenal – it was electric. And the crowd; their old ground, Highbury, was an old-fashioned stadium. People said that it was a tight pitch but apparently it was the same size as most other pitches. But we seemed to have less time on the ball and their fans were almost literally on top of us. It made for a great atmosphere.

We've not seen the like since – that bitter rivalry. There isn't as much physical contact in the game now. Clubs are buying a different kind of player – technically gifted, but not fighters. But maybe it was just the timing. It wasn't just myself and Patrick; there were so many rivalries all over the pitch. I see players in the tunnel today, hugging one another before a game. I don't think any of the United lads would have disagreed with me; they hated Arsenal. And the Arsenal lads hated United.

Which of us was the better team? You couldn't call it. We were like two heavyweights battering each other. Patrick was the new kid. He's five or six years younger than me – not that he looks it. He was a physical player. He was an important player for them, and I was important to United. There were always going to be fireworks. The way we both played, it was never going to be friendly. That would have been impossible. It wasn't as if we were both right-backs, and we'd never come into contact with each other. We were in the centre of the park and we were hitting each other at pace. That was going to lead to confrontation. It could be pointed out that I had a short temper but the way we played – it had nothing to do with temper. We were both trying to control the pitch, and the game. We were leaders, and if a leader is given to heated confrontation, other players will respond. It's normal. Patrick is six foot four – a big six foot four. He's a big guy. But I always tried to look at his height as a disadvantage, for him. When it came to getting little breaking balls, I was sharp; I could read the game a little bit better than him. My anticipation and touch were a bit better, I think. But, in a run for the ball, he was quicker than me. He should have had the advantage on me for headers, but I had a good spring on me. I'd had my running battles with Arsenal before Vieira arrived, right back to my days at Forest. I'd have had run-ins with Ray Parlour and Martin Keown. There was Paul Davis, John Jensen, David Rocastle. None of them were choirboys.

We lost our first game of the new season, 1–0, to Chelsea, at Stamford Bridge. You always want to get a few wins under your belt, to build a bit of momentum early doors. But now, straightaway, we were playing catch-up. I played centre-half that day, which also indicates a bad start to the season. If it had been February or March, fair enough; the squad would have been stretched. But playing out of position on the first day of the season – it wasn't a good sign. It said something about a lack of strength in depth.

It was Mourinho's first game in English football. I remember the goal, and the importance of it. A win against us – Mourinho was already the Special One. It gave them that bit of early momentum, and confidence. Remember: they'd finished second the previous season, before Mourinho arrived. For the goal, I think I could have done better. When Gudjohnsen went to finish it, could I have taken his head off? Maybe.

Chelsea were stronger that day, but we were unlucky. The game reflected the season ahead. We were nearly there; we weren't bad. But we were always behind. Chelsea had spent a fortune. They had Carvalho and Drogba, and Makelele, and we'd slipped behind them. But we always put up a fight. They only beat us 1–0, but that can tell a lot. They were solid; they were going to be hard to break down. But there was also the feeling that Mourinho wouldn't be staying around for long. I didn't think he'd be another Ferguson or Wenger; he wasn't going to be building a dynasty.

Chelsea were very strong, but I also knew that Rooney and Ronaldo would be getting even better over the next year or two. There was no sense of panic. I always thought we'd bounce back; we'd get one or two more players in. And young players had been coming up through the academy – Darren Fletcher, John O'Shea, Wes Brown.

We were in a transitional period. As a senior player, I was aware of that. It wasn't that the manager was saying anything like that to us – or to *me*; he wasn't. But I'd been at United for more than a decade, and I realised that things were in transition. 'Let's hang on in there, and see what happens.' But the changes couldn't take too long; there was always that demand to win trophies. We weren't in the dressing room, going, 'Don't worry, lads, we're in transition; let's lose to Fulham.' There was always an urgency. Fans don't want to wait till next year. And we were still a good team.

Fans always get a lift when a big signing comes, and so do players. When Wayne Rooney walks into the dressing room, it lifts everybody. He arrived for the start of the '04–'05 season. He was a top, top player – immediately. I knew that from the first training sessions. And we'd played against him; his ability was easy to spot. I probably didn't warm to him as much as I had to Ronaldo. Wayne was a bit more streetwise; he was a Scouser – 'All right, lads.' He was straight in with the crack. Ronaldo was a bit more innocent. He acted like a seventeen-year-old, while Wayne seemed older. The only time I had a disagreement with Wayne, it had nothing to do with a pass he should have given me, or a tactical switch.

We were in a hotel, the Friday night before a game – I forget where. The team would always sit down and have a meal together, at about seven in the evening. There was a big TV in the room. I was into rugby league, and there was a big game on. I went to the toilet, came back and someone had changed the channel to something else – something stupid; I can't remember what it was. A few of the players were sitting there, giggling away.

I said, 'Where's the rugby league?'

I knew Wayne was up to something. I could tell by his face.

I said, 'Where's the remote control?'

He said, 'I don't know.'

I said, 'You fuckin' do.'

I didn't exactly storm out, but I couldn't be bothered trying to get the remote control back, so I decided I'd watch the rest of the match up in my room.

I came down the next morning for the pre-match meal and, obviously, I'm very good at letting things go – and Wayne was brave enough to come up to me.

'Did you ever find the remote control, Roy?'

I think I told him to go and fuck himself.

It was the only disagreement I ever had with him. I think he later claimed in one of his books – he has a deal to write ten – that I sent a security man to his room to get the remote control, but that's bullshit.

Alan Smith came in from Leeds, and started really well. I got on well with Smudge. One thing that struck me about him was that he never drank. That made him stand out, a bit. He'd still have a late night with us, and a crack and a laugh. He'd stay to the bitter end. I'd stopped drinking by this time, so we'd often end up chatting together. We were the only two left capable of holding a conversation.

He moved from being a striker to playing in midfield. I think he was struggling to get a starting position as a striker. The manager might have been looking at him as an eventual replacement of me, but I never felt my place was under threat from him. I remember playing against him in a few practice games, and thinking, 'Yeah, he has a chance.' But he never quite kicked on. It wasn't that he didn't reach his potential; he just didn't get the breaks. Or the breaks he got – injuries – were the ones you'd never want.

Gabriel Heinze was another good guy. He was a nasty fucker – nasty in training. I picked up an injury one day. A lot of it was my own fault. It was a Friday. We were playing Spurs at home the next day, and we'd always have light training the day before a home game. But it got a bit nasty and it ended up with myself and Gabby having a few tackles on each other. He kneed me on the side of my leg and, being the hero that I am, I kept my mouth shut. I didn't want to go in for treatment, but I was in agony.

I left the house the next day, limping.

I said to my wife, 'Well, I won't be able to play. I'll just go in and tell them.'

I got to Old Trafford and limped – literally – to the dressing room. I got a few painkillers, and played. My wife said it was the funniest thing, hearing my name being announced on the radio, after she'd seen me limping out of the house that morning.

But I liked Heinze. He picked up a bad injury too, later – his cruciate. A lot of the lads who came into the club at that time – Smudge, Gabby, Louis Saha – they were all very unlucky with injuries.

The dressing room was changing. Younger players create energy. They can be raw; they're not fearful. An older player losing in a semi-final is devastated; a younger player thinks he'll be getting to finals for the next thirty or forty years. They bring that arrogance into the dressing room. I became jealous of that as I got older. The longer you've been around, the less chance there is of winning something, the less chance that your contract will be renewed, the more chance there is of being injured. The young lads don't have those hang-ups yet.

More players arrived. Gerard Piqué was a good lad and a good player. But he wasn't getting a run of games and he wanted to go back to Barcelona. He's done all right there! I don't think anyone could have predicted just how much he'd achieve. This theory that he isn't a good defender – he's one of the best. He knows how to defend.

Giuseppe Rossi was a really good lad. But he had a difficult time at United. He was an attacking player, and had difficulty getting into the starting eleven. Giuseppe is Italian-American and one of the first times he trained with the first team I gave him a bollocking – I think because he didn't pass the ball to me when I was in a better position. And he looked at me – he said nothing. But I knew what he was thinking: 'Why don't you fuck off?'

I turned away, and I thought, 'I like that.'

If he'd said anything, I'd have run at him. But he looked right through me and the message was clear on his face. I nearly went over and shook his hand. I liked him from day one.

I tried to sign him when I was managing Sunderland, and not succeeding is one of my big regrets. I was doing my Pro Licence when we eventually got permission from United to speak to Giuseppe. I had a lecture that evening and I asked for permission to go to Altrincham, in Manchester; I'd made arrangements to meet Giuseppe. I met him at an Italian restaurant. He turned up with about eight agents. Three of them were Italian. His dad turned up, too. It was like a scene from *Goodfellas* – and I mean that in a nice way.

I was at the head of the table, trying to persuade Giuseppe to sign for us.

They were going, 'Sell us Sunderland.'

And I gave him a line – it was either going to be very cheesy or he'd love it. We'd just been promoted. We'd agreed to pay eight or eight and a half million for him, which was a lot for a lad who hadn't done too much yet.

I said, 'Look, Giuseppe. I've got a good orchestra up at Sunderland. But I need a conductor. And you're the man.'

They were all whispering, talking among themselves.

I was thinking, 'It's either gone down really well, or he's not coming.'

We finished the meeting. I was really delighted with it.

He goes, 'I've got to look at my other options.'

A few days later, he signed for Villarreal.

He contacted me and said, 'Roy, thanks for everything.'

Villarreal or Sunderland? I understood his decision. Villarreal were making noises now, and, as Diego Forlán had told me before, it was twenty minutes from the beach.

We drew three of our first five games, and they weren't good draws – Blackburn, Everton, Bolton. We beat Liverpool, and Tottenham; then two more draws, against Middlesbrough and Birmingham. The signs weren't great. It wasn't League-winning form. You can always have a sluggish start, but we weren't used to draws. A draw against Chelsea would have been okay, but there were too many. It's all about winning.

We beat Arsenal at home, 2–0, and ended their unbeaten run of forty-nine games. I wasn't playing.

That summer I'd gone to a detox clinic in Milan, with Ryan Giggs and a couple of his mates. I think David Bellion might have been with us, too. It was recommended to us by some of the French players. The regime was strict; you starved yourself for three or four days and they educated you about diet. I was going through my health freakish phase at the time. Giggsy had been there before, and he'd warned me that we wouldn't eat. I didn't believe him; I thought we'd have to eat something. But I'd paid out quite a lot of money so I could fuckin' starve for four days. I never ate – nothing. The first night, I wanted to leave. But I stayed. I think it was the second or third night when they gave us some carrot juice. The dietician decided that I was eating too much red meat, and I needed to cut back; I needed to eat more fruit and vegetables.

I came home, and went on the new diet. I wouldn't be mixing carbohydrates and protein. Typical me, the man of extremes, I went too far. I stopped eating red meat. I was almost divorced, because I wouldn't eat what everyone else in the house was eating. I'd only eat the healthy stuff, and I stopped eating treats. My wife would be cooking for five kids and I'd be going, 'I need to have fish – and salad.' As I've said, I'm not a lover of fish so I was trying to eat food I didn't particularly like. There was even one time my wife gave me a little trifle and I asked her to take the cream off the top. My body fat went down to 3 or 4 per cent; I went too skinny.

A couple of days before we played Arsenal, I couldn't get out of bed. And I've never been one for being ill – never. Mike Stone, the club doctor, came to my house. I just couldn't get out of bed – no strength, no nothing. I knew I wouldn't be right for the game – and I must have been pretty bad to miss any game, let alone the Arsenal game. Mike asked me what I'd been doing over the last few months and I told him about my detox in Milan. The decision to go there had been independent of the club, in the summer; Mike wouldn't have been aware of it.

He asked me, 'What have you been doing with your diet?'

And I told him, 'Well, the woman told me to cut back on red meat.'

And he said, 'And what have you done?'

And I said, 'Well, I've cut it out altogether.'

He did some blood tests. And I missed the Arsenal game. I was in bed for three or four days, when the test results came back. My iron levels were gone; I'd no iron in my system. Mike told me I'd have to get back to eating red meat, and eating things that I enjoyed.

I think I was trying to eat and live like an Italian or a French player. But I'm Irish. My mother came over a week or two later and she had a right go at me, as only mothers can do. Any pictures of me then, I look gaunt. I was cold all the time; I just wasn't myself. I'd gone too far. I had the body fat of a long-distance runner. But I was a midfielder, playing in tough games, where you need protection.

I was gutted that I'd missed the game, and all the fighting that went on in the tunnel afterwards. I couldn't even go to the game. There was pizza being flung around in the tunnel, but I wouldn't have eaten it; it wasn't healthy enough for me.

I was well enough to go on as sub in the next league game, against Portsmouth, at Fratton Park. Phil Neville had played in my position while I was out. I remember the manager told me, 'Listen, I'm putting you on the bench. Phil's done well for me the last few games.'

I said, 'I think I've done okay in the four hundred and odd games I've played.'

I could see his point of view; I wasn't annoyed. But I sat on the bench while we lost 2–0, and I thought, 'I should be playing.' But I wasn't kicking up a fuss. I accepted the manager's view. But United were a better team with me in it. You have to think that way.

In late October, we were seventh in the table. That's a sacking offence these days.

Missing the Arsenal game because of my diet was unusual, but I'd always accepted injuries as part of the game. You expect mid-fielders to get injured.

I'd had two hernia operations, hamstring injuries, maybe for not stretching properly in my younger years. I'd had broken ribs, stitches in the head – what I would class as normal midfielders' injuries. And, of course, the cruciate. Being out of the game for so long, eight or nine months, gave me a chance to grow up a little bit. Because I was drinking quite heavily at the time. I was twenty-six or twenty-seven – even a touch younger.

The injury that would eventually stop me from carrying on

was my hip. I'd been in Dublin the night before – this was in 2001, I think – doing a gig for Diadora. I'd had a really late night, drinking – a right session. I was training back in Manchester the next day, doing a little bit, going on a jog – and feeling something in my hip. It didn't feel like a massive tear but it did feel a bit strange.

I carried on playing for months afterwards but eventually it took its toll. I saw a specialist, Richard Villar, in Cambridge. Because it was the hip area, it was almost an unknown as a football injury. The standard injuries are hernias, broken legs, knees, ankles, even cruciates. But the hip was a worrying one – an 'Oh, you don't want to go in there' type of operation. It was a bit taboo; you associate hip problems with older people. But the pain was unnatural. I was needing a lot of painkillers to get me through matches.

It was probably wear and tear, all the twisting and turning, the way I played the game, quite physically. But all that drink in Dublin the night before hadn't helped. Maybe my running pattern was different that morning, and I hadn't slept much, or properly, the night before.

Eventually I had the operation. There was a flap of cartilage that had to be shaved off. I remember the surgeon told me that he wasn't sure if I'd be able to play again because of the cartilage damage. The way he described it to me, he said that when he put the scalpel under the cartilage, it was coming away like carpet underlay. He showed me photographs, too, and it *did* look like underlay. I recovered, came back – but I was still in a bit of pain. I knew I wasn't right.

When you come back from a bad injury you know, in medical terms, that the injury is healed. But you still have to deal with the battles in your head. The surgeon had planted a few seeds: 'There's a lot of damage in there, a lot of cartilage damage, and you want to be careful.' I was due to have more surgery on it a few years later, but I changed my mind, I just decided, 'Nah, I'll try and get on, the way it is.'

Funnily, I think being stiff suited me. I had tight hamstrings; it was just the way I was. That tight feeling suited my personality; I don't think I was meant to be too flexible. I'd see some of the foreign lads doing stretches, touching their toes. Mikaël Silvestre could put his head on his toe; I'd injure my hamstring just looking at him. I could never touch my toes. I started doing a bit of yoga towards the end, but I think that kind of made me loose. I persuaded myself that I was more flexible. I'd known my limitations but now I thought I was a gymnast. As with the food, I was trying to be somebody I wasn't. And I still ended up getting injuries. The hip was affecting the quality of my day-to-day life – simple things like picking up my kids or getting out of the car. When I came back after my cruciate injury, people would ask, 'How's your knee – the cruciate?' But I'd stopped thinking about it. The hip was the only injury that had, and has, long-term consequences.

If the weather's cold or I kick a ball with my son, it's sore. Or if I'm in the wrong driving position, or in a plane, I'll be stiff. Chances are I'll need a hip replacement but, if I look after myself, I can avoid it for a long time. Any exercise I do has to be straight – swimming, cycling, walking. No twisting and turning.

We had four wins in a row – Newcastle, Charlton, West Brom and Southampton. You still have to go out and win them, but these were games that we would have expected to win. Although I always had a bit of hassle against Newcastle. I'd been sent off twice up there. I'd had my battles with Shearer and Rob Lee. I always thought they were an arrogant bunch, for a club that had won fuck all. We always got decent results at St James' Park; it wasn't a bad place to play. But as for the Toon Army, the Geordies, the hostile reception – I never fell for all that crap.

We drew with Fulham, away, but then we had another run of four wins in December and over the holiday period. We beat Crystal Palace, Bolton, Villa and Middlesbrough. We were third in the table on New Year's Day, behind Chelsea and Arsenal.

I'd met Brian Kerr, the new Ireland manager, just after he took the job, in 2003. We'd talked about the possibility of me playing for Ireland again. There were six Euro qualifying games left. I'd eventually decided against, because I felt I had enough on my plate trying to get back to full fitness; this was just after my hip operation.

Sometime later I met Brian again, at the Alderley Edge Hotel, in Manchester. I'd been doing some promotional work for the Irish Guide Dogs and I'd mentioned in an interview that I felt there was unfinished business. I was feeling fitter, and stronger, by now. I think the suggestion for the meeting came through my solicitor, Michael Kennedy. We discussed me going back for the 2006 World Cup qualifiers. I knew I'd be under massive pressure from United not to do it. I was at an age where the manager would have thought my priority should have been Manchester United, particularly with my history of injury problems. Also, going back to play for Ireland, the added games, and after all that had happened after Saipan – all the hassle and negativity – it would be putting a lot of extra pressure on me. United were paying my wages; I could see their point of view.

The decision was straightforward – but emotional. I did feel that there was unfinished business. I was thinking about my family. I'm proud of being Irish and being from Cork. I think that feeling has got stronger as I've matured. I think when you go and live in a different country – even though England is only across the road – you can lose a sense of where you're from. It's natural – you adapt and integrate. You change your ways and ideas. My kids were born and reared in England. They often tease me about how they support England. But as you get older, there's a point – maybe a feeling – where you go, 'Don't forget what it's all about; don't forget where you come from.' I didn't want to let the family down.

If I'd looked at it coldly I wouldn't have gone back. There was my age; I was thirty-three. Physically – and mentally – it would be another burden. I'd be playing in the middle of the park; the demands would be huge. People would expect miracles. And I knew there'd be consequences at United. I knew there'd be a price to pay. The manager wouldn't talk to me. But he – they – couldn't stop me.

There were no problems when I went back into the squad. I didn't bat an eyelid. I'd had no disagreement with any of the players.

I like Brian, and the only thing I found a little bit strange was that I wasn't the captain. I'd been captain before, and we'd had success; we'd got to the World Cup finals in Japan and Korea – and, of course, I was the captain at United.

But Kenny Cunningham was the captain. I'd played with Kenny over the years. He was popular with the players. He'd always be organising card schools and quizzes and whip-rounds for the bus driver and for the woman who'd served us tea in 19-fuckin'-52. But most of the lads liked him.

I'd always been a bit blasé about the captain's role. I'd often said that it was only about going up for the toss. I think I didn't want to talk the job – or myself – up: 'Oh, the captain's role is vital, look at me.' But as I got older I realised that there was more to it than that. The captain's role isn't just important; it is vital. And it isn't just an English tradition. Look at the great captains in

Italy and Spain – Maldini, Dino Zoff, Zanetti, Raúl, Puyol. They're inspiring leaders. When, say, the Barcelona captain has to leave the pitch before the end of the game, he puts his armband on the player who is taking the job for the rest of the game. During the last World Cup, the Dutch captain, van Persie, put the armband on Arjen Robben's arm when he was being substituted.

Bryan Robson, Steve Bruce, Cantona – great captains I played with. They led in different ways. Robbo led by example, in the way he was physically demanding, and in his attitude to training. He was also a really good guy, and liked a drink. Brucie was very friendly, and great with the families. He always had a nice way about him, always had time for you. He was good with tickets, if you needed a few extra for family or friends. It was almost a political role. Brucie dealt with it very well, and he's brought that into his management. Cantona led by his presence more than anything else – his charisma. A captain doesn't have to be loud; Eric rarely said a word.

In my early years at United, there was a players' pool, and each of us would get about £800 out of it at the end of the season, for the work we'd done for the in-house magazines, the club videos. It was before all these things were built into the players' contracts. We were all on decent money, and eight hundred quid wasn't going to make or break us. So one time – we were in the dressing room – we decided to put all the cheques into a hat, and the last cheque out whoever's name was on it he got to keep all the cheques. To save face, we all put our cheques in, except a couple of the younger players – I think it was Becks, and Gary and Phil. They opted out; they were new on the scene and didn't have the money to spare. But Scholesy and Nicky Butt put their cheques in. Last name out wins all the money – great crack in the dressing room. Lads sweating – and I was fuckin' sweating; I used to think of that sort of money in terms of the amount of pints it would buy me. I think I was the third last name out, so I got a run for my money. But the last cheque out – Eric Cantona. He'd won about sixteen grand.

He came in the next day. There was plenty of banter.

'Eric, you lucky bastard.'

'Fuckin' money to money.'

He'd got somebody at the club to cash the cheques. He'd split the money in two, and he gave it to Paul Scholes and Nicky Butt, because – he said – the two of them had had the balls to go into it when they really couldn't afford it. The two lads took home about eight grand each – which upset me even more.

But I just thought, 'What a gesture.'

Nobody else would have done it.

Stuart Pearce was captain when I was at Forest – a brilliant, brilliant captain. I loved the way he played and trained, and he was the captain of England at the time. I've been lucky when it comes to people leading by example. Stuart defended me a couple of times. There was once I was having issues with my contract at Forest and I was getting a lot of criticism. Brian Clough had said that I was being greedy. He was trying to put pressure on me through the media, trying to get me to sign a new contract. There were comments from some of the players in the dressing room – and it wasn't banter.

I remember Pearcie saying, 'Listen, lads, are you all happy with your deals?'

They all went, 'Yeah.'

And he went, 'Well, fuckin' leave him alone.'

When I became captain of United, I knew if I made a balls of it I'd have no one to blame except myself. I'd learnt from Cantona, Stuart Pearce, Robbo, Brucie. I found the off-the-field responsibilities – tickets, the crèches for the kids, paying for Christmas dos – a pain in the arse. But it had to be done, and people expected you to do it. I organised a Santa Claus one Christmas, and I noticed – when it was too late and the pictures were being taken – that Santa had tattoos on his knuckles. It wasn't one of my better moves.

The captaincy is important, but squad numbers can have an importance, too. At United, '7' was the iconic number. When Eric Cantona left there was debate about who was going to be the next captain. I was quite relaxed about it. But there was his number, too – '7'. Bryan Robson had had it before Cantona and, of course, it went back to Georgie Best. The manager pulled me into his office and said that he wanted me to wear the '7'.

I said, 'No, I'm not bothered.'

And he said, 'I know Becks will fuckin' want it and I don't want him to have it.'

The little power battles.

I'd had '16' since I'd signed for the club. I was comfortable with '16'. I think it might have kept me on my toes, being outside the '1' to '11'. I didn't think I was a number '7'.

I said, 'Give it to Becks.'

Becks got it, and it suited him – and Cantona. Ronaldo had it after Becks.

The captaincy of a great club is almost a brand – a brand within the brand. After I stopped playing football, I often noticed that people abroad were more impressed with the fact that I'd been the captain of United than the fact that I'd played for them for nearly thirteen years.

The captain is the leader. I think you need someone at the front, at the top of the tunnel, who'll inspire the thought, 'I'll follow him – everyone's going to follow him.' I think I should have been Ireland captain. But I didn't want to put that on Brian. I didn't want it to seem like an ego trip: 'I'll only go back if I'm the captain.' But I should have brought it up in the conversation.

I think Kenny enjoyed the media side of the role. We'd come in at the end of a game, and Kenny would come in after us, because he'd been talking to the TV people. That would piss me off, a bit. Don't forget your place; it's about the team.

My first game back was a friendly against Romania, at Lansdowne Road. We won 1–0; Matty Holland scored. It was good to be back, really, really emotional. I'd always loved the bus journey to the games. Kids waving flags – I used to love all that. The police sirens. And the rebel songs on the bus – I enjoyed them; it was tradition. We were on the bus going to Lansdowne, and we got stuck in a bit of traffic, not far from the hotel. I was sitting by the window, and there was a young kid outside, looking up.

And he said, 'Welcome back.'

It was like he'd been planted there.

I said to myself, 'It's good to be back.'

The game itself, the national anthem – all emotional stuff. I always hated the hanging around and the travelling. But the bus journey and the game – if it had just been about those two things, it would have been perfect.

I was glad to be back, but the consequences of the decision were about to bite me in the arse. I made myself available to play away to Switzerland, in the second qualifier, in September '04, although I'd fractured my ribs. I'd done that a few weeks before in a Champions League qualifier, against Dynamo Bucharest. I'd played in our next Premiership game against Norwich but my ribs were at me. I'd been ruled out for four or five weeks but, after two or three, I felt better. The club doctor said it all looked fine. But I hadn't played for United. So I rang Alex Ferguson and told him I thought I'd be all right to play against Switzerland.

He went fuckin' mad.

'You're not fit enough to play for us!'

But I went and played against Switzerland. We drew 1–1.

That was the second of the qualifiers. The first had been against Cyprus, at Lansdowne. We won 3–0, but I'd missed it because of my fractured ribs. I didn't want to risk it in a game we'd probably win. And I was placating United a bit, too, by not playing in the less important game. We drew 0–0 with France, in Paris. It wasn't the old French team. A lot of the men who had won the World Cup in '98 had retired. We should have won that game in Paris.

We were unlucky. We were 1–0 up against Israel, away, and they equalised in time added on. In the return game, in Lansdowne, we were 2–0 up, and ended up drawing 2–2. I know: you make your own luck. But you need a few breaks and Brian Kerr didn't get any.

We played the Faroes a couple of weeks after United had played Arsenal in the FA Cup final. I'd got injured in the first few minutes of that final, and ended up with a torn groin. I picked up a silly yellow card in the Faroes game – I think it was for arguing. I shouldn't have been playing, because I was injured. But I was suspended for the next game, at home to Israel. I ended up watching that one in the stand. I'm not a gambler, but I had a bet on that Ian Harte would score the first goal – and he did. It was twenty quid, I think, and I got back a couple of hundred. That was the game we drew 2–2. I like to think that if I'd been playing we'd have won. I could have had that impact on the game.

We'd drawn with France in Paris but, by the time they came to Dublin, a lot of their best players had come out of retirement.

I spoke to Mikaël Silvestre about it before the game.

'I can't believe they're all coming back.'

And Mikaël said to me, 'I think there were financial incentives.'

They beat us 1–0.

We didn't qualify. But I liked working under Brian. He should have been given more time, another crack at qualifying for the Euros. We were so close – the two draws against Israel killed us.

I played in six of the ten qualifiers. I was injured or suspended for the other four. I'd enjoyed being back, although not qualifying was disappointing. And I knew: there wouldn't be another campaign for me.

At the start of the new year we were still doing okay. We beat Liverpool and Villa and drew with Spurs, and we were still third when we went to Arsenal.

I didn't see it as a big deal at the time. It was just a bit of argy-bargy. The circumstances, the rivalry, gave it significance. And the cameras in the tunnel – that's standard now, but I think it was quite new at the time. I was told later that the fans outside were seeing what was happening on the big screens. I didn't know that, but it was all part of the build-up, and the story.

But, really, what's mad about the whole tunnel episode is that it had nothing to do with me.

Gary Neville had come to see me just after the warm-up; it was an evening kick-off. We'd just come back into the dressing room. Gary told me that some of the Arsenal players had said something to him in the tunnel, that they weren't going to take any nonsense – they'd be waiting for him. They said there'd be none of the carry-on that had gone on in the game at Old Trafford earlier in the season. There'd been a lot of kicking and argy-bargy during that game, and afterwards. Phil had played instead of me that day, and he'd been running around like a kamikaze pilot, running into everybody. I think Gary was now suffering the consequences of Phil's actions.

But I didn't pay much attention to what Gary said.

'Whatever, Gary.'

I was getting into the zone myself. I was concentrating on my job, getting ready to go out on to the pitch. I wasn't one for shouting and roaring in the dressing room. I'd be geeing myself up, in a calm way. The last thing I wanted was Gary in my earhole, going, 'They've been shouting at me in the tunnel.'

My attitude was, 'Fuckin' deal with it. You're not eleven.'

But he'd planted a seed in my head, warning me.

I was always one of the first out to the tunnel. As captain, I'd be leading the team out. The Highbury tunnel was a strange one, like a little alleyway. Very tight. It was hard to avoid contact with people, even if you were trying to. There was always a lot of tension there. And night matches always created more tension anyway.

I'd forgotten my captain's armband – simple as that. So I turned to go back to the dressing room.

'Go down, lads, I'll be with you in a minute; I forgot my armband.'

And I went back, past our own players. Albert, the kit man, had the armband and he was putting it on me.

'All the best, Roy.'

As I walked to the front I heard something going on at the top of the tunnel. All I could see was a few fingers, pointing at Gary.

I lost it.

Five seconds earlier, I'd been perfectly calm, in the zone, ready for the match. But, because of what Gary had said to me, I just went, 'The fuckers – they *are* waiting for him.'

I'd thought they might have booted him out on the pitch. But in the tunnel? I just thought, 'The fuckers.' They were trying to bully him. They were a big team and, in the tunnel, they were even bigger.

So I said to myself, 'All right. Let's go.'

I went down there. I'd lost it, but I wasn't zoning out; I wasn't forgetting about the game.

I said, 'We'll see you out there.'

I just felt they were bullying Gary. I don't think it was

intimidation; it was bullying. There's a difference. If Patrick Vieira had come up to me and said, 'I'm going to have you', that would have been intimidation. It would have been a clash between equal personalities. But Gary was quiet – I think they were going for one of the weaker players in the team. By 'weak' I don't mean it as it's usually understood. Gary was an established international; he'd sixty or seventy caps; he'd played in World Cups. He'd won the Champions League, and League titles. But his personality was wrong for this. If they'd been having a go at Nicky Butt or Wes Brown, I wouldn't have said anything. I'd have walked past them, probably whistling. In football, intimidation is legitimate but bullying isn't. I never went looking for a full-back who'd never done anything to me. I'd look for people who were in my position or were physically important for their team. I'd always thought, 'They can give it back to me.' I never went for a tricky winger or a small full-back.

'I'll see you out there.'

I meant it. I love the game of football. We'd sort it out on the pitch – no hiding places.

I'd read something in the match programme about the charity work Patrick supported in Senegal, where he'd been born. He'd mentioned how much he loved going back to Senegal.

I said, 'If you love Senegal so much, why don't you fuckin' play for them?'

I think he said something smart to me about Ireland and the World Cup. It was grown men, bitching.

The referee, Graham Poll, was good – 'Just leave it, just leave it.'

'I fuckin' am. Just let us out.'

What was important: it didn't interfere with my perform-ance that night and I don't think it had an impact on the game. Although it might have thrown them more than us. We went out and played like Brazil. We won the game, 4–2. But the tunnel incident was all part of the TV drama. It became entertainment, although I wasn't aware of the cameras. I was there to do a job. 'Win the game – get in and get out.' But it was a bit like the build-up to a boxing match – the weigh-in, the press conferences – when people forget that there'll actually be a fight.

But I still feel that I was defending one of my team-mates. I know what's right and what's wrong, and their behaviour that night was wrong. If it had come to an actual fight, Patrick could probably have killed me. But it was unacceptable.

I think that football might lack that energy now, a bit – that tension. It was great. But years later, people bring up the tunnel and they don't remember the match that came after it.

After the game, we'd moved up to second, behind Chelsea.

I scored in our next game, a win against Birmingham. It was my fiftieth League goal. Scoring a goal – the best feeling ever. The jubilation. It was nice to remember where the back of the net was. We beat City and Portsmouth. We were still second.

We'd had to qualify for the Champions League group stages, because we'd finished third in the Premiership the season before. We got past Dynamo Bucharest, when I fractured my ribs. We were drawn with Sparta Prague, Fenerbahçe and Lyon. I didn't play in either of the Fenerbahçe games. This probably marked the start of my accepting that I wouldn't be playing in every game. I was part of the squad rotation, and it took a bit of getting used to. I was fine about missing certain games, but not the big ones. We ended up second in the group, behind Lyon, although we'd drawn with them away and had beaten them at home. But Fenerbahçe beat us 3–0 in the last game, so we finished two points behind Lyon and drew Milan in the next round.

They beat us twice, 1–0. In the home leg, Roy Carroll couldn't hold on to a shot. It wasn't a bad, bad mistake, but Hernán Crespo got to it; like all good strikers, he was sniffing out the chance. He scored again in the second leg. Milan were a top team then. There was no shame in going out to a team that had Nesta, Maldini, Pirlo, and Kaká in it.

We weren't quite there yet; we'd slipped behind – just a bit. The panic button would have been pressed if Fenerbahçe had knocked us out, but not Milan.

Bill Beswick made the point: 'Sport is all about disappointment.' It's about dealing with the disappointments. It's not the highs. There are so few of them. It's the defeats, the injuries. Great careers carry massive disappointments. It's how you cope with them. You have to look forward, home in on the positives. Take the positive out of every negative. Look to the next game.

But it's difficult. It was one of my biggest weaknesses. Dealing with the disappointment, and the self-loathing that comes with it. I didn't get over it quickly. I couldn't. I'm not sure that the greatest sports psychologist in the world, working with me twenty-four hours a day, would have had much of an impact.

But I am open-minded about sports psychology. Bill worked at Sunderland when I was manager there. But it was always optional. I think that's very important. Whether it's yoga or diet, it shouldn't be like school. The message at United was always that Bill was there if we wanted him.

I would speak to Bill about the sending-offs and the rage, and he'd say, 'Your first target is to stay on the pitch for ninety minutes.' I appreciated that; it was common sense. It was one of the best pieces of advice I'd been given. I'd been advised before to count to ten. That was never going to work for me. 'Just a second, I'm angry – one – two—' So Bill's advice was good, very practical. And towards the end of my career, he nudged me towards ideas that were helpful.

I watched the 2005 Champions League final in Dubai, at about two o'clock in the morning. It was the mad game, AC Milan against Liverpool. I never had a hatred for Liverpool, although I wasn't exactly jumping up and down on the balcony when they won. I remember thinking, 'Milan, you fuckin' idiots', when they threw it away.

We had a dip in form in the League – two draws, two losses, two wins. If you know you're not going to win the League, you lose your edge a little bit. It went back to the first game of the season, when Chelsea beat us. They went from strength to strength and we were always just behind them. We finished third, behind Arsenal. Chelsea had won a record number of points and were already the champions when they came to Old Trafford. We had to applaud them on to the pitch. I didn't like that. I'm not a big fan of that ritual, even when other teams had to applaud us. The applause is insincere; you don't mean it. I was cursing them under my breath, and I'd like to think my team-mates were doing the same. 'Bastards – cunts—' I wouldn't have thought any less of the Chelsea lads if they hadn't applauded us, if the situation had been reversed.

We beat Southampton, 2–1, at St Mary's, in the last game of the season. They were relegated after that result, and West Brom stayed up – Bryan Robson, my old captain, was managing West Brom. I didn't play; I was on the bench. I got into a bit of hassle after the game. When a game is over, players who were on the bench do some running and stretches after the lads who played have gone down to the dressing room. We were doing strides and stretching out on the pitch. There was a bit of tension, a few Southampton fans hanging around. I think they shouted, 'You Irish fucker!' – something like that.

I turned, and said something like, 'Well, you're going down anyway.'

There were only a few people there but they started kicking up a fuss. It seemed it was all right for them to abuse me but I wasn't allowed to say anything back. A few security lads came over and asked us to get off the pitch. They ushered us off. It meant that we wouldn't be able to do our running; some of the players were pleased with that. But I didn't give Southampton's relegation a thought. Although I'd experienced it myself as a young player, with Forest. It was dog eat dog.

The Glazers bought Man Utd around this time. There was a lot of hostility towards them, from fans. But from the players' point of view, I don't think it bothered us too much. I had a few shares in the club, as part of my contract. So the Glazers coming in was worth a few bob to me.

We played Arsenal in the FA Cup final. We hammered them that day. Rooney and Ronaldo were outstanding. We should have won. But Arsenal hung in there – it's a great trait to have; I admired them for it. But we had so many chances. I had a shot blocked by Patrick Vieira near the end of the second half. It was still 0–0 after extra-time. I scored my penalty. But Paul Scholes missed his. Vieira took their last penalty. He scored. But that was Patrick's last game for Arsenal. He went to Juventus during the summer.

I got a really bad knock in my private parts in the first few minutes of the game. I carried on, but I got a scan about two weeks later, after I'd played for Ireland in the Faroe Islands. I'd a torn groin. I'd never had an injury like it before. I slipped into a tackle, and Patrick literally kneed me – right in there. I was cut.

It was bad enough we'd lost the Cup final, but I was in agony as well. I couldn't even sit down at the do that night. I had to go to bed at about ten o'clock. Aside from that, I was quite calm after the match. I remember thinking, 'We played well. We were brilliant.' It was that Arsenal thing; we battered them but they beat us on penalties.

I understood sport. You could play well and still lose. You have to look at the man in the mirror, but there was no shame in losing, once you'd done your best. Garth Crooks was looking for an interview with me, for the BBC, as losing captain. I said, 'Not today', but I should have done it. Ronaldo and Rooney had been the two best players on the pitch. I should have said, 'Watch those boys go. I'd rather be in our position than Arsenal's', even though they'd just won the Cup. They were hanging in there that day. It was another nine years before they won the Cup again. But I wouldn't begrudge them it. I still have that admiration for Arsenal and Wenger.

I think the manager could have been a bit braver; he could have put Tim Howard on for Roy Carroll. We only used two of our substitutions. If he'd just done something a bit mad – changed the goalkeepers, they might have thought, 'Fuckin' hell, he must be good at saving penalties.' Mind games. I'm not saying Tim would have been better than Roy, and I don't think a goalkeeper had ever been substituted in that way, although I've heard that other managers had thought about doing it if the circumstances were right. Martin O'Neill told me that he was on the verge of doing it in a play-off when he was managing Leicester, but they scored in the last few minutes of extra time so he didn't have to. And then, of course, van Gaal made the decision to put on Tim Krul for the penalty shootout when Holland played Costa Rica in the World Cup quarter final. But I think it crossed the manager's mind. I remember seeing Tim Howard getting warmed up, and thinking afterwards that it would have been worth the gamble. It's all hindsight.

The signs were good for us. I should have said it at the time publicly. But it's hard for a player to look at things in the long term. You've just played a hundred and twenty minutes, and lost. But if you looked at both teams that day, and wondered which of them was going to go on and win trophies, it was United.

FOUR

I'm walking up the stairs – we're all walking up in our training kit, like a load of kids being called to the headmaster. I'm walking up and I'm thinking, 'Here goes.'

The first real murmur that something was wrong came when I went back to pre-season training in July 2005. It seems so trivial now, but it was a pretty big argument. Because of a villa in Portugal.

We had a week's pre-season training at a place called Vale do Lobo, in the Algarve. We brought the families with us. We'd never done it before, brought the families. It was almost unheard of. I'd already been there, in the Algarve, for a week with my family, very close to the training camp. The rest of the team were flying in on Sunday, and training would start on Monday. So we drove down there on Saturday, to move into our villa.

A lady there – she was a resort manager, I think – took me up to the town house that my family was to stay in. I looked around the place and I told her, 'I've got five kids. This is too small.'

There were three bedrooms, and there was a plunge pool, which I thought was dangerous; we had five children, and the oldest was ten. I just wasn't comfortable with it.

She told me that no one had mentioned to her that I had five kids. She understood what I meant, I think. She told me it hadn't been designed for families. She even pointed out the glass tables, the sharp corners. They probably have to go through that routine for insurance reasons. The place just wasn't suitable. My wife is very placid and even she was saying, 'We can't stay here, it's not designed for kids.'

The woman brought me to look at a second villa; my wife was waiting down at the first place with the kids. The second place was nicer but, in the meantime, I'd rung the people we'd just hired the previous villa from, where we'd been staying the week before, and I asked if we could stay there for another week. It was literally down the road from the training camp, five minutes in the car.

Carlos Queiroz, United's assistant manager, arrived while I was at the second villa. Carlos is Portuguese – I think he was born in Mozambique – and there was some sort of a connection with the resort people; he had organised the camp for the team.

He came up and said, 'Ah, it's fine.'

And I said, 'I've just got word that we can stay in the villa we were in last week. I'll pay for it myself. I'd rather my family be comfortable while we're training.'

But we had a disagreement. It wasn't heated; it was just a disagreement. I knew I was there for pre-season training, but it was my wife and children's holiday. But I think Carlos might have felt a bit put out; he wasn't happy. And I knew that this would be going back to the manager.

Anyway, we moved back to the villa we'd stayed in the previous week. The rest of the players came in the next day, and so did the manager. He made a big fuss about what had happened, started ranting and raving in the dressing room after the first training session. The dressing room was empty but all the other players were right outside; they would have been able to hear everything that was going on.

'What is the big deal?' I said.

I just thought it was an overreaction.

'I'm just staying down the road.'

The way the place was set up, there was a restaurant where all the players would eat at lunchtime and the families could gather and eat there in the evenings. Ironically, I was the only player who turned up every day with his family. We were never isolated. It was a big resort. Everyone was scattered around.

But something happened there. Whatever had gone on, whatever Carlos said – I don't know. Maybe he felt embarrassed; he'd organised the camp for the club. Whether they felt I'd insulted the owner somehow, I don't know.

I carried on training – we trained for the week. And it was brilliant. The mix – training, then the afternoons spent with the families – was perfect. Pre-season is about training, recovery, and bonding. Recovery just means relaxing after you've trained. Sitting, maybe watching TV or, if you're in a place like the Algarve, sitting by the pool. There's a discipline to that, which I probably wasn't very good at – actually resting. So having my family there was great. And the facilities were fantastic.

One day the manager came on to the training pitch and said, 'I need some senior players tonight.' He was doing this not-talking-to-me routine. It happened regularly, if I went playing a friendly for Ireland or went too soon after an injury. He wouldn't speak to me for a week or two. It was childish, but I'd probably have been the same; I'd have been annoyed with any player who I thought was risking his fitness. He didn't talk to me, so I didn't talk to him; we were both being childish. Anyway, he wanted some players to go for dinner or something with the owner of the resort. We were all there, stretching, and he was going, 'Giggsy and—', choosing his players, and ignoring me. I was the captain and the lads were looking at me, laughing. I was sitting right there in front of him

– such childish stuff. I think it was Giggsy and Gary Neville who had to go to dinner.

Back in Manchester, still in pre-season, I hurt my hamstring, training. I wasn't doing anything too strenuous. We were just stretching, and I felt a tweak. A badly torn hamstring is torture but mine was just a slight tear. So I missed a couple of games, and the pre-season tour of Asia.

When you're a first-team player coming back from injury, you train for a while with the younger players, the reserves, to get back up to speed. You ease your way back to fitness. The reserves wouldn't be at the same level as the first team, so you don't put any extra stresses on your body. There wouldn't be the same intensity, so you can make your mistakes, get the rustiness out of you. Whereas when you go back with the first team there are no shortcuts; there's no messing about. You'd have a game in mind, in a couple of weeks, say, and you'd have a discussion with the medical staff; you'd agree a target, a timetable. As an experienced player, I knew my own body. I was ready to come back – 'I should be ready Monday week' – but I was being told, 'No, no, not yet.' Carlos, for some reason, was reluctant to get me back into the first team. And when he eventually did, he treated me very badly.

There was often a practice match at the end of training, ten v. ten, or eight v. eight. This time, I ended up being the last man standing, the last player to be picked. Carlos looked at me, and I said, 'Carlos, what—?'

He had a bib – and I'll always remember this like it was yesterday, because I'm surprised I didn't knock him out. He just threw it at me. The other players were looking at me and he went, 'Oh, you just stand up front.'

I was a midfielder; I didn't play centre-forward. It was like he was saying, 'You stand up there, so you won't do any harm.'

That got my back up, and rightly so. But I wasn't one for arguing with staff on the training ground. I could count the number of arguments I've had with staff on the training ground on one hand. But I was thinking, 'Am I missing something?' And I concluded, 'Probably.' But I wasn't thinking of the villa in Portugal at that time.

A couple of days later, I was talking to the manager and I said, 'Carlos has been a bit strange, you know. He's reluctant to get me back in the group.'

And the manager went, 'Yeah, I know he can be a funny old sod, but leave that with me, Roy.'

The season started okay. We won our first three games, against Everton, Villa and Newcastle, and we drew at home to Manchester City, which I would have classed as a bad result; we should always beat City at home. But then I broke my foot. In a tackle, at Liverpool. Steven Gerrard stood on my foot. Gerrard was wearing those new bladed boots, and I'm convinced they did the damage. I carried on playing but it was sore – fuckin' very sore. I was tackled again later, by Luis García, and I limped away from that one, so people often think it was García who caused the injury. But it was Gerrard and his blades.

I went off with a few minutes to go. Liverpool have an X-ray machine right next to the dressing room, so they X-rayed my foot and came back straightaway with the news; I'd broken it in – I don't know – five or six places. So that was me out injured again. I remember thinking to myself in the dressing room, 'This is bad timing.' For all sorts of reasons.

The problem with a foot injury is that it's a dead slow recovery. Your foot is in a medical boot, and the blood flow is slow. It's bad, because there's not much you can do. You have to be very patient. It's always a four- or five- or six-week job, no matter how fit you are. I'd already been injured, I was into the last year of my contract, there'd been the awkwardness with Carlos – the insecurities were queuing up.

As part of our contractual deal with MUTV, United's television channel, each player had to go into a studio now and again, to discuss the latest game – the match we'd just played. There was a rota of players, and my turn would come up two or three times a season. About a month after the injury, I think we were playing Spurs at home and I was supposed to cover it for MUTV. But the manager gave me a few days off.

He said, 'Why don't you go and get a bit of sun for yourself?'

I was off the crutches at this stage, and I think the boot – you wear it to keep the weight off the foot – might have been off by then, too. So I was pretty mobile. Coincidentally, my family had already booked a holiday in Dubai, before I got injured. So I just thought, 'The timing's perfect. I can join them.' They went out a couple of days before me; I flew out alone, and came back with them.

A swap was done. I think it was Gary Neville who covered the Spurs game for MUTV, instead of me. And the producers asked if I'd do the next game, away to Middlesbrough, when I got back from the holiday.

So I was in Dubai, getting a bit of sun and putting my foot in the salt water. I suppose I could have gone to Ireland, to Youghal, for that, but I was in Dubai; it's slightly more romantic. I knew the Middlesbrough game was on TV. I thought to myself, 'I want to watch the team anyway, and I'll be doing the analysis when I get back to Manchester.' So I decided to watch it in the hotel bar.

They lost 4–1 – disaster; United were awful. And that just happened to be the game I'd be doing!

Fucking hell.

Later on, I'd think, 'If I'd just done the Spurs game the week before', 'If I hadn't broken my foot', 'If I hadn't gone to Dubai', 'If United had beaten Middlesbrough.'

Ifs and ands, pots and pans.

I came back to Manchester from Dubai and MUTV people go, 'It's your turn.' And I had to do it. United were poor. And I was disappointed with the players. But it was MUTV; it's the in-house channel, propaganda for the club. All the top clubs have channels like it. If things are going bad, they get some positive news out there. Forget about that bad result, some young player's doing well out on loan. If we got knocked out of a cup, the next day they'd announce that some player had signed a new contract, or that share prices were up. That's the game – it's part of the game. So I did the interview. 'He was poor' – 'poor defending' – 'he's got to do better than that'. I was annoyed, I remember, but I wasn't edgy about it. The idea that I was in the studio, ranting and raving – no, it was quite calculated. The message was, we weren't good enough and we could do better.

I think it was the next day, I was told that the interview was being pulled and that they couldn't believe what I'd said.

I was, like, 'I don't think it was too bad.'

We'd lost 4–1; I couldn't say we'd played well. When we'd been beaten before, I'd often said, 'That wasn't good enough today.' Now, it was as if you weren't supposed to say that. It was all too delicate. I just thought everyone was overreacting.

But the news got into the media, and I knew it didn't look good for me. People were starting to say, 'Oh, they've had to pull this video.'

I'm pretty sure that someone at United leaked it. I'd insulted the team, I'd been disloyal. They were building a picture: I was this loose cannon, slagging off everybody. It was back-page head-lines, in all the papers. When it comes to Manchester United, everything is extremes. You win a game, you're the greatest; you lose a game, you're the world's worst. But this was so over the top it was untrue. I was looking at it, going, 'There's something going on here.'

It was even more intense in Manchester, where I live, because it was about Manchester United. I couldn't help thinking, 'This is going to end in disaster.' When I'd stepped out of line before, the PR people at United had always been good at managing it, giving it a bit of balance. But there was nobody giving me a dig-out this time.

I wasn't worried about the dressing room, because I think the players knew my form. But all sorts of stuff was coming out now – that I'd spoken about players' wages, for example – something that I would never do. Usually, when there was anything in the media about any of the players, or a member of the staff, we'd nip it in the bud by going, 'Listen, we're used to it, we're Man United, everything is going to be exaggerated.' It was par for the course. But this was getting a bit silly. And United had just been beaten by Lille in the Champions League, which didn't help the atmosphere. Or the manager's mood.

So, eventually, I got the players together in the dressing room and I said, 'Look, lads, I need to get this off my chest. You've seen all this stuff in the media. Just to let you know, lads, that it's fuckin' nonsense. I would never go into stuff about players' wages or people not trying. I might say a player had a bad game but—'

And they were all going, 'Yeah, yeah—' as I spoke. Not one of them had an issue – not one.

But at the back of my mind part of me was thinking, 'What *did* I say in the video? I might have said something pretty bad, for them to pull it.' And even now – today – people still say, 'This video had to be destroyed.' Like it was a nuclear weapon or some-thing. Did someone drive out to the countryside and bury it in the fuckin' ground? Or did a bomb-disposal unit come and explode it? It had to be destroyed!

Anyway, by now we were talking about the quality of our game, and how we'd taken our eyes off the ball a little bit; we'd had one or two bad results. It went on for about an hour. Instead of going out training, we ended up having this chat. All the players were getting involved. I've spoken to some of them about it since, and Ole Gunnar Solskjær, who's a man I have a lot of respect for, still talks about the conversation I started that morning, about how we needed to refocus, and how we shouldn't let ourselves be distracted by off-the-field stuff – boot sponsors, magazine interviews, too many media commitments. And Ole still reckons it was exactly what we'd needed. No ranting or raving, no finger pointing – nothing like that. And we spoke about training, too – 'Lads, we need to sharpen up. Remember what we're about. It's about what we do – football. Winning football matches.'

We'd been talking for quite a while by now, maybe an hour. So I went up to the manager's office to tell him why we weren't outside training.

He said, 'Well, I'm coming down.'

I knew from his reaction that he wasn't happy.

I went back down ahead of him, and I said to the lads, 'I'm not sure this was such a good idea.'

He stormed in and said, 'What's this all about?', and he asked me if I was going to apologise.

I said, 'Well, I've got nothing to apologise about.'

'What about the video?'

And I said, 'I think the video's fine.'

And he went, 'I'll tell you what. Up fuckin' stairs now, into my office. Everyone. Let's go and watch that fuckin' video.'

So I'm walking up the stairs – we're all walking up in our training kit, like a load of kids being called to the headmaster.

I'm walking up and I'm thinking, 'Here goes.' Because I'm still not 100 per cent sure what I'd said.

We watched the video, some lads standing, some sitting down. More than twenty international footballers. Scattered around this massive office. This was only a couple of years after Saipan. Talk about *déjà vu*; I'd been down this road before. I was getting used to it.

We watched, and I was still thinking, 'I could be the one in for the shock here. "Oh, by the way, lads, I forgot to mention that downstairs."'

But it ended, and I was very relieved because it tallied with what I'd told the players. There were no shocks or contradictions. Thank God.

So I went, 'Look, lads. Have any of you got a problem?'

They were all, 'No, no, no.'

I said, 'Fletch?' – to Darren Fletcher.

I'd said something about my wife tackling better than him, for one of the goals. But I could tell from his expression that he was fine with it; Fletch knew my form. The mood was still good between me and the players.

But Carlos and the manager were in the background, steam coming out their ears.

I said, 'Lads, I told you what I said. But we got beaten 4–1, you know.'

And they were all – every player – 'No, we're okay with it; yeah, we're comfortable enough with it.'

But the manager went, 'No, it's a disgrace – this fuckin' video!'

I said, 'None of the players have got a problem with it.'

With that, van der Sar, who'd been at the club a few months, put his hand up and said, 'Do you know, Roy, I just think you could've used a different tone.'

Edwin. Dutch international – six million caps.

So I said, 'Edwin, why don't you shut the fuck up? You've been at this club two minutes and you've done more interviews than I've done in my twelve years. It was MUTV – I had to do it.'

So he took that; he accepted it.

But then Carlos turned and said, 'You've not shown any loyalty to your team-mates.'

He was just on my right shoulder; how I didn't fuckin' hit him again— I was thinking, 'The villa in Portugal, not treating me well in training – and he just used the word "loyalty" to me.'

I said, 'Don't you talk to me about loyalty. Don't you fuckin' talk to me about loyalty, Carlos. You left this club after twelve months a few years ago for the Real Madrid job. Don't you dare question my loyalty. I had opportunities to go to Juventus and Bayern Munich. So don't you question me about loyalty. And, while we're at it, we spoke about training downstairs. And we were just on about mixing things up in training a bit.'

And he went, 'No, Roy, we need repetition – that's what we need. Repetition.'

And I said, 'Carlos, do you always make love to your wife in the same position?'

And I think he went, 'What – where is this going?'

I said, 'You change the position, don't you? Sometimes you have to mix training up a little bit. That's all I'm saying. That's coming from all the players. It's not a personal thing.'

I haven't a clue why I said that – and still don't.

But the manager went, 'That's enough of that. I've had enough of all this stuff.'

And I said, 'You as well, gaffer. We need fuckin' more from you.'

And I mentioned the horse deal as well. I can't justify everything I said that morning; I was just annoyed. The manager had wanted to get us involved in a syndicate, to buy a horse with him.

This was a few years before. He'd taken us up to some stables, on the way to Catterick, I think. We were all to put money into the syndicate – out of the players' pool. We used to earn extra money for MUTV appearances and other media work, and we'd put it into the pool. Christmas dos, trips to the horse racing – they were paid for from the pool. It was like a kitty, but a pretty big one. The whole thing had annoyed me at the time, that we would have put money into this syndicate but would only have got one-sixteenth between us. As it was, we never got involved in it.

I said to the gaffer, 'You wanted us to go into that syndicate years ago, and we'd only have got one-sixteenth. What was that all about?'

When I go off like that, when I let loose, I'm in the zone; it's like I'm somebody else. It was almost a relief – some sort of freedom. Consequences were the last thing on my mind. I wasn't a Manchester United player now, or a professional footballer. I was a human being, fighting my corner. Not one player interrupted, or tried to take the heat out of it. Maybe because they'd seen how I'd responded to Edwin. They were all in quiet shock, I think; they felt they shouldn't have been in the room – like we were neighbours arguing and they were looking over the wall at us, going, 'Next door are at it again.' It was unfortunate for them.

I said to the manager, 'We need a bit more, gaffer. We're slipping behind other teams.'

And he said, 'I've had enough of that', and I think he said, 'Shut up' – something like that.

I said, 'Well, I've had enough of this meeting anyway. I'm fucking off. I'm going out to train.'

And I left the office. I went down the stairs. I turned around, and I saw Mikaël Silvestre coming out, but he didn't follow me. Ole has since told me that when I left the room, the manager said, 'Well, what about that?'

76

According to Ole, Rio agreed with me, that they'd played poorly at Middlesbrough. All the players started talking, and Ole and Paul Scholes said they were leaving because they didn't want to talk about me when I wasn't there. I love that – that they showed me that bit of loyalty. When Ole got up to leave, he was told by the manager, 'Don't you follow him' – in no uncertain terms.

According to Ole, Carlos called him into his office the next morning and told him to apologise to the manager for leaving the room, or he'd be sacked.

I went out to training and eventually the rest of the players came down.

It was Saipan Mark 2. A heated discussion – nothing unusual in sport, and what should have been a private conversation – all out of control. There was probably no going back.

I was beginning to feel like a dead man walking.

I trained for a few days. Neither the manager nor Carlos was speaking to me. I was due to play in a reserve match, at home to West Brom, as part of my return from injury, and I was preparing for that.

In the meantime, the club had sent me a letter; they were fining me £5,000 for my MUTV interview. And I appealed it; I spoke to my solicitor, Michael Kennedy, and I asked him to write a letter back. I'd been fined before, and I'd never appealed. I just felt this time it was wrong. But I think that annoyed the manager. I think he thought I'd go, 'Okay, I'll take my five grand and we'll move on.'

The team sheet for the West Brom game went up but my name wasn't on it. I spoke to Rob Swire, the head physio, and I asked him, 'Why amn't I in the team for the reserve match?'

'Oh, the manager doesn't want you playing.'

So I went, '— all right.'

I went up to his office and I banged away at the door, and he went, 'Come in.'

What I loved more than anything else – and the manager would have known this – was playing. By not letting me play in the reserve match he was preventing my recovery. The atmosphere in the room wasn't good.

I said, 'I'm supposed to be playing in the reserves. My recovery, you know.'

And he said, 'No, you'd better speak to Michael Kennedy.'

It was Dave O'Leary who had put me in touch with Michael Kennedy when I was on my way to United, back in 1993. Michael did that first deal with United, and every other deal for me, in and out of football, for more than fifteen years.

'— oh,' I said, '— all right.'

I went down and got into my car and I rang Michael.

And he went, 'Yeah, I've just had a call. They want me up on Friday.'

I said, 'They're going to try and get rid of me.'

'But—'

'They're trying to fine me.'

'Yes, but that's not grounds for you moving on.'

'— anyway— We'll see.'

I met Michael at Manchester Airport on the Friday morning. It was 18 November.

He went, 'What's all this about, Roy?'

I just knew they were going to tell me it was time to move on. I was ready for it – but not prepared.

We drove to the training ground for the meeting, at about nine o'clock. The manager was there, in his office. David Gill, the chief executive, was there, too. I hadn't been expecting him.

I went, 'So, what's up?'

And the manager said, 'Look, Roy, I think we've come to the end.'

As simple as that.

And Michael was going, 'What?! What's this? I thought this was just about the fine!'

Michael is a very good mediator, and negotiator; they would be Michael's strengths. He has negotiated with top teams in Italy, and with Real Madrid. He has vast experience. If I had done anything really bad, I'd have been fined two weeks' wages, or even sacked. But a £5,000 fine was, in the bigger scale of things, nothing. So, from a £5,000 fine to what the manager had just said – Michael was nearly falling off his chair.

But I said to the manager, 'All right. Yeah, yeah. I agree with you.'

Then David Gill said, 'And while we're at it, we've prepared a statement.'

They had it all ready. It was another little hand grenade they threw at me. Not an hour later, or two hours, or after the severance negotiations – it was already written.

Usually, I'd guess, a player in my position would have been advised to say, 'All right, I'll go. How much will you give me?' I'll fight my corner for money, but it wasn't the first thing that sprang to mind now. I could easily have said to Michael, 'If Manchester United want me to go today, they fuckin' have to pay me.' My reputation was ruined; it was going to be in shreds. But I wasn't thinking about my reputation, or the PR side of things. I just thought, 'Yeah, he's right. It's over.'

David Gill had a copy of the statement, and Michael leaned across and took it. We were both reading it when David Gill said, 'By the way, Roy, you're also injured.'

And I went, 'David, I broke my foot. My foot – it's broken from playing for Man United.'

I suppose the thinking was, 'Let's try to get him out as quick as we can. Let's not drag this out till next week.' This was Manchester United, one of the biggest media companies in the world. They spent a fortune on the image. And I was reading, 'We'd like to thank Roy for his eleven and a half years at the club.'

But I'd been there twelve and a half years. And now I was thinking, 'The game is up – no problem with that. But fuckin' do it properly.'

I went, 'You've got eleven and a half years there.'

The two of them were looking at each other.

And I said, 'I've been here twelve and a half.'

'Oh, is it twelve and a half, Roy? Oh, I wasn't sure— Was it '93 you came in? I can't remember.'

'Yeah,' I said. 'The first year we won the Double.'

And David Gill said, 'Oh, right, we'll fix that.'

Michael was going, 'I need to discuss this with my client.'

David Gill said, 'Do you want five minutes together?'

And we said, 'All right.'

So they went out, the manager and David Gill, and left us alone.

I said, 'Come on, Michael, I've had enough of them – fuck'm. We've lost respect for each other.'

But Michael was going, 'What—? What are you talking about? I can't believe it. The contract— Your family—'

He was emotional about it; he was upset. Also, I was his client, and he was probably thinking, 'This isn't right, this isn't fair.'

They came back in, and David Gill asked, 'Is that enough time?'

I said, 'Yeah, yeah, yeah, I think you're right. We've come to the end. But I'm not sure about— Where do I stand on my contract? Can I play for another club straightaway?'

That was what I meant about being ready for this, but not

prepared. It was the worst thing I'd done – or not done. I'd known for a few days that they were going to try and get rid of me. I could have rung the PFA – the Professional Footballers' Association – and got legal advice. What were the consequences if my contract was ended? There was the transfer window, in January. This was November. Could I sign for another team, immediately, outside the transfer window? And if I signed, would I be allowed to play immediately? For all my experience and for all the good advice I'd given to people over the years, I hadn't taken heed of it myself.

I said to Ferguson, 'Can I play for somebody else?'

And he said, 'Yeah, you can. 'Cos we're tearing up your contract.'

The secretary's office was just across the corridor, and I thought – for just a second, 'Before we shake hands on anything, or before I walk out or storm out, I'll go across to find out where I stand contractually.'

But it had gone too far. Deep down, I didn't give a shit.

So I thought, 'All right— I'll get fixed up.'

I knew there'd be clubs in for me when the news got out.

I said, 'Yeah – I think we *have* come to the end.'

Michael still couldn't believe it.

I just thought, 'Fuckin' pricks—' and I stood up and went, 'Yeah. I'm off.'

I left Michael to it. I'd gone in there at about nine o'clock; I think I was in my car by a quarter to ten. Maybe it was my way of coping, getting out as quickly as I could. Was it a childish way of coping? Was it my 'I'd better get out of here before I fuckin' kill somebody' way of coping? I don't know. I didn't want to see the players – they'd all have been coming in by then. I didn't want to be saying my goodbyes.

So maybe it was just my immature way – or mature way – of dealing with it.

I got into my car and drove out of the training ground. I pulled over just outside and cried for a couple of minutes. I just thought, 'It's over.'

I drove home.

I kept thinking, 'We could have done this differently, surely.' All this trivial stuff could have been managed much better. Not just by me, but by the manager and the club. There was a picture being painted that I was some sort of head case. If you were on the outside looking in, you'd be going, 'Saipan, now United – he *is* a head case.'

I was thinking about my family in Ireland. I knew what Cork was like. The news would be all over the place. In ten minutes. My family in Cork are big United fans; the effect on them was going to be massive. You'd have thought they'd have been used to it after Saipan. But my parents – it was going to be torture for them. All that media intrusion again. Outside my house. Outside my parents' house. People going, 'Oh, right, he's gone off on one again.' And I remember thinking, too, while I was driving home, 'Ah, I've got the club car here – I'll have to give it back.'

It was an Audi A8 and I really liked it, and I was going, 'I have to fuckin' give the car back.'

If I'd known more about the consequences, if I'd known that I wouldn't be able to play again until January, I would have stayed. I'd asked the manager if I could play for another club. This was the man I'd worked for, for twelve and a half years. I'd like to think he'd have known his stuff, and I do think that he had a responsibility to know what he was letting me in for. Or, he could have said, 'Roy, I'm not sure. You'd better ring the PFA before you leave here today.' But he'd gone, 'Yeah, yeah – 'cos we've torn your contract.'

When I got home I rang the PFA and they said they'd look into it and they'd let me know after the weekend. That worried me – my head was spinning.

'Fuckin' hell, Roy,' I thought. 'That was another clever decision' – walking out without my position properly clarified. Not that it would have changed my mind; I think I'd have gone about it the same way.

I should have said, 'I'll train and Michael will do the negotiating. We'll see how it goes. And, in the meantime, I'll ring the PFA.'

I would have been a good pro, I wouldn't have been awkward. I'd have done my training. But I also thought, 'The manager knows me.' He might have said to David Gill, 'Show him that statement' – to get my back up. He knew my character as well as anybody.

The hours were going by. I was at home. Michael rang: 'Look, Roy, we're struggling here. They reckon there are cash-flow problems in this.'

Ferguson has said since that they honoured the contract. But they didn't. I lost a lot of money that day. I was on a million pounds' incentive if I played in 50 per cent of the season's games. I wouldn't be getting that now. They said they agreed a testimonial. But that had already been agreed months before. There was a confidentiality agreement, but I wasn't paid for that either. My silence cost them nothing. There was no benefit to me financially. They were going to pay my wages. But not in a lump sum, just normal wages. I'd have liked whatever money I was due up front, a lump sum, instead of still being on the wage bill till the end of the season. A clean break – that would have been good. But Michael was now talking about cash-flow problems, so I knew it wasn't going to happen.

THE SECOND HALF

I remember saying to Michael, 'Michael, I'm not fuckin' interested in the money side of it.'

He came to my house later that afternoon. He was as white as a ghost; he still couldn't believe it.

I said, 'Michael, it's for the best.'

And he went, 'Well, I believe you, Roy.'

I had to put up a front, in front of Michael and my wife and family. I was the tough guy; I had to play the role that day – even though I'd been crying in the car a few hours earlier. I was trying to hide my hurt from my wife, although she'd have seen right through me.

There was also an element of relief; it was almost over.

I said, 'No, it's for the best.'

And, actually, it *was* for the best. Whatever happened or was said afterwards, the timing was right. We'd come to the end.

But I still don't know exactly why it happened. If the manager thought I'd been out of line with the villa incident, or the interview, he surely could have said to me, quietly, 'Look, Roy, be careful – you stepped out of line there, boy. You're out of order.' He'd done that before, when I'd been drinking or I'd been arrested, or after I'd committed a bad tackle, or when I'd chased the referee Andy D'Urso, There'd been times when he'd take me aside and say, 'Hey, you fuckin' crossed the line there', and he'd have a go at me. I was his captain.

I think back to Portugal and I wonder 'Was it that?' The whole thing might have been a bit awkward, but I'd been looking after my family. It was no big deal. It was only a villa, the house we were going to stay in. As team captain, I'd always pushed for team spirit. Family get-togethers, the Christmas dos, match tickets for families – I'd sorted all that. Myself and my wife would go out of our way for any of the players, particularly the foreign lads.

Then there was pre-season, and Carlos not wanting me back

84

after I'd hurt my hamstring, and throwing the bib at me. Was I missing something? Did Carlos see me as some sort of threat? And, if so, did the manager feel he had to back him up? Carlos had been away at Real Madrid for a year, and then he came back. He might have felt that I was a bigger presence in the dressing room. But I didn't go looking for that status; it comes with games, appearances, trophies. It just comes your way. But when Carlos came back, he might have felt, 'Mmm, what's this guy about?' Even though I'd worked with him previously and got on well with him. But I was intelligent enough to know that if the manager felt that this was between myself and Carlos, then he'd have to back his number two.

I knew when I got into the argument with Carlos, when I said, 'Do you make love to your wife in the same position?', I knew he wouldn't like it. To be honest, I didn't use the words 'make love'; I think I said, 'When you shag your missis, do you change positions?' I think some of the lads were going, 'Fuckin' hell, where did that one come from?' In the heat of an argument, you go, 'Here, you fucker—', and say things you might not normally say. And why did I bring up the horse syndicate with the manager? I'd like to know. But I wasn't going to sit back and be passive. You know – you fight your corner.

I've thought since that I should have insisted they show the interview on MUTV; I should have checked if I could do that, legally: 'Show the video. 'Cos you're tarnishing me. You're making out I've said something really bad. And I haven't.'

Apparently, I described Kieran Richardson as a lazy defender. But Kieran Richardson isn't a defender. Some players, out of position, defend lazily; they don't get back quickly enough. So the comment was taken out of context. I signed Kieran later, when I managed Sunderland. I was critical of Darren Fletcher. Apparently, I doubted why people in Scotland raved about him.

I might have said something like that, almost tongue in cheek. Sometimes you're rated more highly in your own country than you are in any other. I always rated Darren and I used to push him. I think the lads I was really critical of were the ones I rated. 'I think you've got a chance of being a top player – I think you could do better.' There's always a compliment in that. The players I didn't want to speak about, they were the ones who should have been worried. I went to Old Trafford not long ago; United played Liverpool in the League Cup. The first player to walk over and shake my hand was Darren Fletcher. Darren knew that I would have backed him to the hilt.

A lot of the comments I've been expected to defend over the years, I'm not actually sure I made them. I'm supposed to have said about Rio Ferdinand, something like, 'Just because you're paid a hundred thousand pounds a week and play well for England doesn't make you a top player.' But I don't believe I ever said that. I don't think I've ever mentioned a player's wages in any interview, in my life. And, again, when we had that chat in the dressing room, Rio and Fletch were there, and they were the two I was supposed to have hammered. Fletch took me the way he knows me. And that was – I meant well. And remember, I said it all in an in-house studio. Could they not have just edited the stuff they objected to? If they thought it was so bad that it had to be destroyed, why were they fining me £5,000? Why weren't they going, 'A week's wages for that. You're bringing the club into disrepute.' Or, why didn't they just say quietly, 'We're not going to use it'? I think the video – the interview – was just an excuse.

It's been said that I brought up the Rock of Gibraltar affair, the manager's legal dispute with the horsey crowd – Magnier and McManus – at the same time that he showed the video to the other players in his office. But I didn't. I'd had that conversation a couple of months earlier, in private. Somebody I met in

Ireland had told me to tell him, 'You are not going to win this.' I mentioned it to him. And I told him I didn't think it was good for the club, the manager in a legal dispute with shareholders. I felt I was entitled to say that. He was just a mascot for them. Walking around with this Rock of Gibraltar – 'Look at me, how big I am' – and he didn't even own the bloody thing.

I'd done an interview on MUTV earlier in the season, and I'd mentioned that, come the end of the season, it might be time for me to leave. This was after the Portugal incident. That might have annoyed the manager. He'd said before that when players got to thirty-two or thirty-three he'd discuss their contracts at the end of the season. He'd said it in a radio interview; I remember I was driving when I heard it. That irritated me a small bit. Because other older players had signed deals well before the end of the season, in the past. I felt as if I was back on trial.

As for the idea that I thought of myself as the manager, it was nonsense. I knew my boundaries. I came into work every day and I did my best, and that included pushing the players. That was my job. Leading by example. I think it was one of my strengths. Pushing people, and patting them on the back. I was the captain; I managed the dressing room. It was the job. When you become a manager and you speak to other managers, one of the first things they complain about is lack of that leadership out there among players. Nobody's taking the lead roles. They want the manager and the coach to play the game for them. I didn't. We had a good dressing room and we sorted out the problems; we tried to make the manager's job easier for him. I worked with top players – Ronaldo, Scholes; Laurent Blanc, when he came to United. I knew how to treat these men, how to speak to Laurent Blanc, a player I had massive respect for. Or Darren Fletcher, a young Scottish lad; or John O'Shea, a young lad from Ireland. I knew how to speak to people, in different ways. The Dutch boys – the arrogance of some of them. But I got on well with them. And we were winning trophies. There were good characters in that dressing room. Ferguson was clever enough to know that, whenever I was gone, there'd be enough senior players and leaders still there; it wasn't going to crumble.

Chelsea were strong at the time. They'd won the Premiership the season before, 2004–5, and that was going to continue; they were looking even stronger. Ferguson might have been looking at the team, and thinking it needed a drastic change. He was rising to Mourinho's challenge. But when you're a player and a team like Chelsea come on the scene and – this is a personal point of view – you're thirty-three or four, you start to think, 'I'm past it. I'm not like the player I was.' But Ferguson wasn't an ageing player. He'd just have seen it as a challenge.

Things were changing. Rio had come to the club, and Ronaldo and Rooney – all decent lads, top players. But the game was changing slightly as well. I would make a point about the lads being on their phones and their PlayStations: 'Come on, lads. This is a dressing room, you know.' Maybe that was me being an old fuddy-duddy – I don't know. They were younger than me. I knew I wouldn't miss the players that much when I left. I'd miss them, but there was no one in there who'd make me go, 'Oh, he was one of my best pals.' Those men had left. It's what happens with football clubs. Different characters come and go.

My leaving the club, the way I look at it now, it was definitely for the benefit of Manchester United. If the manager and Carlos felt that I was up to whatever they thought I was up to, if there was that awkwardness, then it was best for everybody that I go. And let me suffer the consequences. Let me cry in my car for two minutes. If it benefited Manchester United, so be it. I think it was for the best. Not from a football point of view, the playing side of it; I could still have contributed. I could look after my body. They knew my body as well as anybody; I would have played fewer games. But from a club point of view, if they felt I had crossed that line – and, again, I don't think I did – then it was for the best; forget about payments and statements.

When the paperwork had finally been sorted and I'd given back the car – this was three months after the last meeting, so I got an extra three months out of it; I drove some fuckin' miles in that car; every little victory is vital – I went to see the manager and Carlos, and I apologised.

But now I kind of wish I hadn't.

Sometimes you feel a justified anger; sometimes you feel you've done something wrong. I apologised: 'Listen—' But afterwards, I was thinking, 'I'm not sure why I fuckin' apologised.' I just wanted to do the right thing. I was apologising for what had happened – that it had happened. But I wasn't apologising for my behaviour or stance. There's a difference. I had nothing to apologise for.

There probably isn't a good way to leave a club. But is it always the player's fault? It can't be. A lot of people left United on bad terms. Good players – Beckham, Van Nistelrooy, plenty of other names. Deep down, I might have accepted that it was not going to end well. Whether it was the video, or if we didn't have any trophies at the end of the season, or if my contract wasn't renewed – it was coming to an end. I was getting older. But I think the best way the manager could have dealt with it, given his experience and man-management skills, would have been to take me aside, and go, 'Listen, Roy, we're having issues with you. But keep your head down, play a few games and, come the end of the season, we'll say that it was best for you to go.' Not in mid-November, when I'd been injured, and I couldn't play for another team until January. It wouldn't have been champagne and 'Ah, he's leaving', but they would have shown a bit of class. But they didn't show it.

I loved everything about United. From the day I signed for them. I just think it suited my personality. I loved the team, I loved the way we played. I liked all the lads, I liked the training, I liked the way we travelled. I liked the pressure. I liked the United fans. I thought they were pretty switched on, even when we lost – they'd be going mad, but a nice mad. I liked the demands. The kit. The badge. The history. I liked living in Manchester. I got on well with the manager. There was trust there – a big word in football. I liked the staff. Everyone at the training ground. The groundsmen. The different coaches over the years. Brian Kidd. Jim Ryan. Steve McClaren. Walter Smith. Carlos Queiroz. Micky Phelan. And winning – I enjoyed the winning.

I still have that soft spot for United, and thank God I do. I took my son to the Champions League final, between Bayern and Dortmund, at Wembley, in 2013. He was going on about different teams, and I asked him, 'Which team do you support?'

He said, 'United.'

He would have known I still had that little bit of resentment.

So I said, 'Why do you support United?'

And he said, 'Well, I was born in Manchester and I'm not going to support City, am I?'

I said, 'Okay.'

That was a good enough reason. And I thought to myself, 'I'd better get us some season tickets.'

We went to see them recently, and I was going, 'Come on—!'

Fuckin' hell – come on.

I want them to do well.

When I moved to Celtic I used to get an early flight up to Edinburgh or Glasgow, and I'd hire a car and drive from there to the training ground. I'd stay a couple of days up there. One morning, a taxi driver picked me up, to bring me from my house to Manchester Airport. I got into the taxi at about six. My flight was at seven. In the middle of winter. And the taxi driver asked me, 'Do you miss being at United?'

It was six in the fuckin' morning; it was freezing – black outside. I looked at him and I went, 'What do you think?'

We laughed.

The tackle on Håland in a match against Manchester City. Was I going around for years thinking, 'I'm going to get him, I'm going to get him'? No. 21 April 2001. (Mirrorpix)

Man United playing against Sporting Lisbon. I saw how good Ronaldo was that day. 6 August 2003. (VI/PA)

I was in the dressing room when Ferguson kicked the boot. Beckham had to have stitches. (Martin Rickett/PA Archive)

Above left Alex Ferguson consoling me
after I came off injured. Charlton Athletic
v. Manchester United, 13 September 2003.
(Andrew Cowie / Colorsport)

Left Against Leicester, 27 September 2003.
I didn't score as many goals as I used to.
My role in the team was changing.
(Adrian Dennis / AFP / Getty)

Above With Ferguson after winning the
FA Cup match between United and Arsenal
at Villa Park, 3 April 2004. (John Peters /
Manchester United / Getty)

Right Peter Schmeichel. He would come
out shouting at players, and I felt sometimes
that he was playing up to the crowd.
(Mark Thompson / Allsport / Getty)

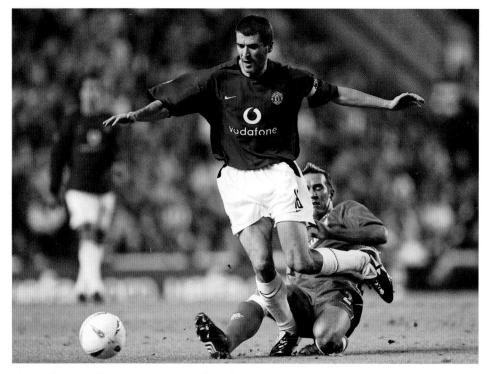

Playing for United against Rangers in the Champions League – 22 October 2003. It was brilliant. (Alex Livesey/Getty)

Diego Forlán playing for United. I remember when Diego Forlán came in, and it wasn't quite happening for him. If a player tried – and Diego did – we'd drag him with us; we'd try and help him. (Manchester United/Getty)

Against Millwall, 22 May 2004. It was the only time I've played in a Cup Final that I knew we were going to win. (John Peters/Manchester United/Getty)

We wore replicas of Jimmy Davis's top when we were going up to collect the trophy and our medals. (Action/Darren Walsh)

Playing again for Ireland, against Romania – 27 May 2004. It was good to be back.
(Reuters/Paul McErlane)

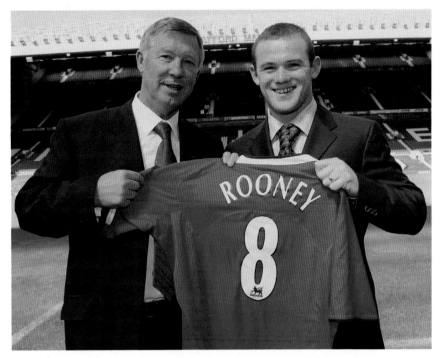

Rooney joined Man United in August 2004. When he walked into the dressing room, it lifted everybody. (John Peters/Manchester United/Getty)

I went on a new diet. Typical me, I went too far. I missed the game against Arsenal. I was well enough to go on as sub in the next league game, against Portsmouth – 30 October 2004. (Reuters/Kieran Doherty/ND Reyters/Action)

Arsenal v. Man United, 1 February 2005. The tunnel incident with Patrick Vieira was all part of the TV drama. I'd lost it; but I wasn't zoning out. (Rex/Graham Chadwick/Daily Mail)

Southampton were relegated after we beat them 2–1 on 15 May 2005. There was a bit of tension after the game, a few Southampton fans hanging around. It seemed it was all right for them to abuse me but I wasn't allowed to say anything back. (Paul Ellis/AP/PA)

Game against Liverpool, 18 September 2005. Gerrard's tackle resulted in my broken foot. (John Peters/Manchester United/Getty)

FIVE

I lay on the bed. And my hip – I've never known pain like it. My hip was fuckin' screaming.

I was going for bike rides around where I live, trying to keep fit. I'd no one to train with, in terms of kicking a ball and twisting and turning – the type of work I needed after being out injured. I was even kicking a ball against my garage door. Inside the garage, striking the ball against the door. It was like being a kid again, back in Mayfield, kicking a ball against a wall. I'd a punchbag in the garage, too, and a skipping rope – I'd do some skipping. And I'd do a few press-ups. It was basic boxing training – anything to make me feel a bit better.

Michael Kennedy started ringing me; there were clubs interested in talking. I'd have choices. But, instead of enjoying it all, I was thinking, 'I'm starting all over again. Back to the beginning.'

But another part of me thought, 'A new dressing room; I'll learn something a bit different.'

But I wished I'd had a few games under my belt. I hadn't played for five or six weeks, and I couldn't play again until January. It wasn't ideal. People at a new club might think, 'We're signing fuckin' Maradona', because of what I'd done at United.

Real Madrid offered me a year and a half year deal. Everton, on my doorstep, wanted me to go to them. I met their manager, David Moyes, at his house, and I was impressed by what he said. Bolton – also on my doorstep; I met Sam Allardyce, too. But I went to Celtic for fifteen grand basic a week. I know it was a lot of money but I'd been earning a lot more. It was a massive pay cut.

When a club is interested in you, the manager generally sells it to you: 'Listen, we'd love to have you here.' But I met Gordon Strachan, the Celtic manager, in London – I met him in the majority shareholder Dermot Desmond's house – and Gordon told me, 'I'm not really too worried if you sign for us or not. We're okay without you.'

So I said to myself, 'Fuck him, I'm signing.'

I think it *was* one of the reasons I signed for them – to prove Gordon wrong. To be fair to Gordon, they were doing well in the League and he already had Neil Lennon playing in my position, and Stiliyan Petrov; he had a good team. So I wasn't sitting back, shocked, going, 'Show me the love.' I thought, 'All right. That's the game.' He was letting me know they weren't desperate for me; he was being a bit coy and I was fine with that. But there was a bit of defiance there, too; like, 'You might be fifteen points clear but, if I join, you might go twenty points clear. You might even need me next year in Europe.'

Michael had been over to Madrid and he'd negotiated a deal with Real. They spoke to me, too. Butragueño rang me. Emilio Butragueño – what a player he was. Michael had given me a heads-up that Butragueño would be phoning, so I took my mobile everywhere with me. And – how's your luck – he rang me when I was sitting on the toilet. He said, 'Look, Roy, we'll be glad to have you.' The club's board just had to sanction the deal; it was standard procedure.

I was going, '— okay', hesitating.

Michael was going, 'What are you doing, Roy?'

Then Real needed time to rubber-stamp the deal – this was a few weeks before Christmas – and I just ran out of patience.

I should have appreciated Real's offer more. It was the most attractive challenge in front of me, but I didn't accept it. With hindsight, I should have said to myself, 'Go. Go to Spain, live there for a year and a half, learn a different language, learn the culture. You might end up loving it. You might even stay there.'

I took a negative approach, I think, instead of saying, 'This is amazing, what a chance for me.' It could have been great for my kids. The weather and the training might have given me another lease of life, another two years of playing; I might have picked up new techniques for my stretching. But instead – as usual – I was looking at what might go wrong. 'Hindsight' is a fucker of a word. At the time, it felt like the right decision.

I didn't want to move to Spain. As much as anything else, it was fear that decided me – fear of the unknown. And I threw excuses in front of me – family, language, the kids' education. I could imagine myself going to Madrid, and into the dressing room. I'd be starting all over again, and I was in no mood to be doing that. I'd had a tough career. Physically, I was struggling.

It's no good playing for a club; or, it's not just about playing for them. It's about having an effect on the club, having a big influence. That was one of my concerns when I left United.

I was thirty-four, an experienced player. Real Madrid might just have wanted someone to do a job, sit in the middle of the park for a few games. But I wanted to go in and have an effect on a team. Yes, it was Real Madrid but, to me, football is still the same; it doesn't matter about the level. Would I go back to Cobh Ramblers next week? No, because I wouldn't be able to affect the team. When I hear people say, 'I played for United', or 'I played for Sheffield Wednesday'; lots of men have played for these clubs, but it's about affecting them. Affecting their history. Having an impact. Some of the top players can do that. Rooney, Ronaldo, Messi. Or Cantona and, at Forest, Stuart Pearce – all top players who had an effect, in their different ways. I could affect games with my presence, by breaking play up, imposing myself, even in the tunnel, before we went on to the pitch. But I was thirty-four, and I played a hard, physical game. I'd watched older players going to new clubs and it hadn't worked out.

Actually, it wasn't really about which club I should go to. Forget about Madrid, Everton, Celtic, Barcelona, Inter Milan and the reasons I should or shouldn't have gone to any of them. The fact is, the morning I left United I lost the love for the game a little bit. I could have had every club in the world ringing me but it wouldn't have given me that buzz, that satisfaction, that 'Here we go'.

I thought I could make a bigger impact at Celtic than I would have at Everton or Madrid. To be honest, I thought it might be a bit easier at Celtic. I knew they would dominate a lot of matches. 'I'll go up to Celtic, and I'll maybe do a job for a year, a year and a half.'

But when I arrived, I still felt like I was starting all over again. Trying to prove people wrong.

I signed for Celtic on 15 December, although I couldn't play until January. The press conference was chaotic the day I signed. I felt like putting a dampener on it. 'Listen, lads, I am thirty-four, my hip's hanging off.'

Outside Celtic Park, with the scarf over my head, for the photographs. Hundreds of fans on the steps of the stadium. They were really good to me. They gave me a great welcome – everybody at the club. And it was nice to get the Celtic kit on. I was glad to be there. They were letting me get back to what I was about, playing football. And Gordon Strachan and his staff, Garry Pendrey, and, of course, Tommy Burns – there was a very good atmosphere, good banter. Tommy was a really good guy, God rest his soul. If I'd gone to Madrid, I would never have met Tommy. John Clark, the kit man, was one of the Lisbon Lions; he was part of the team that won the European Cup in 1967. The kit man is vital; he's almost the hub of everything, a link to everybody. He has to be good-humoured and upbeat. You have to be glad to see the kit man in the morning. He reflects the club, in a sense. I think Clarkie got a bigger buzz out of me signing for Celtic than anybody else at the club; he appreciated what I'd done in the game. He couldn't do enough for me.

I met great people up at Celtic.

Their training, particularly their warm-ups – it was all about rotational stuff, movement of the hips. First and foremost, there was always a ball. If there were sixteen players, there'd be eight serving the ball to eight players in the middle. You'd always be working on the ball, and your recovery was when you were the server; you'd be throwing the ball for somebody in the middle. It was all about flicking the ball back, with the outside of your foot or your instep. All rotational stuff. The stressful part for me was flicking the ball back – and that was only the warm-up.

After the warm-up, I felt like going in. I was thinking, 'That's me done. I'm struggling.' But I actually liked it, getting a feel for the ball. And there was a bit of banter thrown in, because some lads couldn't do it. So I enjoyed all that – but my hip didn't. I hadn't trained properly, with a ball and other players, in more than two months. Knocking a ball against a garage door is no substitute. We trained for an hour and a quarter or an hour and a half. I didn't feel too bad immediately afterwards; it was all new – I had that extra bit of energy.

I got back to my hotel in Edinburgh. People had advised me

to stay in Edinburgh – 'Live in Edinburgh, keep away from all the hassle.' Rangers fans, even Celtic fans. It made sense; I'd have more privacy. But, really, I should have stayed in Glasgow. (Later on, I rented a small flat in the West End of Glasgow, and it was fine.) But anyway, I drove back to the hotel; it was about an hour's drive from Glasgow. Lovely hotel – lovely suite.

I lay on the bed. And my hip – I've never known pain like it. My hip was fuckin' screaming. Just from the warm-up, from the training. It was all that movement; I hadn't moved properly in months. I hadn't been twisting, holding other players off. And it wasn't as if I could ease myself back to fitness. I'd be going back on the pitch in two weeks; I was going to be thrown straight into a game.

I lay there, thinking, 'I don't want to go back. But I need to – I have to.' I was an experienced professional, I'd played more than six hundred games; I could deal with anything.

My hip was screaming. Not aching – screaming. 'What have you done?'

I couldn't budge. I thought to myself, 'You should have retired. You should have just packed it in.'

But I couldn't leave after my first day. Imagine how that would have looked. Celtic fans, with their scarves and jerseys. 'No, I've got to go to work.' Could I go in and tell them that my hip was at me? Would it be better tomorrow? I'd have a forty-five-minute drive the next morning, maybe an hour, back to the training ground. 'I'd better leave a bit earlier – I'll hardly be able to drive.'

It was my own fault. No one had forced me to stay in Edinburgh.

But the hip – fuckin' hell. I should have just packed it in. I should have been braver. Sometimes you have to be courageous enough to say no. An Irish friend of mine once told me, ' "No" is a sentence.' One of my strengths earlier in my career had been my ability to say no to people. I'd be very clear about not over-doing things, and knowing the limits of my job.

Then there's the shame. I was under contract. People had bought jerseys with my name on them. I didn't want to let anyone down. And the feeling that I wouldn't even be able to play. Not long before – less than a year ago – I'd been in the Highbury tunnel, imposing myself on the game before it had even started. Now I was lying on a hotel bed, wondering if I could get through training.

I had to go in the next day. Of course, I had. It was my job. I needed to train. I had that game coming up in a couple of weeks.

My attitude, throughout my career had been: you train how you play. I should have adapted. I should have taken it easy in training. I wasn't going to win plaudits for training on Tuesday; I'd get them if I played well on Saturday. I don't think I felt old, in football terms, but, physically, I was. My body was old. But I was new in the dressing room and I wanted to impress; you have to. The player's job, every day at training, is to impress the manager and his coaching staff. Gordon had never seen me train before. Tommy Burns had never seen me train. They'd seen me play, but they hadn't seen me train.

The training didn't get any easier. Before he took charge of Celtic the teams Gordon had managed had always been up against it. Southampton, Coventry – always fighting for survival. His teams were always hard-working, and his training was designed around that. I liked it. I just wished that I could have coped with it better.

You'd get changed at Celtic Park, and you'd get in your car and drive to the training ground up the road. It's different now, but this was when I played. The biggest challenge was – whose car were we going in. We'd be sitting in the dressing room.

'Whose turn is it?"

Because after training you'd have to drive back and nine times out of ten the rain was pissing down, so a gang of players would be getting into your car, covered in muck.

I enjoyed that, the bit of banter.

'Listen, lads, I've a Bentley. Nobody's getting into it with their fuckin' boots on.'

I got to know the lads in the car. I'd go with Dion Dublin, or Petrov. We'd only be in the car for five minutes, but we'd have the crack. I had the United car for the first few weeks, so I invited everyone into the back of it, boots as well.

I ended up leasing a Golf – to keep my own car clean, but mostly so I could get around discreetly in Glasgow.

At around that time I was asked by somebody in Celtic's administration if I'd mind not being paid until after January, because I wouldn't actually be playing until then.

I said, 'But I've signed my contract, and I'm training, and you're selling jerseys in the shop. I want my wages from when I signed.'

The glamour of it – the fuckin' glamour of it.

Michael had begged me not to sign for Celtic. He wasn't happy with the negotiations, or their 'take it or leave it' approach. But I still think that if I hadn't signed for Celtic I would have regretted it. They'd offered me the least money of any of the clubs. I read somewhere that I went to Celtic for forty or fifty thousand a week, but it was fifteen basic they offered me. I wasn't motivated by the money – or, just the money. I think there might have been a bit of guilt about that, when I left United – the amount I'd been earning there, and earning so much for something I loved doing anyway.

I'd said once or twice in interviews over the years, 'I'd like to play for Celtic one day.' I'd said it casually but now I felt I couldn't go back on my word. And I wanted to play against Rangers, in an

Old Firm game. For the atmosphere, the buzz – the experience. I'd played for United against Rangers, and it was electric. I remember thinking, 'If it's as good as this when it's Rangers against United, what must it be like when it's against Celtic?' I'd been up to see Celtic play Rangers several times, at Ibrox, too. They were massive games. Celtic were going to play in my testimonial at United the following May; it had already been agreed before I'd left United. So I wondered, 'If I don't sign for Celtic, will that be awkward?' But, more than any other consideration, I just thought, 'I want to treat myself here. I'm going to go where I want to go, and fuck the money.' I wouldn't have called it a dream, but I'd always liked Celtic. And the Irish connection would have been in the back of my mind; I felt a bit of loyalty to them. Usually, when you're making a decision about your career, you consider everything – the challenge, family, location. But this decision was a purely selfish one. I just wanted to play for Glasgow Celtic. Celtic is a special club.

My first game was against Clyde, away, in the third round of the Scottish Cup. We were beaten 2–1. It was a nightmare. I wasn't happy with my own game. I did okay, but okay wasn't enough. After the game – the disappointment. As I was taking my jersey off, I noticed the Nike tag was still on it. When I got on the bus, John Hartson, a really good guy, was already sitting there and he was eating a packet of crisps – with a fizzy drink. I said to myself, 'Welcome to hell.'

We went back on the bus to Celtic Park. A lot of fans were waiting, having a right go at Gordon and some of the players as we got off the bus. Being knocked out of the Cup by Clyde – it was a massive shock. But Tommy Burns – I take my hat off to him – stood on the steps and had a go at the Celtic fans; some of those lads were ready for a bit of action.

'You're not Celtic fans,' he said. 'You've got to get behind the team.'

I remember thinking, 'This is a good start.'

My first game, and already the fans were up in arms and one of the staff was on the steps of Celtic Park, having to defend the manager. So that was a nice, gentle introduction.

My first Old Firm game was at Ibrox, and we won 1–0. It was brilliant. It lived up to all of my expectations, probably because we won. 'Magic' Żurawski, a Polish lad, scored the goal. The start of my Celtic career hadn't been great – losing at Clyde, and angry fans. But then, not long after, we go and win at Rangers, and I'm thinking, 'This is what it's all about.'

The atmosphere was brilliant, fuckin' electric. The hatred – I enjoyed all that. I got a yellow card for a foul on Pršo and they were baying for a red card. Physically, I must have felt good. I was Man of the Match, and that was a little moment of satisfaction, another tiny victory. The dressing room afterwards was great. Again, it's what football is all about.

But, at this stage, I was taking painkillers before every match. An injection in the bum – Diclofenac, or Voltarol. The cause of the pain was a labral tear of the hip, and I understood that playing on could worsen the tear. I was taking an injection before the game and one at half-time, just to get through. And you do get through, but the consequences arrive the day after, and the next day. I'd be in bits. Mind you, I'd have been in bits, anyway; the Rangers game was a physically tough one.

I doubt if painkilling injections are as regular now as they used to be, because of the advances in sports science. I don't think players would put up with it.

The painkillers just hide the pain, and they wear off. So there was the double whammy: I was going to suffer anyway, and then the hip would be at me, too. I could justify taking the painkillers for the game against Rangers because I knew it was going to be tough. But now I was taking them for every game. That was when I thought, 'This is not good.'

I'd been taking them in England, but only for the big games – Arsenal, City – when I knew I'd have to be physically at my best. Now, common sense was telling me that my days were numbered.

We played Hibernian a few weeks later, away, at Easter Road, and I remember feeling a bit caught out. I'd done my homework on Rangers but I didn't know much about Hibs. I remember thinking, 'Fuck it, this is hard.' They had a couple of lads in the middle of the park. Kevin Thomson was one of them; he went on to Rangers and Middlesbrough. They were both excellent. We won, but it was a bit of a shock. I thought that I should have been dominating these two, or any Hibs players. But my mind was lying; they had very good players.

We won the League Cup in March, against Dunfermline. But I went off injured. Running around like a madman, I tore my hamstring, making a forward run. We won, but I didn't really feel involved in the celebrations. I was embarrassed.

I'd come on as a sub in the semi-final in the last minute of the second half; I played for about ninety seconds. It wasn't a great experience, but I was coming back from injury – another one. It led to my only real disagreement with Gordon Strachan. After most games Gordon would let me go home to Manchester to do my recovery. But he'd organised a practice game for the next day. I was still getting my fitness up, and I think Stiliyan Petrov was also coming back from an injury, so he'd organised this game, eleven v. eleven.

I said, 'I usually head straight home after a game.'

He said, 'I'd like you to play in the game.'

I could see why he wanted that. But then he said he needed to see what I could do.

And I said, 'Have you not seen me play six hundred and odd games down in England?'

And he said, 'No, no – I just need to see you.'

I stayed over and played the next day and, actually, I enjoyed playing the practice game. But that was where my career was now, playing practice games, showing the manager what I could do.

We beat Hearts at Celtic Park in early April, and won the League title. I was injured that day. I remember going into the dressing room. It was hard to join in the celebrations. I hadn't played enough.

I won League and League Cup medals with Celtic, but I never really contributed. Celtic won the League, but they were about fifteen points clear when I signed for them. I got Man of the Match away at Rangers and that pleased me, a little bit.

I look back at my time there and I'm a bit embarrassed by it. I didn't play too often – twelve or thirteen games, I think. I was on the bench four or five times. I tore my hamstring twice. And the reason you get injured a lot is your body's not right. I wasn't fit. My hip. My strides – I was trying too hard to impress. I was trying to play like a twenty-one-year-old – 'Look what a player you've signed.' I was in cuckooland.

I would have been a bit cleverer if I'd still been at United. I would have been thinking, 'I've earned my stripes here. I know my position. I don't have to be running around like a teenager.' But at Celtic, I thought, 'They've signed me, the fans all think they have a top player.'

I think I was a top player, but I hadn't sprinted in years. At United, I just read the game and was in the right positions. At Celtic, I was going, 'I'd better start getting the odd goal here, to impress them.' A childish attitude – stupid.

Why didn't I go to Everton? I would have regretted not going to Celtic, and I couldn't go to both. But Everton would have been good. I spoke to Phil Neville, who'd moved there earlier in the season. I knew that there were good fitness people there who could have helped me. I liked David Moyes, their manager. The chairman, Bill Kenwright, was very good with Michael in the negotiations. They offered me a lot more than Celtic were paying me. But I think I might have found it hard playing for another English team. Which is stupid, I suppose, because it's business. Although I would never summarise my years at United as business. It wasn't business to me.

Everton might have given me another lease of life; I might have had two or three more years there. The system they played would have suited me. I would have been a proper sitting midfielder.

It doesn't keep me awake at night.

And I'm not knocking Celtic; it's a brilliant club. I've no regrets. Even though it didn't work out. I go up to Celtic quite a bit, and I enjoy it as much as anything. I should be embarrassed because I hardly kicked a ball for them. It's almost like a family up there. 'You played for us; you're one of us.' I feel lucky to have played for Celtic.

Maybe I was just putting off the inevitable decision. I was frightened of saying to myself, 'I've retired.'

My testimonial was on 9 May 2006. A player's testimonial can be very rewarding financially. But I think it's tradition that makes it such a big day. You're thanking the fans and they're thanking you. It was a chance for me to say goodbye to the United fans – a huge incentive for me.

I felt a bit bad going to Old Trafford with Celtic. I was thinking, 'I've only been with them two minutes.'

An important part of the testimonial is the presents, for both teams. The Celtic lads were at me – I'd better buy them something good. If the player who's having the testimonial doesn't give the teams decent presents he'll be criticised – privately – for the rest of his life. So, at the end of the season I was wondering about my career and my future, but the pressure I was really feeling was coming from the Celtic lads, and having to choose a present for them. I ended up buying fifty Omega watches, twenty-five for each dressing room. They were good watches, so I reckoned they wouldn't be slagging me off.

Celtic love going down to United; they like playing against English opposition. A testimonial is a friendly game; it's a celebration, but they still want to win. And the Celtic fans love it, too.

The atmosphere was brilliant that night, very special. I had my family with me. It was nice to be back.

It had been arranged that I'd play a half for each team. I played for Celtic in the first half. I went into the Celtic players at half-time and I told them, 'Lads, I'm going to play with them in the second half.'

There was plenty of banter with the Celtic players. I always enjoyed the crack in the Celtic dressing room. Stiliyan Petrov is a good lad; Neil Lennon and John Hartson – all decent lads. And Dion Dublin. Myself and Dion went out for a few meals together, and I generally ended up paying for them. The testimonial just about covered my food bill.

So I went back into the United dressing room. The kit man, Albert, was there – 'All right, Roy?' – and plenty of banter from the lads. I put the United kit on. I felt ten feet tall. It was like I was putting an old jumper on. 'This is my kit.' I didn't want the feeling; I was fighting it. But I couldn't help myself. I remember thinking, 'We'd fuckin' better win.' I was with United.

We won 1–0; Ronaldo scored, and I thought, 'Now I've got to

go back into the Celtic dressing room and take more stick from them.'

But it was so frustrating.

I kept wondering, 'Why did it all go pear-shaped?'

That self-destruct button.

Anger has always been part of my personality. I don't see it as a bad thing or a bad word. My reputation has always been, 'Oh, he's angry, he's always grumpy', and I probably played up to it when I was a player. But a lot of my sending-offs wouldn't have been because of anger; they were caused by frustration. There's a big difference. I don't ever remember getting sent off when we were 3–0 up.

When I have been angry that's been me defending myself. I think the man upstairs has designed me in a certain way, and this provides me with a form of energy, a form of self-defence. I drop my guard sometimes, but when I do, and become more laid-back, it can backfire on me. I see my anger as a useful tool. Me expressing my anger – not every two minutes – I'm releasing something. I can control it better now than in the past.

It's a family trait. Without a doubt, I get it from my dad. You can see it – a lack of patience, low tolerance levels. It's probably one of my many contradictions: I don't get as angry as people might think. But it helps me. As soon as I walk into a room, I know people are apprehensive; I know they are. They are expecting some sort of skinhead thug. So I've a good way of disappointing them. I think I treat people pretty well. I've got friends I've known for thirty years. If I was some impatient thug, I think they'd keep their distance from me.

I've looked at my anger for what it is. It's just anger; I won't beat myself up about it. Anger is an energy and when you lose a lot of energy it's just like after a football match: you're drained.

There's a massive drop. Someone once said to me – an ex-player, and it's going back to my drinking days – he said that going out with me was like going out with a time-bomb. The reputation probably keeps people away from me, and that often suits me – although I'm not saying that's a good thing.

So anger is a useful trait. But when I'm backed into a corner, when I get into situations, professional or personal, I know, deep down, that when I lose my rag, and I might be in the right – it doesn't matter – I know I'm going to be the loser. I will lose out. Saipan and the World Cup – ultimately I lost. Or when I left United, when I could have stayed a bit longer if it had been handled differently. I was the one who lost; I know that. That's the madness of me. When I'm going off on one, even when I might be right, there's a voice in my head going, 'You'll pay for this.'

That's the self-destruct button. I don't know if it's low self-esteem. Things might be going really well, and I don't trust it: 'It's not going to last', or, 'Why am I getting this? Why are things going well? I'll fuck things up a little bit, then feel a bit better, myself.' I might be buying a car: 'Who do you think you are, buying a new car?' And I'll fuck it up. I'll drag things down around me, and then I'll get started again. When I get back up to the top, I look and see that there were things that I wasn't happy with, and I could have managed differently.

That self-destruct button is definitely there. And I suffer for it. With my drinking, I used to go missing for a few days. I think it was my way of switching off, never mind the consequences. It was my time. It was self-destructive, I can see that, but I'm still drawn to it. Not the drink – but the bit of madness, the irresponsibility. I can be sitting at home, the most contented man on the planet. An hour later, I go, 'Jesus – it's hard work, this.' When I go back to Cork, I can fall back into that old routine: 'I'm going to go off on one here.' It doesn't worry me. I kind of go in, have a look around, go, 'Nah', and come back out of it. But sometimes I don't know what's best for myself and that's why I've got great faith; the man upstairs looks after me. I just have to trust Him a bit more. I've learnt to say 'Sorry' pretty quickly, if I think I've been out of order. Or, sometimes I can just say 'Sorry', to move on.

Maybe 'self-destruct' is too strong a phrase. Maybe I play games with myself. I have great stability in my life. But, then, that worries me. I like my home comforts, but then I want to be this hell-raiser – but I want my porridge in the morning. I want my wife and kids around me. I've dipped into the madness, and I don't like it that much. I like walking my dogs in the morning. Maybe I'm like every man on the planet – I don't know; I want a bit more than what's on offer. My mid-life crisis has been going on for years.

I'd never really let myself self-destruct. I want to have my pride, and I like nice things in my life. I don't want to be another fallen ex-star. I'm quite good at living in the day. Really, what is cool for me is sleeping well at night and having people around who I love.

There's a difference between anger and rage. With anger – when I've been angry – somebody with me, or even myself, can pull it back. There's a comeback – I'd be able to pull myself back in, if I was angry. But with rage, I've gone beyond all that; it's beyond anger. It's rare – even more so, now that I'm not playing football. And I'm not sure that I ever felt pure rage on the football pitch. All the times I was sent off – it was frustration, or a controlled anger. There's no control with rage. It's not good – especially the aftermath. You're coming down, and it's a long way to go. The come-down can be shocking in terms of feeling down, or embarrassed by my behaviour, even if I feel that I wasn't in the wrong. I haven't felt real rage in a long time, thank God.

*

I was in Barbados with my family when I decided to leave Celtic. This was a few weeks after the end of the season. I just thought, 'I can't go back' – because of my hip. I'd seen the specialist Richard Villar at the end of the season, for an update. And he said, 'Basically, Roy, the more you play, you'll do more damage to the hip.'

He followed up the meeting with a letter:

In essence, your right hip is, clinically, a little worse than it was when we first met. The MRI scan, now it has been reported, demonstrates some slight damage within the labrum (cartilage of the hip) but also some early degeneration within the articular cartilage (gristle) of the hip. In essence, this implies early osteoarthritis of the joint.

Under normal circumstances, a joint such as yours would not be something I would expect to interfere with life too greatly. Clearly, however, when you are stressing your right hip enormously, changes such as I have outlined above do become significant. In terms of a feature of the hip such as this, it is obviously very difficult to be sure. Nevertheless, it is likely that the rate of deterioration of your joint will be in proportion to the amount of strain which is placed through it. At the same time, one should be aware that degenerate joints do not always need to be totally rested. In fact, a certain degree of movement is a very good thing for them.

I realise that you have an enormously difficult decision to make and I do not envy you or the situation at all. However, I do hope that our discussion in clinic, combined with the letter I have written, helps you towards reaching a satisfactory conclusion and, as I am sure you know, I am always here to support you should you need further advice.

I was embarrassed about the decision to retire. Really, I'd only just arrived at Celtic. Even when I was at United I'd be embarrassed going to work and saying, 'I'm injured.' The shame of it.

The hard part was making the decision – just that; coming to the conclusion. I'd had a chat about it with my wife, with the kids playing around. It wasn't a committee meeting. I didn't talk to anyone else. I'd made my mind up.

I rang Gordon Strachan and said, 'Gordon – it's about coming back. My hip's playing up and— D'you know, I think I'm going to have to call it a day.'

And Gordon went, 'All right, yeah – okay. Yeah – it's for the best.'

And I was saying to myself, 'Try and persuade me, for fuck's sake. At least pretend.'

I was relieved.

It's about making the decision. I can procrastinate about lots of things but, once I make the decision, it's made. Let's get on with it.

I think I'd been frightened of accepting that I was going to retire. And it might have been why I didn't like Barbados. After I made the decision, and after I spoke to Gordon, there was still fear, but a nicer fear. Even excitement. What was going to happen?

Now life starts.

SIX

He had the penthouse in Sydney Harbour, and the Lamborghini, all the women. A hard life. But I knew he loved football. He loved the game and he liked a challenge.

I said, 'D'you fancy coming back to Sunderland?'

Measuring yourself after football – it's difficult. You lose your identity. You lose what you stand for. For years you strive to be a footballer. Then you have it. You're like an actor, every Saturday. Then it's gone.

You feel like you're starting out again. It shouldn't be a surprise because, when you start out in your career, you know it's going to finish at thirty-four or thirty-five. You know it is. But I'm not sure that your emotions know it. Your head tells you lies, and there's a fear of accepting, 'This is it.'

Then there's that big question – 'What do I do?' I had a few bob in the bank, but I had a nice way of living. And it wasn't cheap. Football had been brilliant to me, mind-boggling, but all those bills were still coming in. I wanted to go on nice holidays; there was my family to look after.

There was that excitement – 'What's next?' But I also knew that whatever I did it would never be as good as playing football. Never.

When I was a footballer I was doing exactly what I wanted

to do. But that stopped. I was a footballer and then I was an ex-footballer, whatever the 'ex' covers. What I stood for at United – the winning, playing with injuries, the red cards: I'd loved all that. I remember thinking, 'I shouldn't be loving it this much.'

But I was doing what I loved doing. It was everything. People might say that it was a job, and I do understand what a football club means to supporters, people who travel up and down the country, who pay big money and are often frustrated. I used to be like that at United; I often shared their frustration. I was almost going, 'Fuckin' hell, I can't believe this. I'm going to be found out soon. Somebody's going to say, "Hey, you—"'

I think that was part of it; I think that helped me in my career – the fear of being found out, of getting away with being paid so well for doing something that I loved doing so much. That, and knowing deep down, 'I'll never get that feeling ever again.'

That's the sad part.

When I left the United training ground I should have stopped playing football, because I knew it would never, ever, be the same. That was why it was so hard to leave. That was why I was upset.

No matter what I do for the rest of my life, nothing will replace it.

That's the big shock.

Knowing that, for the rest of your life, everything was going to be disappointment – jobwise. Nothing could come near to it.

I was thirty-four.

The challenge for me now was: don't self-explode.

It was a case of 'What can I enjoy?'

I wasn't afraid of becoming the ex-footballer, where everything is associated with your past. But I don't really live in the past. I like getting people's respect but I don't want to live in their memories.

'Remember that goal you got against Arsenal?'

'— yeah.'

I feel like saying to people, 'You need to move on. That was twenty years ago.'

It's like your identity.

'He was a Man United player—'

And it's still part of mine, whether I like it or not. Wherever I go in the world – 'Oh, Keane, Keane – Man United' – it could be anywhere. It could be China. 'Keane – Man United'.

I could easily have become a walking museum, and I didn't want that.

I didn't miss the training, once I'd stopped. I didn't miss the people – the companionship – *that* much, or the banter. My injuries had been taking a toll on me. My hip had been playing me up, so I saw the last few years as a bonus. I'd just thought, 'Every game's great', every training session.

I think it's the people around you who suffer more than anyone else. My family – parents and brothers, sister, uncles and aunts. For years I had people coming over from Ireland to see me and to get a game in. But that stopped. I felt sad for them, sad that they were missing out on the buzz that football and my career had brought them.

My wife and kids were fine. They'd always stepped back from the public side of my life. They almost knew, more than I did – even the youngest ones – that it wasn't going to last.

You miss the money. You've had a very good standard of living; you miss those wages coming in, hundreds of thousands a month.

It's about adapting. You have to kind of grow up. And accept it. When you're at a top club everything is done for you. You end up living in this little bubble. Wherever you go, people are looking after you, and everything's VIP or upgrades. All of a sudden, that stops. I had days when self-pity kicked in. 'Why me?' and 'Poor me'. The United stuff, how it ended – I hear myself complaining. It happened. Jesus – count your blessings. Grow up, and take responsibility for what you're going to do next, like most other men out there. Most other men who lose their jobs, or who work for twenty-five years and get a poxy watch at the end of it.

The answer to the question, 'What are you going to do for me?' should start with, 'Well, do it yourself.' Maybe I'm being arrogant, because football was good to me financially. But I think there has to be that starting point: take responsibility for yourself. Find some work, or adapt your lifestyle. Downsize your house. Have fewer holidays. Hold on to the car for a few extra years. It's about everyday things, your lifestyle.

I sat down with the kids and gave them the news, about how things were going to change. It wasn't anything too drastic. There'd be fewer holidays, and so on – 'Those days are over.' I was trying to put the frighteners on them, a little bit. But kids pick that up. They were looking straight through me, going, 'Get on with the lecture, we want to watch the TV.'

I began to realise that I'd enjoyed the luxuries – the holidays – more than anybody else. A few months later, we said we wouldn't be going away for one of the school breaks. I remember saying to my wife, 'Why did I go on about cutbacks?', because I was the one who wanted to go on holiday. I'd almost been putting the onus on the kids. Even going back – 'I don't want to go to Real Madrid because of my children.' They'd have upped and left in two minutes. The kids can become scapegoats – blame the kids.

'Hey, kids – everyone together—'

'Ah no, another Keane lecture tonight.'

I had done a certain amount of preparation. I'd been doing my coaching badges.

There's no actual badge. It's a certificate – an award. I'd gained my UEFA B award in 2004. It's like any education; you start at the bottom. In the B course you have to show basic organisational skills – say, a session with four or five players, or a drill; setting up cones, laying out bibs, everything. It's so basic, it's difficult. You've been playing at a professional level, and now you've to work with kids or lads who rarely kick a ball – it isn't easy. A lot of players who've spent ten or fifteen years trying to get to the top struggle with it. I found it hard. It's almost like having to go back and do your driving test. I can drive, but I'm not sure I can tell you the rules of the road.

I was starting the next step, my UEFA A badge, in 2006, the summer I stopped playing. You go up a level; you're organising full training sessions, eleven v. eleven. And there's more on tactics – say, how you prepare a game against a team that plays 4–3–3. I found the higher level much easier; it was more familiar. Still, though, you're in charge now, not just part of it. You're not a player any more.

The next step is the Pro Licence. It's a requirement to manage in any of the top leagues. It's not cheap; I think it was six or seven grand. There's a discipline to it, which is good, and you meet top people. And it's nerve-wracking. It's about working at the top level, and not just coaching – dealing with club boards and chief executives, budgets, handling media. They'd set up mock press conferences; you'd be challenged, and advised on how to deal with different questions.

There were session plans to be written, and you had to log your coaching sessions. This can be a problem for a lot of ex-players; writing of any type is torture. Some of them wouldn't have been great at school – I know I wasn't. As a player you'd have been involved in thousands of training sessions, with different coaches. But now you had to become the teacher. It was difficult. And standing up in front of a group. That wasn't too bad for me, because I'd been the club captain and I had some experience of that, and some sort of leadership qualities.

The badges are hard work but there's big satisfaction, too, in getting them done. I'd wanted to get started on the courses while I was still a player. I started the first, the UEFA B, when I was thirty-one or thirty-two. It's the mistake a lot of ex-players make; they wait until they're thirty-four or thirty-five before they decide to start their coaching awards. Quite often, players don't do it while they're still playing, because it's time-consuming and they'd have to sacrifice part of their holidays. The expense is off-putting, too, especially if you want to get to Pro Licence level, although the PFA will contribute 50 per cent of the fee.

While you're doing the courses you're networking; you meet nice people. I ended up working with some of the men I met when I was doing my coaching course. I met Ian McParland and Gary Ablett, who both worked with me later at Ipswich. And it was Gary who put me in touch with Antonio Gómez, who became my fitness coach at Sunderland. You end up meeting people you'll work with – or against.

I knew I'd have to be ready. Actually, in a way I'd been ready since I was a kid. I'd been lucky, but I'd made my own bit of luck. I was playing League of Ireland football, and I was doing a FÁS course; there was nobody ringing me to come over to England. As much as I lacked confidence in some things, there were other areas of my life where I went, 'Give me a go at that—' I wrote to a number of clubs in England, looking for a trial. I offered to pay part of the cost, although I didn't have a penny. I got a letter back from Forest saying that if I was good enough I'd be spotted.

I *was* spotted – by Forest. When I went there for my trial I knew I wouldn't be going back to Cork. There was nothing there, and no prospects. In my first week at Forest they put me with the kids; no one saw me. I was eighteen or nineteen. They apologised and asked me to come back; they'd organise a game. I said, 'Just give me the game.' I wasn't one for going around cones – 'Give me a game.' They told me there'd be a game at the City Ground, and Brian Clough was going to be there, and I thought, 'Brilliant.' I didn't go, 'Is he? Oh, fuck.' I went, 'Brilliant.' When it was over and they told me they wanted to sign me, I wasn't cocky enough to say, 'I knew you would.' But I thought it. It was what I'd been waiting for since I was a kid, since I was eight years of age, at Rockmount. Even back then, I played for Rockmount instead of my local club, Mayfield, because Rockmount had the better players. And I knew that at eight or nine years of age. Mayfield would have been convenient, but 'convenient' was boring; I needed that challenge. Good players – good people around you, pushing each other. When I was thirteen or fourteen, Eric Hogan – a decent lad, he still plays for the over-35s in Cork – he wouldn't go training one night because he got a new skateboard. I fell out with him; we didn't speak for a year because he wouldn't go training. I always had that drive. 'Stick your skateboard.' As I matured and the situations got bigger, I'd think back to the skateboard. 'Stick your fuckin' skateboard.'

Sunderland should have been a nightmare. It had seven or eight Irish owners! There'd be a lot of interference; they'd all feel they owned the club. I'd have too many people to answer to.

But it was the opposite. Because there were seven or eight of them, no one felt he was in charge. Niall Quinn was the front, the public face. The Sunderland fans loved him, and he answered to the owners. And the fact that they were Irish turned out to be fine. You could have a bit of banter with them. They trusted myself and Niall to get on with it; we were the footballing people.

Sunderland had been relegated at the end of the previous season, '05–'06. Then Niall formed a consortium, Drumaville, made up mostly of Irish property developers, including Charlie Chawke, the Dublin publican. They took control of the club in July. But then they went into pre-season, and the start of the season itself, without a manager. Niall had to take on the job temporarily, while they kept looking. They lost their first four League games.

They'd met me earlier in the summer, soon after I'd stopped playing. Niall had contacted Michael Kennedy. I wasn't *that* surprised. Football's a small world and they would have known that I'd stopped playing and, probably, that I was doing my coaching courses. As for the history between myself and Niall, Niall would have been trying to do what he thought was right for the club. He would have been big enough not to let it get in the way.

They sent a helicopter over to Manchester and flew me to Dublin. They were trying to impress me, of course; I was crossing the Irish Sea in a helicopter, but I was wondering, 'What am I in for here?'

I'm not sure where the meeting took place. Some estate, a manor house outside Dublin. All the lads in the Drumaville Consortium were there, and Niall was, too. As the helicopter landed I saw that he was a few feet away, beside the helipad, waiting with the other people. I got out of the helicopter, kissed the ground and blessed everybody.

'The Pope has arrived.'

No, I didn't.

I got out of the helicopter, walked across to Niall and we shook hands.

He said, 'Do you want five or ten minutes to ourselves before you go in?'

It was the first time I'd spoken to Niall since the World Cup. I don't think the conversation would have happened if Niall hadn't been involved in the consortium. So it was an opportunity to let bygones be bygones.

We went into a room together, and I said, 'Listen, the Saipan stuff. Whatever happens with Sunderland now, we need to move on, anyway.'

He agreed, 'Yeah, yeah.'

And that was it.

I went in and met the lads. It was all very casual. I had a suit on but I didn't feel like I was being interviewed or that I was under any pressure.

They asked me would I be interested in the job.

I said, 'I'm not sure what I want to do yet, lads. I'll have a think about it.'

They spoke about what various players were earning, contracts and wages, and about getting players in and out.

I was going, 'One step at a time; let me have a think about it.'

They were basically giving me a plan. They seemed keen. I thought the job might be mine, if I wanted it. They'd just taken over the club, and you have to have a manager in place before the start of pre-season. If only to save face. Mick McCarthy had gone in March, before the consortium took over the club; and Kevin Ball had been the caretaker until the end of the season. They'd been relegated with one of the lowest points totals ever.

I went home and I told Michael a few days later, 'It's not for me.'

I wanted to focus on finishing my coaching courses – I was about to start the UEFA A; I didn't want to jump into a job too quickly. Sunderland were disappointed and, over the next month or so, they couldn't find anyone to take the job. Which still amazes me. I heard that Martin O'Neill and Sam Allardyce had turned it down before they'd spoken to me.

At that stage, I wasn't 100 per cent sure what I wanted to do. I genuinely wasn't certain if management or coaching were for me. There was a stricter divide between the two roles back then. The courses weren't exactly whetting my appetite for coaching. I'd often thought, 'Well, this is a pain in the arse.' There's a coaching expression, 'Being out on the grass'. I wasn't sure that that was what I wanted. But I understood that the courses had to be done. I thought I'd be more interested in management, and running a club. But, if I did take a job, I didn't want to be doing the courses while I was starting. Paul Ince and Gareth Southgate had had to do that. If things didn't start well, I didn't want the accusation thrown at me, 'Well, you didn't finish your coaching badges.' And, financially, I didn't have to jump into a job.

I started my UEFA A course that summer, then I went on holiday for a few weeks in August. I was in Portugal when the season started, and I watched a few matches on television. Sunderland were struggling badly. They played Bury away, in the League Cup, on a Tuesday night. And they were beaten. Niall was interviewed after the game; he was their temporary manager. He looked about a hundred.

My sister texted me: *Did you see Niall Quinn? You need to help him out.*

I looked at Niall – and I rang Michael Kennedy the next day. I asked him to get in touch with Sunderland: 'If they still want me, I'll go for it.'

I'd been with my family all summer. It had been great, but I didn't want to be with them all the time. I'm a dad; I needed to go out and earn a living. I wanted my kids to see me going to work.

The consortium came back: 'It's there for you if you want it.'

And I decided I'd go for it. My best decisions are always the quick ones. I wasn't thinking about staff, or tactics, or 'We'll need ten players.' No master plan. It was just, 'I'll go for it.' One step at a time.

From a business point of view they knew what they were getting. Obviously, I was way behind Martin and Sam in terms of experience. I'd never managed a team before. It was a proper gamble for them, and it was a gamble for me. But they'd have been thinking about ticket sales, too. I think if you'd asked Niall at the time, he'd have said, 'We're not too worried about the coaching credentials; we need a boost.'

They'd lost their identity, lost their spark. They probably thought, 'He's the man.' I was the marquee signing, and I don't shy away from that.

Five defeats in five games – it was a shocking start, especially for a team that had just been relegated. Bury, who knocked them out of the League Cup, were the lowest team in the League – ninety-second. But Sunderland weren't as bad as the results were suggesting. A lot of those players had just been in the Premiership. It didn't matter to me if they'd been relegated with one point or thirty-five, they were still a Premiership outfit.

On the other hand, I wasn't thinking about promotion.

I wasn't associated with the club; I'd no loyalty to them – unlike Niall. I was able to go in cold; I'm very good at living in the now. And my reputation as a player probably helped. There was a certain fear – 'What's he going to do?' But I know what I'm good at, and I thought, 'I'll be good with these players.'

What helped me make the jump from player to manager was the experience I'd had at United, and my responsibilities as captain. I had a bit of common sense to me. But I hadn't given the prospect that much thought, and it had never been a dream – I don't think you'd grow up dreaming of being a manager! I just thought, 'Let's give it a go. We'll see what happens here.'

The complications of the job – board meetings, getting staff organised, even meeting the parents of young players; I was gung-ho about facing all that – 'We'll see how that goes.' If I'd sat down and considered every aspect of it, I might never have gone into management. But if you keep that childlike love of the game, you're inclined to think, 'I'll adapt to that, and I'll have good people around me. From Monday to Friday, my job is to try and get a result on Saturday.'

Sunderland were playing West Brom at home the following weekend, after I'd phoned Michael. I was back home in Manchester by then, and I drove up to watch the match, with Tony Loughlan – Tony was going to be my first-team coach. Nothing had been announced yet. I wanted to have a look at the team, and the training ground. There were 14,000 people there, in a stadium with a capacity of 42,000.

They won 2–0 – but I don't claim credit for that. It was what I'd expected; they were a half-decent team. I remember thinking, 'They're not bad, these.'

They'd just been having a hard time – a few injuries, confidence. It was exciting, watching the team I was going to manage. I knew the potential was there.

Niall showed me around the training ground, the Academy of Light, the next day, and introduced me to the team.

Michael was handling the negotiations. We knew they would be straightforward, and that we were in a great position. It wasn't going to be a case of, 'Ah, I've got you now, lads', but I'd been seen at the West Brom match; there was talk around the place. There'd been a bit of embarrassment about other possible managers. They'd be lynched if they didn't get the deal done with me. Niall had had a bash at the job, and it hadn't gone well. He knew it was hard work. So I thought I'd get a little bit of grace.

Everything fell into place. I got a brilliant contract, over a million a year, a lot of money for a Championship job – and my first job. I suppose what usually happens is you're offered a short contract, you ask for a longer one and you meet in the middle. But Sunderland offered me a five-year deal and I said I only wanted to sign for three. I was confident enough, but I wanted to see how it would go. I was still thinking like a footballer – a shorter deal and keep your options open. I should have been thinking of job security and the financial consequences of being sacked.

I've learnt since that, contractually, the day you take over at a club is the day you start to leave. Most of the contract details are about what happens at the end; you're already negotiating your settlement. It's such a negative way to go into a job. You should be upbeat, but most of the negotiations are about how much it will cost to get rid of you.

The distance from my home to Sunderland was about two and a half hours in the car. The plan was, the family would follow me. We'd move house, up to the area, and we'd find a Catholic school for the kids.

Myself and Tony took training for the first time the day after I'd signed my contract. I knew Tony at Nottingham Forest. He was a player there when I arrived. He only played a couple of first-team games before he left, because of injuries. We were together a few years at Forest, and I'd always kept in touch with him. I'd kept in touch with a few of the Forest players, Tony, and Gary Charles. When I came to Forest I didn't have a car and Tony would bring me to play snooker, and Gary Charles used to drive me around sometimes; we'd go to the pictures together. They were nice to me – simple as that.

Tony did his coaching badges when he was twenty-one or two, at Forest; he did them on Sunday mornings with some of the other players. I'd be lying in bed, hungover, hearing him collect Gary Bowyer, who I was sharing a house with, as they were heading off to do their coaching course, and I remember saying to myself, 'Idiots.'

Tony had a lot of experience at this stage – he was coaching at Leicester City's academy – and when I did my own courses, he helped me a bit with the session plans that I had to hand in. I'd always thought if I got a management job I'd ask Tony to come with me – a good coach and a good friend, and someone I could trust. We enjoyed each other's company. I don't remember us laughing, but I'd like to think we did. He's coaching at Burnley now, with Sean Dyche and Ian Woan, two ex-players who were also at Forest when we were there. That's how the game works.

We took training, and we started looking at the staff and players. I thought, 'My God, there's a lot of work to be done.' They weren't great; they were nothing like a promotion team. But they were near the bottom of the table, so there was only one way to go.

I loved it from thereon. From the very beginning, I thought it was brilliant. Niall trusted me to get on with it.

We had to spend money, although not as much as was often reported. We were heading towards League One; we'd got used to losing. Throughout the season, we invested roughly three and a half million in players, taking into account players coming in and going out. But now we only had a couple of days to get a few players in, before the transfer deadline.

The transfer deadline makes people panic. That's why transfer fees go through the roof. Agents are holding guns to the heads of chairmen. It backfires on everybody. We identified six or seven players – which is a lot. Meeting the players, medicals to be organised, personal terms. But Niall and the chief executive, Peter Walker, were brilliant; they got it done for me. I asked for six players and they came back with six. It made sense, of course; we were all after the same thing – success. I knew my arrival would give us a bit of a boost, but we had to keep it up.

I brought in six. Six players I'd played with. Six good characters. They'd all played for their countries. I'd had them at the back of my mind, although I didn't know if they'd be available.

I only had three days. But I think, on this occasion, it worked well for us. If I'd had a couple of months, I'd have had people bouncing off me, people moving the goalposts, agents going, 'We've another club waiting.' But this time the players and their clubs had a quick decision to make. I had to make offers for them. 'But you'll need to make your mind up, because you'll have to have a medical tomorrow.' No one was taking a pay cut. We'd no one coming in from AC Milan. We were paying decent money for that level. Not thirty or forty thousand a week, but twelve or fifteen – something like that. Graham Kavanagh and Dave Connolly were at Wigan, and that helped. We weren't dealing with six different clubs, for six players. We'd the two lads from Wigan, Ross Wallace and Stan Varga were at Celtic, and Liam Millar was being released by Manchester United

It was a great lift. You go out training with one group of players and the next day five or six international players come out with you.

It was Niall who made the calls and did the deals. He rang Celtic's chief executive, and he'd have rung the agent to see if, say, Ross Wallace fancied the move. I've a reputation for being a loner, but I got on well with all these lads. I'd roomed with Graham Kavanagh when we were with Ireland.

I was staying in a cottage at the back of the hotel, so I had a bit of room and privacy. Ross and Stan came, with their agent – he represented both of them. I'd played with them a few months earlier at Celtic, so the conversation was easy.

'Do you fancy it, lads?'

It was very straightforward.

'We're pretty average. But if you come on board – and I'm trying to get another couple of lads in – we'll be all right.'

They went, 'Yeah.'

And I went, 'Brilliant. I'll put the kettle on.'

It was as simple as that. I almost wish I'd kept that approach more. To be myself.

I had to pull a few teeth to get Dave Connolly. Michael Kennedy represented Dave, and I knew he'd play hardball. There was no problem there, even though Michael had represented me; he'd negotiated my contract with Sunderland. But Michael was representing his client here, not me or Sunderland. I knew the business. I needed a striker and Michael would get the best deal for his client.

Dave was going, 'Oh, I don't want to leave Wigan.'

And I went, 'Listen, Dave, compare Wigan to Sunderland.'

I brought in good players, and good characters. They made my job easier. Somebody asked Capello years ago how come he was such a good manager. He said, 'I've been very fortunate. I've always worked with good players.' Never forget that. Never give managers too much credit – but don't knock them too much when things are going bad. I think it was Jock Stein who said 'Football is about the fans and the players.' Never get too carried away about the manager. I'm not playing myself down – but the players did the business.

All these players were signing on the same day, and it lifted everybody. It lifted Sunderland – the city and the club. And we hadn't played a game yet. We weren't signing Ronaldo, but Ross and Stan were both Celtic players – good players. Dave, Graham, Liam – I knew them. You'd have looked at them and said, 'Well, we're heading up the table.'

When you sign a player, you're sending a message – to the fans and to the other clubs in your league.

I rang Dwight Yorke. It was seven in the morning when I picked up the phone at the training ground, because he was in Australia, with Sydney FC; he was their marquee player.

So I rang him.

'All right, Yorkie?'

I'd got on well with Yorkie at United. He had the penthouse in Sydney Harbour, and the Lamborghini, all the women. A hard life. But I knew he loved football. He loved the game and he liked a challenge.

I said, 'D'you fancy coming back to Sunderland?'

And he said, 'You want me to leave this? You want me to leave fuckin' Australia?'

I said, 'Yeah.'

And he said, 'Yeah, I fancy it.'

I thought we'd get him on a free. He was thirty-four. But we had to pay Sydney two hundred and fifty grand. The club wasn't happy. But Yorkie walked into our dressing room. Like an actor. A character, in the dressing room. He'd won the Champions League; he'd played for United.

'All right, lads? What's cooking?'

Yorkie was my best signing. Expectations around the city were high; we were hoping to get crowds of 40,000. Some of the players couldn't cope with it. But Yorkie was, like, 'What's the problem?' He brought an aura to the club that it hadn't had. It's all about characters. Yorkie arrived, and my staff were going, 'He's some man, isn't he?'

And I said, 'Yeah, he's a top guy.'

And a good guy.

I went to a lot of functions with Niall. He was trying to promote the club. We'd lost a lot of fans over the years, and he kept saying that we needed to get season ticket sales up. We were meeting and greeting fans – normally my worst fuckin' nightmare. But I enjoyed it. What I liked about the Sunderland fans was that what happened on the pitch on a Saturday made or broke their week. That's not the case with every football club. So I thought, 'I think I'll love having that responsibility.'

We got off to a decent start, away to Derby.

My first ever team talk was before that game. We were at the hotel. I'd picked my team, and I'd had to disappoint a few people.

'All right, lads. This is what Derby are like.'

We'd done a bit of homework in the previous three days. It had been a bit mad – trying to move to Sunderland, trying to get players in before the deadline. I'd decided the night before that I'd focus on the Derby goalkeeper. He was poor on crosses. But I went on a bit long. Dave Connolly, who I'd played with for Ireland – a funny ol' lad, a strange lad, but he was a goalscorer, so he could be as tricky as he liked – he had his hand up at the back.

I kept going.

'Lads, the first few balls – nail him. He's weak on crosses. He's good with his feet—'

I was keeping an eye on Dave. He still had his hand up.

'What is it, Dave?'

I was wondering did he want to go out for a piss or something. He said, 'Gaffer, you know the keeper—?'

I went, 'Yeah.'

'He was sold a week ago.'

Not injured – fuckin' sold, a week before. And I was supposed to be the big hero coming in to save the club, fans and flags every-where, lifted on to their shoulders.

That was my first team talk.

So, I went, 'Hey, lads, it just goes to show you, you can't get the fuckin' scout reports.'

I blamed the scout.

And, actually, it helped; it relaxed everybody. It was good for me, because it embarrassed me, a bit – instead of trying to be the perfectionist, the sergeant major. It lightened the mood.

Derby were doing well at the time. Billy Davies was managing them; they had good players.

We were 1–0 down at half-time.

If you'd seen the players when I walked into the dressing room – they were shitting themselves. They were expecting fireworks. Good managers have to keep people guessing; you can't be too predictable. Clough did it, and Ferguson. So I walked in.

'All right, lads – relax. You're doing well, we're doing okay. Keep at it.'

Unless things were going really badly I'd let the players settle down at half-time before I'd go into the dressing room. I'd give them a minute or two, to gather their breath, and to let me get my thoughts together. It was my first managerial job, so I wasn't going off on some tactical journey. My plan was to keep it simple.

Brian Clough's advice to me on my debut for Forest, away to Liverpool, was, 'Get it, pass it to one of your team-mates, and move. Can you do that?'

And I went, 'Yeah, of course I can do it.'

I'd been doing it since I was a kid. Pass it and move. I'd made a career out of it. Part of my admiration for Brian Clough was the simplicity of the game he saw. Alex Ferguson's outlook was pretty simple, too.

I was looking at the players and they were expecting me to lose it, because of my reputation. But I didn't want to be predictable. The explosion was in my locker; I think they knew that. In the media, after a press conference, whatever I said, I 'blasted'. '"We could have done better," Keane blasts.' Instead of not smiling, I 'glowered'. It was a cartoon image of me but, now and again, I used that to my advantage.

But that could also backfire on me. When I'd try to be genuine with people, or if I lost my rag just a little bit, it could become exaggerated. Raising my voice would be a big drama. Enthusiasm could be mistaken for anger. If people felt I was angry all the time, it would lose its effect. The picture would be out there that I was constantly at the players, even though I'd made the conscious decision to be calm on the sideline and, more often than not, relaxed in the dressing room.

I hadn't had the players for pre-season, so I wasn't pre-judging them; I was giving everybody the benefit of the doubt. The problem is, the longer you work with players you end up looking at their defects. But at this stage I was wondering if this was a defect in a particular player, or if he was just having a bad game. I was quite nice with them, polite and encouraging. I think it was clear to the players – whether it was my body language or tone of voice, or my analysis of Derby's ex-goalkeeper – that I was new to the job. They were well aware of that. I hadn't made any decisions yet – 'Four of them are going next week' – so they wanted to do well for me.

It was all very innocent. That changes a bit when you start becoming familiar with people. You start picking holes. But my reputation as a player and my lack of managerial experience were both advantages at first.

'You're doing well, we're doing okay. Keep at it.'

We won 2–1. Chris Brown, a big lad, a typical Championship striker, and Ross Wallace, one of the new lads, scored.

I'd been used to winning as a player. This was a different kind of satisfaction. I could carry it into the training ground the following Monday.

But I'd learn, losing was different, too; it carried much more responsibility. It was harder to recover. It took me far too long to get over a defeat. I was the same when I was a player, but this was worse. There has to be a certain amount of suffering, but not to the extent that I put myself through. I wouldn't eat properly; I felt I didn't deserve a good meal. That would have a knock-on effect, because I wouldn't sleep properly. When it came to handling defeats and victories, I had the balance wrong, throughout my career. When we won, I'd go, 'Brilliant, but we've got to win next week.' When we lost, I'd never go, 'Okay, we lost, but we've still got next week.'

The key, I think now, is to move on quickly – if you can. If you're in sport, you're going to lose. We couldn't win every game.

I'd never had an office before. Now I had a secretary. I had a phone – a phone with buttons, and different lines. I had a leather chair that swung around, a swivel chair. For the first few days I used to swing around on it. If any of the players or staff had peeped through the office window and seen me going 'Wheeeh!' The phone would ring, and I'd be pressing different buttons, trying to get the right line.

I didn't take proper advantage of the office. But I didn't really need it at first. The early signings were all lads I knew. I didn't have to bring them in and sell the club to them. They were all eager to come. My initial reaction was, 'What do I do with this? Do I need an office?' I was sitting in my chair, going, 'What do I do?'

Your own office can be a lonely place. I'm not one for hanging up loads of pictures of my family. I had one of those electrical picture frames, where the photos are repeated, but that was it. I remember thinking, 'I'm not going to get *too* comfortable here.' But what I should have done was the opposite. I should made myself comfortable, because you do end up spending a remarkable amount of time there. I should have made it a bit more homely, with pictures of my family. When players came to see me, they could have seen that other side of me. But even when things were going well, I thought, 'If things go badly, I want to be able to clear it out pretty quickly. One box.'

Keep it clean, keep it tidy, and be ready for a quick getaway. I'm not sure now if that was the right way to be thinking, but it stopped me from getting too complacent. And, ultimately, it wasn't my office; it was the club's. But, again, I think I was afraid to enjoy myself too much – the glass was always half empty.

I'd be embarrassed to ask the secretary, Susan, to arrange anything for me. If I had to book a flight or something, I'd do it myself. She used to look after all the players. I'd give out to them sometimes, particularly when we lost: 'Keep away from my secretary. She works for me.'

But she must have been looking at me, thinking, 'I'll be fuckin' unemployed soon.'

Tony had come to the club with me, and I brought in some of my own staff as I settled in over the next couple of months. I brought in Mike Clegg, as our strength condition coach. Mike had been a player at United. Neil Bailey came in, to coach the first team. He had coached the youth team at United. I brought in Antonio Gómez, as my fitness coach, and Raimond van der Gouw, as the goalkeeping coach. I'd played with Raimond at United. Mick Brown came in as chief scout; he'd been at United. Further down the line, I brought in Ricky Sbragia, who I'd also known at United. We'd a good bunch. I felt very comfortable with my staff.

I had to let some other people go. It was horrible. I still feel a bit guilty about it. But later, at Ipswich, I'd feel guilty about keeping some people on. Guilt comes with the job.

Our next game was away to Leeds. It was brilliant; we won 3–0. Kav and Liam Millar scored, and another Irish lad, Stephen Elliott.

I wasn't on a personal crusade against Leeds, because of my past experiences as a player or because of the Alfie Håland episode. We just needed the win, and we played really well. A couple of Leeds fans tried to get at me in the dugout. People coming close to the dugout and shouting abuse is common enough, but these two tried to climb in. It didn't bother me – we'd won.

The atmosphere in the dressing room afterwards was great. I was very happy with the players. These were lads who'd have a go. At the press conference after, I said that they'd shown character, desire and talent, and that I was very proud of them. I knew they'd hear the message. We all like to be praised, and they deserved it. Another away win, and the new lads were settling in. The fans were terrific, too. We had a bit of momentum. We were up off the bottom of the table. That was the priority now; I was thinking like a manager.

Leicester were next, at home. Suddenly, we were expected to win. 'We won at Derby, we won at Leeds, now we'll beat Leicester.' But we didn't. We drew, 1–1; Tobias Hysén scored for us when we were 1–0 down. Which wasn't a bad thing. It was a reality check for us all. I could look at the group of players, and go, 'No, we're still a bit short.'

What I found out quickly was, everything comes to the manager. I was constantly making decisions. Niall and the chief executive, Peter Walker, were brilliant. With experience, I realised that the job of those around you at the club is to help the manager. And Niall and Peter were a proper help to me. We were all on the same wavelength. I didn't come in, going, 'I want us to be Real Madrid', but I did want to change things – the players' suits, the hotels we stayed in the night before matches. That's all money. They knew what I was trying to do, changing the mindset, and they were right behind me. When they didn't agree with me, they explained it well – another reality check, a lesson in economics. Not that I wanted one. I was all about winning, at any cost. Economics was the last thing I wanted to hear about.

A key to management, I think now, is to try and maintain

that childlike love of the game, that innocence – innocence, not naivety. Give people the benefit of the doubt. As the days go by, people start to challenge you – not always deliberately. Kenny Cunningham kept calling me Roy. But I wasn't Roy any more. I had to talk to him, in my office. I felt uncomfortable about it. I'd played with Kenny, with Ireland; he was the Sunderland captain.

I said, 'Listen, Kenny. Don't be calling me Roy any more.'

'I wasn't aware I was.'

I said, 'You were. I'm the boss or the gaffer.'

'All right, Roy.'

That was it.

Probably the longer you stay in management, these issues – being called Roy – become less important. But these small things – I had to nail them. It seems unimportant, but it actually is important. I had to make my mark. I couldn't have Kenny calling me Roy. It was just common sense. But a Dutch coach once said to me, 'Common sense is not so common.'

I never felt 100 per cent comfortable being called 'boss' or 'gaffer'. But I insisted on it because, from the start, they all called me that, and I couldn't have two or three not doing it. I had to be consistent. If I go back into management, it's a tweak I'd make, I think; I wouldn't have them call me 'gaffer'. It doesn't happen in other industries, and I would certainly have felt more comfortable being called by my name. I had people of fifty or sixty, who'd been working at the club for years, calling me 'boss'. I think I felt I hadn't earned the right to be called 'boss'. But even Tony was calling me 'boss'. I felt like saying, 'Don't call me boss. Just call me Roy.' It's the tradition in football, but I like to go against tradition now and again. If I'm comfortable, I'm better at my job. It's more human.

It was hard to get used to the number of staff employed by the club, the sheer numbers. The academy, the canteen, all these people. Trying to get to know people's names – it's trivial, but vital. I found that hard. And I think most managers would tell you the same. Myself and Tony were being pulled left, right and centre, and we had more games coming right up.

'Gaffer, do you want to travel at two or three o'clock next Friday?'

And I was going, 'Ah, Jesus— Let me look at that next week, a bit closer to the day.'

You're being introduced to one of the club staff but your head is spinning a bit, because your priority is getting a result on Saturday.

'My name is Paul.'

I'd think of Paul McGrath, someone I knew, to help me remember the name; I'd think of the staff member as Paul McGrath. I was learning the importance of remembering – and using – people's names.

There were little things I did in the early months that I knew were appreciated. Sunderland is a cold place in winter – nearly all year. It would be freezing. There was a hut down at the bottom of the training ground, and I'd see the groundsmen going in there. I was chatting to them one day, and they told me they had their lunch in the hut.

I said, 'But we've got a canteen. Come and have your lunch with us.'

That was me just being polite. But it had an impact – another little lift.

They started coming in every day.

I'd go, 'Grab your food, lads.'

I wasn't being a hero. It might have had something to do with where I come from; I couldn't sit and eat my pasta, looking out the window at the lads having their sandwiches and freezing to death. I love pork and onion sandwiches myself, but not in a field in the middle of winter. And the groundsmen have the hardest job at a football club.

The games were coming thick and fast. In management, you're supposed to have short-term aims and long-term aims. Our aim, mine and Tony's, was to get through the bloody day. There was one day, two lads came to give myself and Tony a talk about Prozone, the performance analysis package. The club didn't have it, so these two lads wanted to sell us the product.

We were in the players' lounge. There was a big screen in there and comfortable chairs. And both of us fell asleep. The lights were out, to be fair. Afterwards, I asked Tony, 'Did you fall asleep?'

And he said, 'Yeah, yeah – did you?'

We were embarrassed about it but not sure if the two lads from Prozone knew we'd had our little power nap. We bought it anyway.

We watched DVDs of the opposition in that room. Leather chairs – the heat. Years later, after I'd left, I was talking to Seamus McDonagh, who had worked with Martin O'Neill at Sunderland, as Martin's goalkeeping coach.

Seamus said, 'You know that room where you watch all the matches?'

I went, 'Yeah.'

And he said, 'You couldn't keep your fuckin' eyes open, could you?'

'Yeah, we were the same!'

It was a relief hearing Seamus, because myself and Tony thought we were being unprofessional. Mind you, Seamus is well over seventy, so he's entitled to fall asleep.

Having Prozone at a club can be very useful, although it's expensive to set up, possibly over a hundred grand a year. Cameras have to be placed throughout the stadium. They monitor distances covered by each player, crosses into the box, fitness levels, a whole range of statistical information. I was open to all that but I wouldn't be dictated to by it. It was useful if a player questioned what you were saying about his game, or his stats. If we didn't think he was running enough, and he disagreed, we could go, 'Well, we've got back-up here.'

Some players almost lived off the stats. They might say, 'Well, I ran fifteen miles.'

And I'd say, 'Yeah, that's because you kept giving the fuckin' ball away.'

The stats would give you useful feedback, but it was just a tool. Immediately after a game the statistician might come up and say, 'We didn't get enough crosses in.' But I'd have seen that already; I was at the game. Some players love getting the information and watching the DVDs. We found that the defenders, in particular, were keen on looking back over clips of games: 'Can I see where I was when that cross came in?' Defenders think more about the game than attacking players. The forwards tend to be more instinctive.

When I was a player I'd be home at one or two o'clock. If it was two, because I'd stayed behind to do some extra stretches, I'd think to myself, 'I had a long day today.' The length and rhythm of my working day had changed completely – engaging with so many people. It was all new. Decisions coming at me; it took a while to get used to it.

There was one day, a lad called Bill – a big Sunderland fan, the tattoos and everything, a really nice fella; he was the masseur – he came in to me.

'Gaffer, we're travelling next week. What soup do you want for the bus?'

I went to myself, 'Fuckin' soup?'

I had so many things to do.

When I was a player, I was almost wrapped in cotton wool.

Now I was in the real world and it was a shock. I was signing players for millions of pounds, releasing young players, letting staff go – people's livelihoods, knowing they had mortgages.

I was bringing adults into my office and saying, 'I don't like the way you're behaving.'

I was making changes – timetable changes.

'We always train at half ten.'

'Well, now we're training at ten.'

I'd feel conflict, sometimes, from people. A bit of paranoia – 'Who likes me? Who doesn't like me?' The groundsmen liked me because I'd let them into the canteen, but I couldn't please everybody.

The soup almost put me over the edge.

I think I said, 'Fuck you and the soup' – in a nice way.

He took it well. We laughed about it. I think he realised that his timing hadn't been good. And it took me a while to understand that the soup was important. Important to Bill, and important to the club – and me.

The next game, we lost. Three–one, at Ipswich.

It was an important day for me.

I was always looking to see what the staff contributed on match day. It's a day out for some; others like to go out and get pissed the night before – it's a tradition in football. I didn't want it. I wanted my staff in bed at a decent time. I was keeping an eye on all that.

That day at Ipswich, one staff member took charge of the music in the dressing room. It might seem strange, but you find out about characters when you look to see who's in charge of the music. A young lad might want to put on the latest sound; an older player might say, 'I'm the senior player' and put himself in charge of it. But I noticed none of the players were taking

Right Training with Carlos Queiroz, 2005. (John Peters/Manchester United/Getty)

Below Leaving Man United, November 2005. (Chris Coleman/Manchester United/Getty)

Above left Testimonial between United and Celtic at Old Trafford, 9 May 2006. (Laurence Griffiths/Getty)

Above right I swapped sides at half-time. It was nice to be back. (Andrew Yates/AFP/Getty)

Top left Signing for Celtic, 15 December 2005. (Ian Stewart/AFP/Getty)

Left First Old Firm match with Celtic, 12 February 2006. It lived up to all my expectations. (Jeff J. Mitchell/Getty)

Above With Tony Loughlan at Sunderland v. West Brom, 28 August 2006. (Matthew Lewis/Getty)

Left Sunderland training. (Action/Lee Smith)

Above right First match in charge of Sunderland, away to Derby, 9 September 2006. (Warren Little/Getty)

Right Last-minute equaliser by Dave Connolly for Sunderland against Burnley, 16 December 2006. A big turning point for us. (Owen Humphreys/PA Archive/PA)

Right Dwight Yorke playing for Sunderland, 1 January 2007. He had the penthouse in Sydney Harbour, the Lamborghini, all the women. I asked him, 'D'you fancy coming back to Sunderland?' (Clive Mason/Getty)

Below Jonny Evans playing for Sunderland, 24 February 2007. Jonny was unbelievable for us. (Action/Lee Smith)

Top right Celebrating Sunderland win at Luton, 6 May 2007. (Clive Rose/Getty)

Below right A derby with Newcastle, 10 November 2007. My first and it was brilliant. The atmosphere, the relief we weren't beaten. Danny Higginbotham got us the first goal. (Owen Humphreys/PA Archive/PA)

Left Shaking hands with Alex Ferguson at the Sunderland v. United match on 26 December 2007. I got a good reception from the United fans. (Action/Lee Smith)

Below Fàbregas scored an injury-time equaliser for Arsenal, 4 October 2008. It was a pivotal moment in my career. (Nigel Roddis/Action/Reuters)

charge of the music, and this was a concern for me. A member of staff was in charge of it. I was looking at him, thinking, 'I hope someone nails him here.'

If I'd been a player and one of the staff was taking control of the music, I'd have been going, 'Hey, it's the players' dressing room.' The staff have to know their place.

The last song that was played before the players went out on to the pitch was 'Dancing Queen', by Abba. What really worried me was that none of the players – nobody – said, 'Get that shit off.'

I stood back, and thought, 'It's not my place, either. I'm learning.'

We went 1–0 up but we lost 3–1. I don't think it was down to 'Dancing Queen', but after the match I criticised the players; it was one of the few times that I lost the rag. They had to take responsibility, I told them; it was their music.

'What motivates you? This is *your* music.'

They were going out to play a match, men versus men; testosterone levels were high. You've got to hit people at pace. Fuckin' 'Dancing Queen'. I wouldn't have minded if it had been one of Abba's faster ones.

It worried me. I didn't have as many leaders as I'd thought I had.

But even so, I remember saying at the time that I wouldn't want to be working anywhere else but Sunderland. And I meant it. I had a strong feeling for the players and the club. I already felt it was my club.

The Abba fan moved on not long afterwards.

SEVEN

As we went in, Steve was going, 'All right, lads?
All right?' Then he put his head on his desk, and
went, 'You fucking lucky bastards. You fucking lucky
bastards robbed us.'

Nobody can really prepare you for management. I'd done my
UEFA B badge, and was well into my UEFA A. These are stepping
stones. In any other industry I'm sure the stones are of help. But
in this industry, football, they're almost no good to you at all. I
feel a bit bad saying that, because the courses were good. But
when you get into the actual job and you've got players in your
office and they're demanding to leave, or one lad's been drinking
and another one's got gambling problems, or staff are coming to
see you because they've got marriage difficulties, you're going,
'Fuckin' hell, they didn't teach me this.'

I hadn't anticipated that I'd be dealing with personal problems.
I thought my management of the players would be quite straightforward. But saying, 'Just get on with it' isn't enough when there's
a man in your office who is getting divorced, or whose wife has
just had a miscarriage.

'Take three days off, don't worry about it.'

One morning, we were training and the police – two police
officers – came out on to the training pitch.

'We're here to arrest one of your players.'

It was Carlos Edwards, and they were taking him in because he hadn't paid a load of driving or parking fines. He was a really good lad.

I went, 'Can you wait till we're finished training?'

After training, we persuaded the police not to arrest Carlos, that we'd do whatever was necessary to get the fines paid and everything sorted out.

They said, 'Okay, we'll give you the benefit of the doubt.'

As you gain a bit of experience, you end up coping. There were some things – players' problems – that I think I dealt with quite well. I felt comfortable enough talking about drinking or gambling, although I'd never been a gambler – and I tried to give logical, practical advice. But when it came to personal or family problems I felt a bit out of my depth and I didn't want to pretend that I had anything to offer, other than the time off, to try and sort themselves out.

People love giving you information when you're a manager, whether you want it or not – good stuff, bad stuff, players up to no good.

'Two players were out drinking till four in the morning.'

I'd call them in and I'd try to treat them the way I'd like to have been treated. A lot of it is common sense, but it's tiring. Playing had been so much easier.

I lost my temper three times over the season, but never on the sideline. The first time was after the Ipswich game. We'd been 1–0 up, our keeper was poor, 'Dancing Queen' – that was enough.

Sometimes losing my rag just involved me kicking over the tactics board. It became one of my favourites. The kit man, Cookie, enjoyed that one, too. If I came in angry at half-time, I'd say to him, 'Cookie, get the tactics board up.' He'd set it up and I'd kick it over – give it a karate kick. It would let off a bit of steam and, by kicking the board, I was telling the players that this particular game wasn't about tactics. Sometimes you need the board, but my point now was 'This has nothing to do with fuckin' tactics. This is about how much you want it. And they seem to want it more than you.' The Championship is a lot less tactical than the Premiership. It's more about the characters in your dressing room.

Into October, and we lost two more games. Preston beat us 4–1, away. Preston were doing well. Paul Simpson was managing them and they had David Nugent, who I tried to sign the following season. But it was a bad defeat, and our goal – Stan Varga scored it – came when we were already 4–0 down.

Then Stoke beat us 2–1. Rory Delap broke his leg playing for Stoke, only a few weeks after I'd let him go there on loan. I rang him in hospital.

I'd had to let some players go out on loan. Rory went to Stoke, and Jon Stead went to Derby. It was all about trying to balance the books. I'd brought in Dave Connolly, and the club was paying him good money; so I had to let Steadie, another striker, go. If I let a player go I always thought it was for his benefit. Steadie went to Sheffield United later in the season; they were in the Premiership. If the player wasn't getting a game, I wouldn't hold on to him. There was a financial benefit for the club, too, getting him off the wage bill, and there might be a loan fee. That was the business side of it – and I discovered a lot more about that later, when I tried to get some players in on loan.

The defeats – three in four games – worried me a bit. When a new manager comes in there's often a feel-good factor, a honeymoon period. New ideas, and a few new players. That phase seemed to be over. But I'll always remember the Sunderland fans at Stoke, after the game. The away fans' enclosure is near the tunnel, and they gave me a great send-off, even though we'd just been beaten. The Sunderland fans travelled in big numbers, and they were noisy. They were as passionate as the United and Celtic fans. I applauded them – sometimes the applause is an apology – and I mentioned them regularly at the press conferences throughout the season.

We got two good results in a row, at home to Barnsley, then at Hull. Ross Wallace scored in the last minute of the Hull game, then got sent off – a second yellow for taking off his jersey. Removing your jersey is an automatic yellow but a lot of footballers shouldn't do it anyway, and Ross would have been one of them. He was always going to struggle keeping his body fat down below 10 per cent.

'Here, listen,' I joked. 'We don't mind some lads taking their tops off. But not you – you little fat fucker. You'll get my fitness coach sacked.'

I didn't crucify Ross for the offence. He'd scored the winner; it was an emotional moment. At the press conference after the game, journalists kept asking what disciplinary measures I'd be taking against him. I said that I'd have a look at it during the week. But I didn't fine him at all.

We were winning a few matches. We were growing in confidence. And I was growing in confidence. I was thinking, 'Yeah, this is for me, management.'

When you're winning, you don't see yourself losing. We'd moved up the table, to thirteenth, but we were struggling to be consistent. Everyone remembers Sunderland going from the bottom to the top in a couple of months, but it didn't happen that way. It was hard work.

We were beaten at home by Cardiff, 2–1. Cardiff were a good team but, just when I thought we were making progress, we came up short – again. You lose a match, you start doubting your players.

Then we were beaten at Norwich. That was followed by a draw with Southampton. We were 1–0 up, but Gareth Bale scored for them in injury time. Bale played at left-back; he was outstanding, the best player on the pitch. Everything he did had a bit of quality about it. He was seventeen. Even though they'd scored in injury time, I couldn't begrudge Southampton the result. I was grateful for the draw.

We won at home to Colchester. Our results so far – it was proper hit and miss.

In the meantime, my wife was coming up from Manchester with the kids, and we were trying to find a school. A Catholic school was important to us because the kids were already at one; the schools were good and we liked their message. We were looking at houses but we couldn't find a school. Weeks went by, then months, and my family hadn't moved. But I was happy enough with the arrangement. It suited me, the balance between my personal and professional lives. So, I said, 'It's working.'

In the end, the family stayed in Manchester. The travel wasn't killing me; I like driving – I like driving late at night or early in the morning. It was a two and a half hour drive, a nice drive, past Leeds. I'd have two or three days at home. I'd work hard at Sunderland, and then I'd go home to people who didn't really care too much about my professional life.

Funnily enough, they were more interested in my job as a manager. I think they understood that I had more responsibility, and they appreciated the pressure I was under. They were rooting for me more. Before games, they'd go, 'Good luck, Dad', whereas, when I was a player, I'd go, 'I'm off, Daddy's going to Old Trafford to work', and they'd hardly notice.

I rented a flat in Durham, in a student area. I could go into the cafés because, generally speaking, students aren't that interested in football, so they hadn't a clue who I was. I'd be in bed at eight or nine, anyway. I should have decorated the flat a bit more, made it more of a home. I wish I'd made more of an effort. I could have got a good telly, a nice sofa. But I ended up living like a student myself – Pot Noodles and tins of beans.

After a month or two I was worried about the body-fat levels of some of the players, particularly some of the lads who hadn't been playing regularly. I don't mean that they were half a stone overweight. I put an announcement up on the notice board: unless players could get their body fat down to under 10 per cent they wouldn't be selected to play. I excluded the goalkeepers, because they need to carry an extra bit of fat, to cushion their landings. They were pleased with that.

Every now and again you have to change the routine. The notice board was down near the players' dressing room. I kept my distance, as a manager. I didn't go into the dressing room too often. It was the players' area. But I knew that when a notice went up on the board – squads, or trips – it became a hub of activity. The body-fat announcement was just a small idea, something to get them talking. It was fun and games, really; a little threat. I was putting pressure on the players. And it worked. I'd been pals with everybody; I'd played in teams with a lot of them. I just wavered on the niceness a bit. But if a player stayed just over the limit, and he was important to us, I wasn't going to drop him for it.

Mick McCarthy was managing Wolves and he rang me about a player; I think it was Neill Collins, who he wanted to take on loan.

He rang me direct, straight through to my office.

'All right, Roy?'

We chatted about the player, and about this and that. It wasn't an awkward conversation, and I was glad he'd rung me. It had crossed my mind that we'd be meeting during the course of the season. Our teams would be playing against each other, and I was a member of the LMA now, too – the League Managers' Association; there'd be functions I'd have to go to. We were bound to meet.

I think it was Mick who suggested that we meet up for a chat; we both thought it was a good idea.

We met at the Four Seasons Hotel, near Manchester Airport, and it was a bit like the meeting with Niall, a nice anticlimax. I said I was sorry about what had happened in Saipan. I'm not sure I had anything to apologise for. But you try to move on.

But that was that. It was important, and I'm glad it happened.

We were playing Wolves, away, in November, on a Friday night. The media were all over it, and the game was live on Sky. The build-up to the game was all 'Are they going to shake hands?' But we'd already met and we'd kept that to ourselves. So it was no big drama for us. We shook hands before the game, but it wasn't prearranged. We just shook hands. Managers do it before every game. It's standard practice. The only difference this time was that there were fifty cameramen around us.

But that was another night I lost my rag. We were 1–0 down at half-time; we were shocking. I told Cookie to get the tactics board out, and I did a bit of a Bruce Lee on it. I think the players were distracted by the whole Keane–McCarthy stuff. And I have to ask myself the question, was I extra angry because I didn't want to lose to Mick McCarthy's team? I'd hope not. But we were on TV and we were shit. Poor Cookie had to spend ages looking for all the little players off the tactics board.

We drew 1–1 but we were lucky. Our keeper, Darren Ward, kept us in the game, and our goal, a shot by Stevie Elliott, was deflected.

We beat QPR, 2–1, away, then Norwich, the return fixture, at home. We beat them 1–0. Daryl Murphy scored in both games.

Our next game, the following Saturday, was at home to Luton.

I was called to a meeting at the club on Friday night. Niall and the club secretary were there. Three of the players, Chris Brown, Liam Lawrence and Ben Alnwick, had allegedly been caught on video making out with a girl. The club hierarchy was panicking about it because the story was going to appear in the *Sun*. The two lads who were important to me were Brown and Lawrence, because we'd a game the next day and they were both in my team. They hadn't done anything illegal, so I said I was going to play them. But Niall said that the club was insisting that they wouldn't play.

I didn't play them.

It was the first time, I suppose, that I was challenged as a manager. I wasn't kicking and screaming, but I was upset about it. But I could see the club's point of view. We were trying to build a new Sunderland, a new image, new standards. And the club wasn't telling me that the players could never play for Sunderland again.

I told Lawrence and Brown they were out for Saturday's match, but I let them know that they'd be back in the team at some stage. I made it clear to them that it wasn't my decision. I thought it was important that they could think, 'Well, the manager's still all right with us.'

We won without them. We beat Luton, 2–1; Murph and Dave Connolly scored.

The whole thing had annoyed me but I think I'd have been more annoyed if they'd been late for training. I'd been a player myself, and I'd been in trouble; I'd caused the club and the manager grief. So I always tried to be fair with the players. When I called them into the office, say, for drinking, I'd let them know that it wasn't on. But I'd like to think that I was understanding. I wasn't condoning their behaviour, but I was their manager, not their father, or judge and jury – and I'd have a football match coming up that I had to try and win. That, ultimately, was my job. I needed the players. Lawrence and Brown weren't Messi and Ronaldo but they were important to me.

Later in the season I had a falling-out with Liam Lawrence on the training pitch. I had the lads playing eleven v. eleven, and we'd too many there – more than twenty-two. Some players weren't getting the full game, and Liam was one of them. He wasn't happy about it, and stormed into the dressing room. He said he wasn't going to stand on the sideline.

I said, 'See you in my office.'

The two of us were shouting at each other, in the office. I think now that it would have been wise to have someone else present, if I thought there was going to be a confrontation, or a contract issue, or a player wanting to leave – someone to witness the conversation, all the 'he said this, and I said that'.

I told Liam, 'It's no big deal.'

Other players had to stand on the sideline, to give another player a run out. That was all there was to it – as simple as that.

But Liam was going, 'I'm not putting up with all this.'

It was a proper shouting match; it was more than that. It was intense. I think I might have grabbed him – there might have been a bit of grappling, when he started to leave the office. We were alone, but everyone in the other offices would have heard us.

But it was good. Everything had been going well; I'd had the full support of everyone. This was my first real confrontation. I loved it. I thought to myself, 'I want more of this – one of these a day.'

I don't really mean that, but it was good to let off some steam.

It didn't exactly shock me, but I was surprised that Liam was so angry and that I was so angry. Up to now, whatever I'd said, people had done. This was the first time a lad had defied me – and in front of the other players. So I'd had to think fast.

'How am I going to deal with this?'

Liam just lost his rag on the day; there was no bad blood between us. And I kind of admired him for standing up for himself. But, ironically – or maybe not so ironically – we got a call from Stoke the next morning; they wanted to know if Liam was available.

I said, 'Yeah' – but not because of the bust-up. As I've said, when you bring players in you have to let other lads go.

Liam came in just after the call and apologised.

'I'm sorry about yesterday.'

I said, 'No problem. But I'm just after getting a call from Stoke. Do you fancy it?'

He said, 'All right.'

It suited everyone.

Our next game, a 2–2 draw away to Burnley, was a big turning point for us. We were 2–0 down and we were awful. Grant Leadbitter got one back for us, but then we equalised in injury time – Dave Connolly again. We came away with a point, but we could have been beaten five or six-nil.

Steve Cotterill was managing Burnley at the time. After a game, the tradition is you have a drink with the opposition manager, whether you won, lost or drew. Everybody puts on a front.

'Well played.'

'Who have you got next week?'

'I thought you played well.'

I'd speak to the manager, the goalkeeping coach would speak to the goalkeeping coach. This time, we were a bit embarrassed going in. We'd got a point in the last kick of the game, and we hadn't deserved it. We felt like we'd mugged them.

As we went in, Steve was going, 'All right, lads? All right?'

Then he put his head on his desk, and went, 'You fucking lucky bastards. You fucking lucky bastards robbed us.'

It was brilliant; he was being himself – honest. He wasn't going, 'Well done, lads, good game. Here's a Diet Coke, Roy; well played.' We all do it; we go, 'The fucking bastards', but only after the other team have got on their bus and gone home. But Steve did it in front of us.

We all relaxed; we were laughing.

Usually, when you go into another manager's office nobody's relaxed. Everyone's acting; you can't be yourself. If you've won the game, you're buzzing. If you've lost, you're pissed off. But you can't express these feelings in front of the other team's manager and staff. A year later, Blackburn came up to the Stadium of Light. Mark Hughes, who I'd played with at United, was managing Blackburn, and they beat us, 2–1 – they robbed us. Everyone was listening to the conversation between myself and Mark in my office after the game.

He asked me where I lived.

'Durham.'

'How long does it take you to get from Manchester to Durham?'

'About two and a half hours.'

'How many miles is it, door to door?'

I'm not knocking him – I've got time for Sparky. But we couldn't be ourselves.

I answered him: 'A hundred and thirty-eight', I think it was.

When he left, my staff were going, 'What the fuck was that about?'

But it was just awkward, and it was like that every week.

'Who have you got next week?'

'Where did you stay last night?'

But this – Steve losing his rag – was one of the highlights of the season. We'd shown another side of our team, the fighting side. We kept giving ourselves mountains to climb, but the players were climbing them. We were fighting, and scrapping. We'd got a draw we hadn't deserved; we'd scored in injury time, in front of our fans.

We showed a clip of the celebrations to the players, because it had been on the news, on television. Dave Connolly had jumped into the away stand, to celebrate with the Sunderland fans. One or two of the fans fell out of the stand – it was only a small drop but, still, they went head over heels on to the pitch. But it was creating a story, that we were all in this together, the players, the fans, the club – 'We're Sunderland and we never give up. We stay to the end.'

As the season went on, we got a lot of late goals – because the teams we were playing believed we'd get a late goal. It wasn't about us believing; it was about them – dropping back and dropping back.

But it still hadn't crossed my mind that we might get promoted. I just thought, 'It's been difficult, but we're moving away from relegation.'

After the Burnley game I said that we weren't ready for the play-offs yet, and that some of the players weren't up to that challenge. I'd say something like that, occasionally, to test the players' mentality, or as a message to Niall and the board, to bring them – and me – back down to reality. If the board were getting a bit giddy, and thinking that we had all the players we needed, I was reminding them that we needed a few more; the January transfer window was coming up. I wasn't playing games with the board; we *did* need the players if we were going to go further. And, if we had a midweek game, there'd be four press conferences in the week – I had to say *something* to the media. There'd be a press conference on Friday, then again immediately after the match on Saturday. If we played on a Tuesday night, I had to talk to the media on Monday, and after the match. It was boring – the same questions four times a week.

The Championship was full of big, historical names – Leeds, Derby, Leicester, Wolves, Sunderland. But I didn't like that term 'the sleeping giant'. That was why I thought that me going into Sunderland cold was a good thing; I didn't care about the history, at first. The reality was: 'This is where we are', near the bottom of the Championship; let's get the house in order. As I got a feel for the club, I began to appreciate the importance of history. I met some of the ex-players, including Charlie Hurley, who is a massive star in Sunderland, and Dennis Tueart, who'd been in the team that won the FA Cup in 1973. I started to get pictures up on the walls, in the dressing room and in the training ground. The training ground had the feel of a private hospital – brilliant facilities, but cold; the walls were bare. 'Let's get some pictures up.' Bob Stokoe and the 1973 FA Cup, previous teams that had won promotion, and pictures of the fans.

I spoke to the staff about the need to dress well for match days. I was putting my marker down. Bill the masseur had a Sunderland tattoo down the side of his leg. I remember talking to him in my office.

I said, 'I know on match days you wear short socks. Can you wear bigger socks? I've nothing against tattoos but I'm trying to send a message – we're Sunderland now.'

It was a strange one. I kept reminding myself that I was speaking to a grown man.

But he said, 'Yeah, I know where you're coming from. Brilliant, gaffer – you're dead right.'

Bill was a really good guy, a big Sunderland fan. He wasn't going, 'Who do you think you are? I'm proud of my tattoos.' It was a chat that could have gone wrong. He took it in very good spirit, and I think that summed up my time at the club. If I'd said to people, 'Jump,' they would have said, 'How high?'

We were beaten by Crystal Palace, away, and then we beat Leeds, 2–0, at home on St Stephen's Day – Boxing Day; Dave Connolly and Grant Leadbitter scored.

There were over 40,000 in the ground; the atmosphere was brilliant. Leeds brought a load of fans up with them, too, and there's a lot of hatred between Leeds and Sunderland, going back to the 1973 FA Cup final. Dennis Wise was managing Leeds, and Gus Poyet was his assistant. We were attacking, and Gus got a ball from one of the ballboys. He kicked it out on to the pitch and stopped the game. He was sent to the stand. There was proper rivalry between the two teams, so it was a good win for us. Yorkie was starting to look sharper – considering he could have been on Bondi Beach, having his Christmas dinner.

We lost at home to Preston, 1–0. I'd sent ten players out on loan and I was regretting it now. I particularly regretted letting them play against us. The lad Tommy Miller played against us for Preston, and he played very well. I shouldn't have let him play; it was a big mistake. The only loser was going to be me. If the player didn't play well, it was almost irrelevant. But if he had a good game, it was going to be, 'Why are you letting him play against us?', or 'Why is such a good player out on loan in the first place?', because it was a guarantee that he'd have something to prove when he was out on the pitch. In my innocence I didn't want to begrudge the lad a game. I was still learning not to think like a player, and to be a bit more ruthless.

At the end of 2006 we were twelfth in the league. We had thirty-seven points from twenty-six games, and we were ten points behind Preston, who were second in the table. Generally, if you can average two points a game you'll be promoted. We were well behind that.

Our first game of the new year was on 2 January, away to Leicester. Leicester were good but we won, 2–0. Dave Connolly scored again; he was doing the business for us and really proving his worth.

That was the day we took off. The day our surge to the top started – although we didn't know it then. But I began to wonder if we could kick on and get into one of the play-off positions. A top-two place, and automatic promotion, seemed too far off. I didn't think it would happen that year; it was too early. But the play-offs would be progress.

But we had – it's the biggest word in football – momentum. It's like a tidal wave. Southampton, away; we scored in the last minute. Burnley, at home, down 3–2; we scored with the last kick of the game. Derby, at home, it's 1–1; Liam Millar scores the winner in injury time, with a header – and he's the smallest man on the pitch. Momentum – we had it.

We brought in some players in January. Carlos Edwards, from Luton; Anthony Stokes, from Arsenal; and Jonny Evans – we got Jonny on loan from Manchester United. They were all good signings, brilliant, and just what we needed. One of the reasons they worked, I think, is because I knew a bit about them, beyond the stats – something about their personalities.

Carlos had played against us when we beat Luton earlier in the season, and I'd seen what a good player he was. He gave us a right-sided midfielder. He had pace, and he could get us up the pitch; we could counter-attack away from home.

Jonny was a centre-half. He had the qualities of a Manchester United player, and he was bringing them to Sunderland. For such a young man – he was nineteen – he was very mature, and a born leader. Jonny was unbelievable for us. He lived with his mam and dad in Sale, near my home, so I picked him up there and brought him up to see the set-up at Sunderland. I knew I was on a winner; I knew him, and I knew what he was about. I remembered an incident when I was still at United; there'd been a fight in the canteen and Jonny had looked after himself well – I think he knocked the other lad out. I knew Jonny was tough.

Stokesy got us vital goals towards the end of the season. He was a good signing for us, because there'd been a lot of competition for him. Celtic and Charlton, who were still in the Premiership then, were after him. So signing Stokesy sent out another message: we could compete with other clubs. I spoke to Stokesy's dad and, for some reason, he thought I'd be able to keep his son on the straight and narrow – because Stokesy was a bit of a boy.

I can't think of a player who we brought in that season who disappointed. They all contributed. I'd brought in good players, to add to the good players we already had. Regardless of where we finished the season, these players would do a job for us for a good few years.

We were knocked out of the FA Cup in the third round, by Preston. That was a disappointment, because I'm a fan of the FA Cup. A run in the Cup would have been great; I would never have worried about a fixture pile-up. The financial incentives were there, too – a Cup run brings money into the club. But we played Preston three times over the season, and they definitely had an edge over us.

We beat Ipswich 1–0; Dave Connolly again. Then we beat Sheffield Wednesday away, 4–2. Yorkie scored a great goal, a nice little dink over the keeper. But we were 3–0 up and they came back to 3–2. I nearly had a fuckin' heart attack.

That was the third time I lost my rag. Again, there was a message. Everyone in the dressing room was delighted. We'd won 4–2 – but we should never have let them come back. I told them that it wasn't good enough, and that there had to be consistent standards. They couldn't let the other team back into the game; they might get away with it against Wednesday, but not against better teams. It's not a bad idea to be critical of the players after they've won a match. They took the criticism, but they'd still won. And it's not as if I'd lost my temper because we'd lost; that wasn't the excuse, so they couldn't dismiss it.

But the atmosphere among our fans at that game was fantastic. They started singing a version of 'Hey, Jude' – 'na na na na-na-na-na – Keano' – at half-time, and kept at it right through the second half. It carried on for the rest of the season. I took it with a pinch of salt, although I'd never heard supporters singing about a manager like that before. I should probably have appreciated it more. But I didn't want to enjoy it too much, because it can all change so quickly. We were doing well but I knew that we'd eventually have a dip in form. Real Madrid and Manchester United have had dips. At Sunderland, we were going to have a big fuckin' dip. And when that happens, who's the first to get it? The manager. I wasn't a messiah, and I didn't want to be seen as one. Anyway, I've never been a big lover of that song. It might have been different if it had been a song I liked.

I brought in Stern John before the transfer deadline, from Coventry City. He was one of my best signings ever.

I was at home on a Monday night, watching Coventry away to Plymouth. It was pissing down, and it looked like a shocking game. But every time the ball went to Stern John, it stuck – it stuck with him. He couldn't run, but we just needed someone who could get hold of the ball. Dave Connolly and Daryl Murphy were about getting into the box and scoring, but there's a saying in football, 'When it goes up to him, it sticks'; when the ball went up to Stern, it stuck. Brian Clough used to say to his son, Nigel, 'Fuckin' stick – make it stick.' The ball was protected, and we could get up the pitch, or have a breather, or win a free-kick – you had options.

The next day, I went and spoke to my staff.

'I've seen a player – Stern John. We've got to get him. He'll give us something different.'

One of the staff said, 'His knees are gone.'

I said, 'Look at his record.'

He rarely missed a game; he played forty games a year.

He failed his medical, but I said to Peter Walker, 'Do the deal.'

I'd looked at Stern's playing record, and the fee we were paying for him was small; it wasn't a massive investment. And who was going to question me? We were winning matches; everything was going well. We signed him.

I knew he'd be a man, and he was one of the best men I've come across. I knew he could deal with coming up to Sunderland. I knew he wouldn't be coming into my office with, 'Can I have a day off next week 'cos my wife needs a scan?' I knew I wouldn't have to baby-sit him.

A year or so later I was after Kenwyne Jones, and I told Stern, 'I don't want to sell you, but I'm trying to get Kenwyne Jones in and Southampton want you as part of the deal.'

He said, 'Okay, I'll go for it.'

He stood up and shook my hand.

'Thanks for everything.'

And I went, 'That's why I signed you.'

A man.

He was brilliant.

Danny Simpson came in, on loan from United. A right-back – he helped us get promoted. He got us up the pitch. Himself and Carlos played on the right, too, and they struck up a good relationship. We now had plenty of strength and pace down that side. Danny was a likeable lad and he brought United qualities with him; but he was no angel – he had an edge to him.

We had a good mix of players. We'd Yorkie, Carlos and Stern, from Trinidad; we'd the Irish lads; we'd a couple of local lads – Grant Leadbitter and a few other young lads in the background coming up, Jordan Henderson, Martyn Waghorn, Jack Colback. It was a really good mix – lads who got on well together. It helped that we were winning football matches; everything seems great when you're winning.

Our next game was a 0–0 draw, at home to Crystal Palace. We didn't win but we kept a clean sheet. I was happy with that, and I let the players know it.

I'd made Dean Whitehead our new captain. The previous captain, Stephen Caldwell, moved on to Burnley just before the transfer deadline. Dean's fitness levels were very good; he was never injured and I could rely on him – I liked him. He was captain of the team but possibly Yorkie was the unofficial leader.

We beat Coventry at home, 2–0; Yorkie and Carlos scored. Then the same score away to Plymouth; Dave and Stokesy.

Ian Holloway was managing Plymouth. I didn't get a real chance to celebrate the victory because Ian pulled me into a meeting to tell me all about the problems he was having getting training facilities. I was thinking, 'I don't give a shit about your training facilities. I just won a game of football.'

We beat Southend United 4–0, at home – Dave, Tobias Hysén, and Stern got two. When I look back at it now, I think the signings I made that season are even better than I thought at the time.

The crowds were unbelievable. It made me feel I'd definitely made the right decision, coming to Sunderland. We were winning, and the crowds were steadily getting bigger. We'd gone from 14,000 to, eventually, 42,000. Where did the twenty-seven extra thousand come from? I don't think we were doing anything amazing; we were winning.

We were up to sixth.

The Championship is relentless. You don't get a breather. But I'd like to think there was fun. It's horrible, I suppose, but when you win you think, 'We'll have to win next week', or in a few days, if there's a midweek game. And if you lose, you go, 'It's going to be a long week.'

I've spoken to experienced managers. Some of them enjoy Monday to Friday, but dread Saturday. I was the opposite. I wasn't mad about Monday to Friday, but I loved Saturday. I felt a bit like a boxer; the sparring is all well and good, but it's all about the fights. But a good boxer has to spar, and a good team has to train properly. I didn't like it if we got beaten – 'There's pain coming today' – or if we had injuries, but I thought that that was where I'd be judged, on the pitch, on match day.

I enjoyed watching reserve games during the week, or DVDs of the opposition, but I found some of the duties, like writing programme notes for the next home match, a bit mundane, a bit of a nuisance. I couldn't wait for the next game. That changed later on – football will always kick you in the bollocks. But, with this group of players, I knew what I was going to get.

We'd have debriefings on Monday mornings, and plenty of banter. Do you know what? – we *did* have a lot of fun. This was on the back of winning matches. We socialised a lot, three or four of us going into Durham for a bite to eat. The staff and myself were quite competitive, so we'd do a lot of gym work together – or go-karting. There's an outdoor circuit near Sunderland. It's brilliant. I think the go-karting was the highlight of the week for some of the staff, not what happened on Saturday.

We were going well but there were always issues; things were never too rosy. Tobias Hysén told me that he was homesick; he wanted to go back to Sweden. And there were things I was still trying to get used to – not dramatic moments, just aspects of the job. We were trying to move some players. We had too many that we didn't need. I'd be praying for a phone call from another club. I found that frustrating – the waiting. Staff would come to me, asking, say, for time off because of marital difficulties, or problems with their children. I think that was one of my strengths; I think I had a kindness to me. But there was never a day when I'd go into work and come out later in the same mood; there'd always be something going on.

I'd get letters now and again from supporters telling me that some of the players had been out drinking – the standard stuff. It was always the Irish lads – always. I never got a letter about the English lads out drinking late.

Graham Kavanagh and Stokesy got into trouble one night; there'd been a fight.

I think it was Stokesy who said, 'Gaffer, it wasn't me. I was only backing him up.'

I think Kav had head-butted someone.

I'd say, 'Now, lads, watch yourselves.'

I wasn't their parent. I think some managers go too far, trying to be the father figure. When the players came into my office, I didn't come down on them, all the big I am.

I'd go, 'Lads, what are you doing? Just be careful.'

I'd try to be more like a friend – maybe a big brother. Because I had been there myself, and people *will* want to get you into trouble. Ferguson used to call me in and say, 'I found out you were in a bar last week.'

And I'd say, 'Yeah, I was – I was.'

'You left at half two in the morning.'

'Yeah? Was it half two?'

I would go out on a Sunday night, even if we played on a Wednesday, or I'd drink on Wednesday night with a game the following Saturday. But I'd never drink two nights before a game, whatever day the game might fall on. It's not ideal to be drinking even three days before a game but, at the time, I felt I could manage it. It was a standard clause in the contract that you couldn't go out two nights before a game, so I wasn't breaking any rules.

'You got a taxi at half past two this morning, in Sale.'

'Yeah.'

'What were you doing there?'

'I was drinking.'

We were sixth, in a play-off position. But I wasn't going overboard. I stayed in the role, kept up the moody image. I didn't want the players thinking we could relax or settle for a place in the play-offs. And we had three games coming up, in the space of eleven days, against teams that were above us. These were going to be massive games for us.

The first was against Birmingham, managed by my old friend Steve Bruce. We drew 1–1; Carlos Edwards scored the goal, lashed it in with his left foot – almost a trademark Carlos goal. He was scoring some great goals. Birmingham were ahead of us in the table, so I was happy enough with the result.

I've always had good battles against Brucie, when he was with Birmingham and, later, Wigan. He's a good key to learning how to manage upwards – how to manage the owners and chief executives. He was at Birmingham when Gold and Sullivan were the owners, and he got on well with them. Brucie always had a nice way about him, whoever was in his office. He got on well with Dave Whelan when he was managing at Wigan. Now he's at Hull, with the owner who wants to change the name to

'Hull Tigers', and Brucie defends his point of view. He seems to work with difficult people, but he manages it well. During my Pro Licence, one of the things I was told was that the key to managerial longevity wasn't managing downwards, but managing the people above you. I admire the way Brucie has done it.

Next, we had Derby, at home. At the press conference the day before the game I said that, mentally, some teams at the top of the table would lose the plot. I was playing games. That's what you do, especially against the teams ahead of you. We were in a good position, nowhere near the top yet. It was like a horse race: don't get to the front too early. We were coming up slowly, and the teams higher up the table had been watching us for months. Now we were coming up against the Derbys and the Birminghams, managers like Billy Davies and Brucie, men with huge experience. Sometimes I had to throw a couple of hand grenades. If we were beaten, nobody would think much of my quote, or even remember it. If we won – 'Oh, the mind games.'

And we won – Liam Miller's header. The smallest man on the pitch. That was when the crowd really took off. The staff were jumping around, the subs were out on the pitch. And I thought, 'There's something happening here.'

I won Manager of the Month. But I wasn't sure about the point of these awards, and I've always felt that way. I won awards as a player – the Sports Writers' Player of the Year, the PFA Player of the Year, Player of the Year in Ireland. I was at the award ceremonies, and I'd be praying that I wouldn't win. I hated putting myself out there, in that way – going up to collect it. There was a shyness involved in it. I didn't want to go up. But I loved football as a team game, and it gets my back up when I see players, and even managers, being presented as more important than they actually are. A lot of the awards are about publicity for the sponsors. I won Manager of the Month in February 2007.

What good was it to me a few years later? Don't get too carried away, because you're up for a fall. I said at the time that I'd put the award in the garage – and I did.

We beat West Brom, 2–1, away. Yorkie and Stern scored; they were brilliant. It was a great result for us. But afterwards there was a bit of trouble in the dressing room.

Near the end of the game, only a few minutes to go, Stokesy had gone through; he gave a bad ball away and West Brom broke on us. They didn't score, but a lot of the players were still angry with Stokesy and having a proper go at him when I went into the dressing room.

I went berserk. Defending him. Defending a young player who was being bullied. We'd won the game and he'd made a mistake. When I'd lost my temper after the Sheffield Wednesday game, it had been a football matter; we'd nearly thrown the game away. But this time was different. He was eighteen or nineteen – a kid. They were all shouting at him aggressively. Senior players.

I think my exact words were 'Give him a fuckin' break!'

Then I found out that Tony Mowbray, the West Brom manager, had been talking crap after the game, as managers do. He was going, 'We were the better team and if we keep playing like that we'll be all right. We played better than Sunderland.'

I felt he was quite dismissive of us, and me. I was annoyed about that, because we'd deserved the win; we'd played well.

Those three results in a row, the draw against Birmingham and the wins against Derby and West Brom – we were taking off. I remember thinking, 'My God, we might actually go up.'

The next game was away to Barnsley. And three players missed the bus – Stokesy, Tobias Hysén and Márton Fülöp. We'd waited for them at the station in Middlesbrough, where we'd arranged for all the players to meet us.

They rang us: 'We're stuck in traffic.'

I said, 'Well, we can't wait any longer. We're off.'

I left them behind.

'We'll get another few players down.'

I didn't shout down the phone or anything. I understood: they were stuck in traffic. But that was no good to us. So we left without them.

That was another message I was sending out. Lateness was an issue at the club – bad habits. Football is about good habits. It's not about always doing something extraordinary; it's about doing the ordinary things well.

We went to Barnsley and we won, 2–0; Dave Connolly and Grant Leadbitter. It was another massive game. We took 8,000 fans with us, and the place was rocking, absolutely brilliant. The news about the players we'd left behind was going around the fans. And Niall was on the radio – 'We'll stand for no nonsense.' It was a bit hard on the players. I didn't want them to be scapegoated, but it was almost natural that they would be. They'd been late, but a good bit late. We'd waited; I'd given them a chance.

After the game, at the press conference, I said that I was trying to change the mentality at Sunderland, the idea that it was a yo-yo club, that it was acceptable to be late for training or that you didn't have to train hard all the time, or that you could get two or three weeks out of a week-long injury. That was a message for everybody – the players, the staff, the fans, Niall, the board. Everybody. It was nice to be able to deliver these good messages on the back of victories.

The Barnsley Three were at the training ground early enough on Monday morning to bring in the milk. I'd called them in early for a meeting, but only so we could get it out of the way and they could go out to training. They came into my office together, like they were coming to see the headmaster. Which I didn't like.

I said, 'Look, lads, you were out of order. But it was no big deal. You're not going to be made to suffer any more. You'll all be training with the first team.'

I didn't fine them.

I'd take a stance, then say, 'It's over.' I wanted the lads to know that we were going places, and they were still part of it. I wanted them to look at me like I'd looked at Ferguson and think, 'Well, that's fair.' Regarding more personal matters, I could have hang-ups for years. But when it came to players, I had to be a bit more selfish; I knew I needed them.

We drew with Stoke at home, 2–2. We were 2–1 down, then Daryl Murphy scored in injury time. We were poor. Everyone had thought that we could beat Stoke, even though Stoke had beaten us earlier in the season. But Stoke were decent. Murph scored, and I said to myself, 'That's a massive point.'

After the game, I came into the dressing room. Everyone was flat. The players, even the staff. I got annoyed with my staff that night. Two–one in injury time, and we still drew – they're the points that get you up. Never give up.

We beat Hull at home, 2–0; Jonny Evans and Stern. Then we won at Cardiff. A big result – Ross Wallace scored with a free-kick. Jonny was a big player for us – his leadership, and his ability to read the game. He was a tough boy. The Championship is full of men who've been around the block, but Jonny was only just a kid. I liked everything about Jonny.

That was the night Niall organised all the taxis for the fans who were stranded at Bristol Airport. Later, I announced that I was hiring a private detective to dig up some dirt on Niall, that no one could be that good. I'm still working on it.

Since the new year we'd had eleven wins and three draws. Our next game was at home to Wolves. I thought, 'This'll be a good test for us.' It would be a measure of our progress, a little benchmark. Wolves were doing well, too. It was April now, and there were six games left to the end of the season. I knew some of the players would be nervous.

Yorkie had just had his Lamborghini shipped over from Sydney and he brought it into the training ground. A white Lamborghini in Sunderland does stick out a little bit. I was looking out of my office window and Yorkie was pulling up outside, and all the lads – the players – were looking at his wheels. It was perfect. They were focusing on Yorkie's Lamborghini, and the game against Wolves was the last thing on their minds.

The next day we went out and beat them. We won, 2–1. Daryl Murphy scored for us – a rocket. After the game, Mick McCarthy said that we'd definitely be promoted. He was playing games with us, the way I'd done with Derby – putting the pressure on the other team.

The rumour on the street was that we were doing something extraordinary. My training, apparently, was legendary. But we were just doing what I'd done for years. But we were doing it properly. We trained properly and we travelled properly. I made the lads wear a shirt and tie when they went anywhere.

This is vital: we'd trained our fuckin' socks off. I always say, 'You train how you play', with intensity. We always had a game at the end of the session. Not just a few stretches, and a little kick about. If it was a draw, the lads played until there was a winner, even if it went on for hours. There had to be something at the end of training; there had to be a winner or a loser, and punish- ment for the losers – press-ups, or collecting the balls and cones. We were creating a spirit among them. There were bust-ups and fisticuffs – but nice fisticuffs. It wasn't nasty; it was enthusiasm. The players were hungry. They all wanted to be in the starting eleven.

I'd go to the staff, 'Let them get on with it. Don't get involved.'

Winners and losers. Grown men playing like they were kids on the street. There were no draws in street football.

'We can't play any more; it's too dark.'

When I was a kid we'd play till midnight, until there was a result. Even then, we'd go for five more minutes. Never mind blood levels and muscle tears.

I'd be told that it was going on too long.

'It's half twelve. We started at ten.'

The sports scientists will tell you it was all wrong, and that everything should be done by the watch. And I understand that, too; I'm interested in sports science. But I'm also old school.

If we didn't have a midweek game, we'd give them Sunday or Monday off. Tuesday would be hard, a tough session; then Wednesdays would be off. We'd mix it up the odd time. There wouldn't be that much training at this stage of the season, towards the end, because of the number of games we were playing. It was all about games, and recovery. We kept it simple because we were winning matches.

Southampton, away – a brilliant game. We won 2–1, with a couple of great goals. Grant Leadbitter scored one of them. He was a top player for us. He was a good goalscorer, and very rarely injured. A good local lad; he had a nice way about him. He could go off on a rant in the dressing room, and it was very hard to understand him. It was a standing joke among the staff, when Grant went off on one – 'Leave him.' He was a good leader.

I don't think I ever had a conversation with the players or a member of staff about promotion – but I did have the odd glimpse at my contract to see what the bonus was. We just kept winning, and the League table took care of itself. The table never lies. It was one of my strengths as a player – 'Just try and win your next match and everything else will fall into place.' That was always my attitude.

We beat QPR at home, 2–1 again; Dean Whitehead, and another great goal from Grant. I think I praised Nyron Nosworthy after the game because of his attitude. I said it summed up the attitude of the whole team. Nyron was a really good player for us, and a nice lad. I had an incident with him earlier in the season. He was late for training, but he lived about two minutes from the training ground. I called him into my office – and the excuse he gave me? He told the truth.

'I slept it out.'

I said, 'Thanks for telling me the truth.'

I didn't even fine him.

We had three games left.

We went mountain biking in Cumbria. It was great, and a bit mad. I began to wonder if it was a bit too mad. We were on the bikes for six or seven hours. A competition was organised for us – two or three teams. I remember having a go at one of my team because he had a puncture. We were shattered after it – fucked. And we'd a game in a couple of days, against Colchester. We were building up team spirit and camaraderie. It was brilliant.

We went to Colchester and we lost, 3–1. We cycled to Colchester! The players still had sore arses from the biking in Cumbria.

There was a lesson in the result. We'd got back to 1–1, and a draw wouldn't have been bad. But we were on a run, so I thought, 'Fuckin' go for it.' We just kept going, which had helped us in other games, but not this one. If we'd drawn at Colchester, we could have been promoted in the next game, at home to Burnley, and that would have been brilliant – in front of our fans.

Burnley came to the Stadium of Light on 27 April, a Friday night game. It was our friend Steve Cotterill again. Steve had worked at Sunderland as Howard Wilkinson's assistant, and his time there hadn't gone well. So we knew there'd be extra edge to the game. But we won 3–2; Murph, Dave and Carlos scored – another of Carlos's typical goals.

That was our last home game. We ended up being promoted that weekend but we didn't know it yet, because the other teams still in contention were playing on Saturday and Sunday. I was walking my dogs on Sunday afternoon when the news came through that Derby slipped up; they'd lost to Crystal Palace. Someone at the club texted me. I was buzzing – I went home and double-checked my contract!

It was great but I would have enjoyed it a lot more if it had happened just after a match, especially at the Stadium of Light. I'd no one to celebrate with. My wife and kids were delighted but they weren't the staff; they hadn't worked with me. So it was a bit of an anticlimax, sadly. The texts started coming in – *Well done, gaffer*. One of the staff texted from Sunderland – *We're all out*. But I was in Manchester. And I was glad in a way. I didn't want to be in a pub all night with my staff. I think the manager should keep a distance.

I had to leave Danny Simpson out of the side for the last game of the season. The players, no doubt, had been celebrating promotion after Derby had lost, and Danny turned up late for one of the training sessions. He pleaded with me to let him play; he was very emotional. But I wouldn't let him play. The point – the message to the players was 'There's no relaxing. I want to beat Luton.' The season wasn't over.

We went to Luton on the last day of the season. The challenge now was if we won we might win the League. And we did win, 5–0 – another rocket from Murph; he lashed it in. All the final games of the season were being played at the same time. Birmingham slipped up; they lost at Preston. And that got us to the top.

We were Champions. Promotion had been great, and winning

the Championship was the icing on the cake. It had been a brilliant journey for us all.

But they wouldn't give us the trophy that day, on the pitch. And that pissed me off a bit. They said it was for security reasons, because we weren't at our own ground. Lifting the trophy in front of the fans – it didn't matter if it was a replica – would have been great. And the place was bouncing with Sunderland fans. There are great pictures of some of the players, Nyron and Carlos, mixing with the fans, wearing silly hats, hanging off the crossbar.

I went to the dressing room and did my usual thing – played it down a bit. Deep down there was satisfaction. But I was too blasé about it. Everyone was jumping around, singing; there was champagne. I was, like, 'This is what I'd expect.' I wish I'd let myself enjoy it a little bit more. But I was always afraid to enjoy success in case I got too carried away. I was keeping myself on my toes. 'Don't get too grand.' But if you can't enjoy winning, there's something wrong, isn't there?

We were given the trophy and medals a couple of nights later, in a hotel. I gave my medal to one of the lads who hadn't played enough games to qualify; I think it was Márton Fülöp, one of our keepers. During that week before the Luton game I knew the players would be planning a celebration once the last game was over. As an incentive I offered them £5,000 to go and enjoy themselves, if they beat Luton *and* we won the Championship. That night, during the reception, Yorkie approached and asked if I'd also pay for a coach and a hotel for the players. That pissed me right off. I was giving them five grand, and they'd have been on good bonuses for winning promotion.

I found out that Danny Simpson and Jonny Evans, because they were loan players, weren't entitled to bonuses. But I made sure they got them. You've never seen happier young lads. And I think it helped the following season, when I went to sign Jonny again, on loan.

I was getting a million-pound bonus and then a big pay rise because we were now in the Premiership. The financial rewards were great. But it was more about the town. There was a plan for us to go on an open-top bus through Sunderland. Niall rang me and I said, 'No, I'd be ashamed of my life.'

I think it's right to celebrate achievements. But to celebrate promotion a year after we'd been relegated – it was too much. It wasn't as if we were a small club being promoted for the first time in twenty years.

I look back now and I understand that it would have been more for the supporters, and maybe the players and their families. I hope that my decision not to have the bus wasn't arrogance, because I'd won things with United and Celtic. Some of the players said, 'This is the first medal I've ever had.' Maybe I should have been more open to their point of view. But the open-top bus didn't appeal to me – most of the players would have been late anyway. And it would have been fuckin' freezing. I've other regrets, but not that one.

There was a meeting of all the medical staff – a debriefing – at the end of the season. And they told me that we were getting a lot of injuries on Tuesdays; the players were training too long. We weren't performing well, in terms of muscle injuries.

I said, 'Okay, yeah, I get it, lads. But just to remind you – we *have* been promoted.'

We'd scored a bucket-load of late goals. And that was why – because of the way we trained. I'd take a few injuries in exchange for those goals. The players ran, and ran, and ran. There'd be an element of my own character in there – you keep going. The crowd helped there, too – credit to the fans.

I remember thinking, 'The work starts now. We're up with the big boys.'

I'd be starting my first pre-season at the club. I'd have to go to the consortium for more money. I'd have to get some players in. How would I get good players to come to Sunderland?

The connection with Ireland – the number of people we had coming across to watch us – was amazing. There was myself, Niall, the consortium, the Irish players. I liked working with other Irish people around me. I always liked the way the consortium lads spoke to me. It was very Irish.

'Great fuckin' result.'

I enjoy it; I plugged into it. There are Irish traits I think we need to move away from, but not that hospitality and support.

'Fuckin' good on yeh.'

I said I needed a goalkeeper.

'Is there no fuckin' goalkeeper we can get in from the youth team?'

'Ah now, lads.'

At the same time, they were clever business people and I bet they couldn't believe what was going on. It was a proper journey for them. But the Premiership was going to be different. As much as these men were successful, the Premiership was about the Russians and the sheiks and the Yanks. We'd be shopping in a different shop. Up to now, we hadn't been buying where Manchester United go to buy.

People often say that the Championship is one of the toughest leagues in the world. I won it as a manager – I have to say that. No one else ever does.

EIGHT

The disappointments are remembered more than the highs. They're what spur you on, because they hurt. I enjoyed the victories, but took them with a pinch of salt. Especially in the Premiership, you're always going, 'God, look who we've got next week.'
Then it changed.

'Fuck the draws – let's go and win.'

We lost a lot but we won a few we wouldn't have been expected to win. We didn't have many draws – and they're actually vital. The attitude was all or nothing. But it worked. I appreciate that it doesn't always work, but I wasn't thinking that way. It was, 'Let's go for it.' Even when we were 4–0 down at home to United, I was thinking, 'Let's have a go at them.' I knew the players' strength, and the fans wouldn't have wanted us to be defensive.

From a tactical point of view, we should probably have been more cautious. But what had got us promoted, and what gave us a bit of early success, was having a go. You need a feel for your club, and Sunderland was all about having a go. Sunderland really did suit my personality at that time. I was up for it and full of energy and I felt that the Sunderland fans were right behind me.

Getting players in was the most important part of our preparation for the Premiership. But there were other issues, too. Where could we improve? Could we travel better – do we fly to more matches, and stay in better hotels? We were going to London now, and Manchester, and Liverpool. The year before we'd been going to Colchester and Southend. It wasn't arrogance. It was a fact – we'd be travelling to big cities.

Could we get better medical care? Did we change the bonus schemes for staff? Would we want better training kits? The whole club improves – the badge on your kit is now Premiership. The whole package. The excitement of the supporters when the fixtures were published – Tottenham, Liverpool, United in the first five matches. And we'd be playing Newcastle – the derby.

People had told me about it.

'Oh, the derby up there.'

It didn't disappoint. It was the best derby I've ever been involved in, up there with Celtic and Rangers. And we'd be going to Middlesbrough, too – another derby.

As a player I'd had plenty of experience of the grounds we'd be visiting and of the quality we'd be playing against; I'd only retired the year before. And we'd some players with similar experience, like Dwight Yorke and Kieran Richardson. The important thing was not to be intimidated, or worried about the occasion, or even overwhelmed. Expectations were higher now, and the players would have to live with them. You wouldn't hear the Sunderland fans saying, 'As long as we stay up.' They'd have their targets – 'Once we beat fuckin' Newcastle,' or 'We have to beat this team.' The players had to realise that they deserved to be where they were, and not to be overawed.

Our first game was at home to Tottenham, live on Sky. We won. 1–0. Brilliant. Michael Chopra scored, in injury time.

A newly promoted team really does need a decent start. You need points. If you fall behind in your points per games figure – one point a game – it's a fucker. But, straightaway, we'd three points from just one game. We drew at Birmingham midweek, so now we'd four points from two games.

'What's the fuss? What's everyone frightened of?'

This was great.

Then we go to Wigan – 'Fuckin' Wigan?' – and they turn us over, 3–0.

'That's what it's about.'

Wigan bullied us. They were big and strong. Heskey was up front, and Kirkland in goal. These were England players.

Then there was Liverpool.

Then United.

Now we had four points from five games.

Then we beat Reading. Seven points from six. We went to Middlesbrough, and drew. Eight points from seven games. Blackburn. We were robbed. Eight points from eight. Not too bad; I'd have taken that. Then we lose to Arsenal, then West Ham. Eight from ten. We draw with Fulham. Nine points from eleven games – now we were chasing our tail.

We'd played Birmingham the previous season, in the Championship. But this time – our second game in the Premiership – we'd only four players starting of the eleven who'd played for us the year before. It's hard to let lads go when they've done well for you. But it's the game. Characters get you promoted, but you need more than characters in the Premiership. You need skill, talent, pace, luck.

Immediately after we were promoted I was thinking about new players. Even while we were celebrating in the dressing room.

That's the hard side of life for many footballers. It was sad, and I wondered how I was going to tell them. But, then, it's a business, and I wondered if I could get good money for them. I'd have to speak to their agents. Hopefully, there'd be takers for them. It was no good deciding that, say, three players wouldn't be staying if no other clubs actually wanted them. It seems brutal, but they've been part of a promotion team, so it almost guarantees them a good move. It's one of the hardest parts of management – shifting players.

I had five or six weeks off, but I was still making and taking phone calls. In some ways, holidays are a nightmare for a manager. I made the mistake – and I made the same mistake the following year. I was all summer making phone calls. It was pointless, because everybody was away anyway. Agents, chief executives, medical staff – right across football, they're all away. I never got a deal done during the summer. I should have left the phone off, and checked in now and then. I've read since that Arsène Wenger switches his mobile off when he's on holiday, and just turns it on for an hour in the evenings. I wish I'd had that wisdom, or common sense, at the time. But I was thinking, 'I'd better be proactive, I'd better be busy.'

I should have been thinking about the quality of the calls, not the quantity. It was inexperience. I wanted to be keen, and I wanted to do well.

'Oh, if we don't sign this player in July, he could be gone.'

I'd a list of players, lads playing in the Premiership, that I gave to Niall when we were promoted. I thought it would be easy. But it wasn't. They wanted too much money but we weren't giving out mega-money. We'd made progress, but we couldn't go from one extreme to another. We didn't want to go the way of Leeds or, later, Portsmouth. And Sunderland had been in difficulty until the Irish consortium took over. The top player at Sunderland was on less than twenty grand a week. It was decent, but a lot a players were looking for forty or sixty. So I had to start accepting that we weren't going to get the players I'd thought we would.

We got permission to speak to David Nugent. He was at

Preston and I'd seen him, against us, the previous season. He was a decent player, although not a massive goalscorer. I met him at my house in Manchester, with his agent. I thought the house was a better option, less formal. We'd agreed a fee – I think it was four million.

So he's, 'Yeah, yeah – big decision for me – thinking it over.'

Fine – no problem.

I was doing my Pro Licence at the time, and on my way back home a few weeks later I got a call from David Nugent's agent: 'He's undecided. Harry's in for him at Portsmouth.'

This was Harry Redknapp.

So I said there was no pressure but it was only a couple of weeks before the start of pre-season, and there'd come a point when we'd have to make our minds up.

I had to bring it to a head another few weeks later. This was David Nugent, by the way; he hadn't become Messi. But he was a good player and we wanted him.

So I rang his agent.

'Well,' he said. 'Harry's in for him.'

I went, 'Yeah, I'm aware of that. But we've been in for him for three or four weeks.'

And he said, 'Just to put you in the picture. Harry's away this weekend, on his wedding anniversary. He's been married for forty or fifty years and he wants to speak to David when he gets back.'

I said, 'I'll tell you what. I've waited three or four weeks, and now you're asking me to wait because of Harry Redknapp's wedding anniversary? We're pulling out of the deal.'

The joys of management.

We got Greg Halford, from Reading. I shouldn't have signed him. He came in for about two and a half million – a decent fee for a full-back. Reading had bought him from Colchester but he'd hardly kicked a ball for them – not a good sign, but it was a sign I ignored, thinking I'd be different. It was a young manager's outlook; you think, 'I'll be down with it.' You've been playing until recently, so you look at players as a player looks at players, not as a manager. The older you get you realise that the lads who bring baggage bring baggage everywhere. So you can't be bothered with them – unless they're brilliant. Greg had done well for Colchester, against us; he was a talented boy. But I should have gone with my gut feeling. He came into my office in Sunderland, and I didn't like the way he sat down. He was crouched down, too laid-back.

And he asked me a few questions.

'Who else are you buying?'

I should have been asking him the questions. Six months earlier he was at Colchester. He should have walked up to Sunderland. I should have sent him on his way. But we signed him. We'd agreed the fee, and the wages. It's common practice – everything is agreed before the player actually comes to the club to meet you. The player and his agent have the cards. Brian Clough would never agree a deal until he'd met the player – 'We're not having you.' Players did have agents back then but Brian Clough wouldn't have tolerated them. He managed at a time before players' agents had the power they have now. We were newly promoted and Sunderland was a bit remote; we had to dangle carrots for people.

I didn't like him after that. I thought, 'Not for me.' But I signed him! I was finding out slowly that certain players suit certain clubs. And Greg Halford wasn't a Sunderland player. Sunderland people are hard-working, roll your sleeves up – I appreciate that even more since I left – and Greg wasn't that type of player. He wasn't a roll your sleeves up, work your socks off player. He was about dealing with the ball, coasting through the game, and just doing enough. He's had a decent career. I saw him at Forest recently and he played okay.

When I first discussed players with Niall, we were going down the list. But the lads we were after wanted bigger money, or they wouldn't come up to Sunderland. So we moved on to players like Greg Halford. We needed a bigger, and better, squad; we needed more numbers. There'd be more demands, more injuries – the games would be physically more demanding, more intense. You also need a big squad for training numbers. I was hoping that Greg was better than what we already had. In particular, we needed another defender, a right-back. We wouldn't be getting players from Chelsea or United; that might come later on.

Trying to get good players in became very frustrating. The wise thing to do is to step back from it a bit, and this is where you need a good chief executive. I had that at Sunderland, Peter Walker. He got deals done – and Niall. Everything was – and this is a big word for me – transparent.

'Roy, it's not going to happen. He's asking for sixty grand a week.'

'Forget about him. Move on.'

We were after Darren Bent.

'Roy, they want sixteen million. We can't go to that.'

'Okay, let's move on.'

I still think that if we'd bought Darren Bent then, at the start of the '07–'08 season, I'd still be the Sunderland manager. He'd have got the goals. But it was too much money. They bought him later, after I'd left, because they'd had another year in the Premiership so they had more money to spend. The longer the club stays in the Premiership, the bigger an attraction it is to players, and the club can start to afford the higher wages.

There was one lad who didn't even get back to us. The word 'shopping' was used. His wife wanted to live in London.

There was another lad, Matt Taylor. I showed him the Stadium of Light, brought him to the boardroom. He told me he had other clubs interested in him. I walked him to his car, told him to take his time with the decision.

I was walking to my own car when I got a text – from Matt Taylor. I could see him, still in the car park, driving out. *I've decided to sign for somebody else.* He'd been telling me fifteen seconds earlier that he was unsure about what to do. He went to Bolton.

On the other hand, I met Leighton Baines at a hotel in Sunderland. He was leaving Wigan. We'd made an offer and it had been accepted. The first thing he said to me was, 'Roy, if Everton come looking for me, I'll be moving to Everton, because I'm an Evertonian.'

And I went, 'Okay.'

I appreciated it.

We bought Kieran Richardson from United. He was a good signing, but it was tricky. I had to meet his dad a few times. Kieran was making a few demands; he wanted a certain jersey number, he wanted to take the penalties. His ego had to be stroked a bit. He did well for us and scored the winner against Newcastle the following season; so he'll always be remembered for that.

Craig Gordon was the big name. He came in from Hearts for massive money, nine million – a record for a goalkeeper at the time. Craig was the only player I've seen being applauded off the training pitch, in all my career – by his own team-mates. It was after his first training session. Nobody could score against him and, it being his first session, we were all watching. We needed a number one goalkeeper; we were in the Premiership – 'Aim high.' He was amazing.

Brian Clough bought Peter Shilton for big money and said that Shilton had saved Forest twelve points a season. Clemence, Schmeichel, Shilton – top teams have top goalkeepers. I think I underestimated the importance of keepers when I was a player. It wasn't that I took them – Schmeichel or Packie Bonner – for granted. But I expected them to make big saves. But then, when you're not working with a top keeper – 'Fuckin' hell!' – you appreciate them a bit more.

Kenwyne Jones came in from Southampton, for six million, and they got Stern John as part of the deal. Kenwyne did brilliantly for me – and he hasn't done much for other managers since. I think the fact that Dwight Yorke and Carlos Edwards, lads from Trinidad, were already there helped Kenwyne to settle in.

Danny Higginbotham came in, from Stoke. He could play left-back or centre-back. Tony Pulis gave me all the crap – 'Oh, he's my best player', all the silly games, trying to get the fee up. But we eventually got Danny. He could score from set pieces, too; he had a good leap. He got a couple of important goals for us.

Michael Chopra came in. The fact that he was a Geordie was an issue for some, but not for me. He did a job – we got a good year out of him. We paid five and a half million, and he scored me seven goals. That's the madness of Premiership football. A million a goal – but his goals kept us up. That was what we paid for. A player worth fifteen million, who might have got us more goals, wouldn't have come to us in our first season up. We were learning that quickly. I'd say to players we wanted, 'It's not Australia.' But Sunderland is pretty bleak. So is Newcastle, but they were in a position to pay a lot more than us. I'm a footballing man; I didn't really care where I was. But others look at the whole package.

'Will you come up to Sunderland?'

'Yeah, yeah.'

'The wages are decent but they're not mega.'

'Well, I'm not coming up.'

They wanted compensation for the cold and dark nights. We knew that the lads who *were* coming to us were doing it for the right reasons.

And Sunderland was the place to be. The crowds – 44,000

and more – the fans were brilliant. The club ran so smoothly at times I wonder if I'm remembering it accurately. We hear so much now about interference in team selection, and so on. But we had it perfect. Everyone knew their role. I was looking after the football, Niall was looking after the PR and the finances, the chief executive was getting deals done, the medical staff were on top of their job, the players were happy to be playing for Sunderland. Niall knew the game, and he just let me get on with it. There wasn't just one owner – no one person claiming control. The fact that we'd got out of the Championship in my first season meant, I think, that I'd the real support of everybody – and I felt it.

We were beaten by Luton in the Carling Cup. It was a bit of a shock because we'd beaten them 5–0 only a few months before. I'd made a mistake – squad rotation. Squad rotation is fine if you're replacing players with international players, like at United or Chelsea. But we weren't doing that. Also, I overdid it – four or five changes instead of one or two. I thought, going to Luton, I could make the changes. But it only works if you win. And we didn't. So it backfired on me. But I hadn't learnt the lesson yet.

Luton didn't just beat us; they hammered us, 3–0. Their manager, Kevin Blackwell, said that they'd been after revenge, which is fair enough. But that game decided a lot of players' futures. I'd played some fringe players, to give them a chance. You realise that they're fringe players because you don't really trust or believe in them. Greg Halford didn't exactly warm himself to me when he got sent off in the second half. I remember, after the game, I wanted to smash my fist against the dressing-room wall; I think it's the only time I'd ever felt that.

Clive Clarke, one of our players who was out on loan to Leicester, suffered a heart attack that night. The news came through to us after the game. The madness of football: we'd been beaten 3–0 by Luton, a shocking result, but at the press conference after the game I said that football results didn't really matter and I mentioned that Clive Clarke had had a heart attack. And I had the evil thought, 'I'm glad he had it tonight', because it would deflect from our woeful performance. That was the world I was in.

A couple of months later I was asked about Clive's heart attack and I said I was surprised they'd found a heart. It was a joke at a press conference but, on paper, without the context or the tone, it looked less like a joke. I sometimes forgot that I wasn't the only person with parents and children. It was after Clive had said something critical of me – something about me kicking chairs. The lads who were most critical of me were the lads I moved on or the ones who never played.

When you've had a decent career as a player the hard part about going to Liverpool or Manchester United when you're a manager is almost having to accept that you're going to lose, 1–0 or 2–0, and go, 'That's not bad.' It isn't a hiding – five, six or seven–nil – which would have a big impact on your goal differ- ence, especially if you're near the bottom of the table. It's hard accepting the thought, 'It could have been worse.' I struggled with it. It felt a bit like I was robbing our own fans.

We were taking on the big boys. But I don't like that term 'big boys'. It's almost like you're beaten before you start. We were in the same league as them. I think I was quite good at looking at my players' strengths, not deficiencies. When we lost these games, I was disappointed but I never lost the rag. A manager's biggest fear is feeling that his players aren't trying for him. If you have that doubt, that is where your pride is hurt. The beauty of Sunderland was I never felt that. You want your team to play like you. As much as I thought we needed more players and we needed improvement, I never looked at the Sunderland lads and thought they'd let me down. We lost 7–1 at Everton but I knew they'd tried. It was naivety on my part. We were 3–1 down, never going to win the game, and I kept saying, 'Keep going'; we could get back into the game.

I didn't enjoy going to Old Trafford, although I got a good reception from the United fans. But there was too much fuss. Craig Gordon played well. He was justifying his price tag. But Saha scored their goal, from a set piece.

You hear managers going, 'I was particularly disappointed to see us conceding from a set piece', almost as if it's okay to concede a goal from general play. The thinking is you should be organised to set things up. But the opposition can upset that by doing something quickly. And, no matter how well organised you are, it's all about the delivery. The opposition is putting the ball in the box, at pace, and they've players attacking it. At no other stage in the game do you have seven or eight players attacking the ball in the box. A huge proportion of goals are scored from set pieces. 'You should never concede from a set piece' – we've almost been brainwashed into thinking it and saying it.

After the game we went to Alex Ferguson's office for a drink with his staff, but Ferguson never turned up. I thought that was out of order. He called me a few days later, to apologise. He said he'd had to rush off after the game, and he'd waited a long time for me. I told him he should have had a drink with me, like he would have with any other manager, and that he hadn't shown me or my staff proper respect.

That was three league losses in a row – Wigan, Liverpool, United. You're starting to wonder where the next victory is going to come from. You begin to see why clubs can go ten to fifteen games without a win. When you're near the bottom it all makes sense. But I think I stayed quite calm. We'd just been promoted, and I was still new to the job. I was still being given the benefit of the doubt – a bit of breathing space.

Reading came to us and we won, 2–1. A big result. Kenwyne and Ross scored for us. We drew at Middlesbrough. It was a good draw, because Liam Miller scored with the last kick of the game. We were still scoring late goals.

The defeat by Blackburn, 2–1, at the Stadium of Light, was a hard one to take. I was down in the dumps after it; it was one of the games I thought we should have won. Arsenal away – we were 2–0 down after ten minutes, and I was thinking it could end up being seven or eight. But we came back to 2–2, before losing 3–2.

We'd played Liverpool, United, and Arsenal. We'd put up good, fighting battles but we'd still lost the games. Even thinking we'd played well felt a bit of a cop-out.

We weren't invited for a drink with Arsène Wenger after the Arsenal game. Apparently he's not one for that tradition. But I went in anyway. I wanted to meet him. I look at some managers and think, 'The experience they have.' It comes out of their pores. So we walked in. He was surprised but dead nice. Arsenal have that bit of class.

West Ham was a big game for us. It was one we needed to win. The teams in the bottom half of the table – it's like a league inside the league. You had to get your points from these teams; anything from the bigger teams was a bonus. Grant Leadbitter hit the bar; we'd have gone 2–1 up if he'd scored. Kenwyne had already scored for us. But we lost 3–1. One of their goals – Craig dived, the ball hit the post, came back, hit Craig and went in. The fine line between victory and defeat – that was another tough one to take.

We drew with Fulham, at home. Halford was sent off again. I was really warming to him now. Kenwyne scored again. That was late October. He scored again in December, then didn't score again till March. That was Kenwyne. It happens to strikers. We scored on average about a goal a game, so it was a battle every week. A striker in a struggling team needs to get you one or two goals a month. But if they're not delivering you're in trouble.

Manchester City, away, and Stephen Ireland scored for them – a volley – then pulled his shorts down. He was wearing Superman underpants. The 1–0 defeats hurt because you think you're close to a point. You'd almost be happier losing 2–0.

We'd slipped below the point-a-game target. We had nine points from twelve matches and we were stuck in the bottom three. We'd almost got used to it, but we hadn't gone into any sort of free fall. I worried, but I was confident we'd climb out of the bottom three. As a group, I think we felt we'd be all right. Self-belief – it's a great trait to have.

Newcastle came to us in November. It was my first derby and it was brilliant – the atmosphere, the relief that we weren't beaten. Our record against Newcastle wasn't great. But we should have won it. We were 1–0 up – Danny Higginbotham got us a goal. But they got one back. James Milner's cross went in off the far post. Chopra headed against the bar near the end of the game. You come away from a game like that thinking, 'We could have won it', and then we got hammered the following week.

I wasn't a great one for motivational videos or talks but, before we got off the bus at Goodison Park we showed the team a clip from *Any Given Sunday*, Al Pacino's speech at the end. He's an American football coach. His speech was about endurance, keeping at it – 'On this team we fight for that inch.' So we went out and lost 7–1.

Nothing like it had happened to me before. Everton slaughtered us. David Moyes was very good after the match. There was no small talk. It was just me and him. I think he brought me to a private room; he must have known I'd be in a bad way. He was saying, 'Stick at it.' He showed real humanity towards me that day.

The defeat hit me badly. I went home, to Manchester. I hardly left the bed for forty-eight hours. You're advised to move on quickly, but I couldn't. I don't think I even showered for two or three days. I was punishing myself. I hadn't even had the cop-on to take our loss, when we were three or four down; we kept going for it. Take your beating; don't make it even worse. But, no – 'Keep going.' A part of me felt I'd let the players down. I took full responsibility. Bizarrely, we'd had some good chances. Chops missed a great chance when it was 3–1; that would have made it 3–2.

Eventually, I knew I had to go back in to work, but I don't think I went to the training ground till the following Friday.

Somehow – I think – I need that self-loathing. I don't want to wake the next morning and say, 'Ah, well – it's gone now.'

The only time we'd try to be clever tactically we'd play with a sitting midfielder, who, nine times out of ten, would be Dwight Yorke.

There are only three or four systems you can play. That's not to say you can't have an influence. You tweak things, you change things, you make substitutions at the right time. Brian Clough and Alex Ferguson kept it simple. When I managed, I kept it very simple. It's a simple game. Pass it, then move; try and score more goals than them. Win your tackles.

Yorkie had played in that role for his country, Trinidad, towards the end of his career. We'd played him in midfield in our promotion season but, in the Premiership, we sometimes played him with two in front of him – in the Makelele position. We'd do this when we were trying to be a bit more defensive, against the better teams – Arsenal at home, United away, Chelsea – the bigger teams, if we thought we were going to get overrun in midfield. We didn't always do it, and when we didn't it often backfired because we got overrun. I'd play 4–4–2, and say, 'Come on – let's get at them.'

I'd think completely differently now but, at the time, I thought that playing the sitting midfielder was almost like waving the white flag – which is ridiculous. A lot of the top teams do it. But I'd been brought up with the 4–4–2, and there's nothing wrong with knowing your strengths – but we were being found out in a lot of the games. We only won two games away from home all season. That's probably close to the average for a newly promoted team. I could have been more tactical, and gone for more draws, but it's very hard to change your mindset. A newly promoted team at the start of the season – the sun, the new badge, the better hotels – they have a spring in their step. 'Let's go!' The clever response is, 'No – don't let's go – take your draw.' And with a sitting midfielder, you're not necessarily settling for a draw. You can still play on the counter-attack. But there's no point in being too clever tactically if you don't have the players. We were always going to be in a battle. And what we did have was a good dressing room.

I don't remember the game, but we were up against a team who were playing three in the middle, and we only had two, because we were at home. The Sunderland fans weren't mad about three in the middle – 'Too much fannying about – get up and at 'em.' Two strikers, two wingers. So, this time, we were outnumbered in the middle of the park. Yorkie was blowing a bit. He was thirty-four or thirty-five now, and he was up against three in the middle.

Someone was injured, so Yorkie ran across to me.

'Gaffer – gaffer— You know – they've got an extra man. What shall we do?'

I went, 'Yorkie, you need to run fuckin' more.'

He went, 'Right – right', and he ran back out.

That was me at my tactical best. I'm sure he thought I was going to get a drawing board out and give him a master class on how to deal with the problem.

I think, today, I'd be a bit more cautious. It's the problem of being a big club like Sunderland *and* also being newly promoted. It's hard to be cautious. You tend to get carried by the emotions of the crowd. We played with our hearts more than our heads. 'Here we go – take on the world.' When, really, I should have been saying, 'Here, listen – one step at a time. Let's be hard to beat.'

But when you've been promoted you've got into the habit of winning matches – that's why you were promoted. And you try to carry that into the Premiership.

We had ten points from fourteen games. It was, generally, panning out the way I'd thought it would, after the giddiness of the first few games. It was going to be a struggle. It was going to be about survival.

We came straight back after the Everton game and beat Derby. Derby were struggling, too, but it was still a massive victory. We did okay against the teams around us, especially at home – and we had to. Stokesy provided the winner. In time added on. Another of our late goals.

I look back at the fixture list and I can point to three or four games we needed to win to stay up. This was one of them. Derby had sacked their manager, Billy Davies, earlier in the week, and he'd been replaced by Paul Jewell. I thought they'd be kicking on a bit for the new manager. But we won. I rested Craig Gordon – and I mean 'rested', not dropped – after the seven goals of the week before. We won, but Carlos Edwards broke his leg. That was a big loss for us.

We went to Chelsea and lost, 2–0. We worked hard but it was one of those games where you'd take the 2–0. Liam Miller was sent off for a push on Pizarro. We dropped into the bottom three again, although we had thirteen points from sixteen games, not too far off the point a game figure.

I brought Ricky Sbragia to the club. Ricky had experience at Bolton and I knew him from United. I was always thinking of moving things around, and Ricky was more of a defensive coach. I thought he'd help us. I moved Neil Bailey to work with the development squad – what used to be called the reserves. But I should have left the staff the way they were.

We drew at home to Villa. We were robbed. We'd a goal in the last minute; Danny Collins headed in from a set piece. It was disallowed – a disgraceful decision. The extra two points, and the win, would have been massive for us. I read afterwards that I pursued the referee, Steve Bennett, down the tunnel after the game. But I had to go that way anyway, to the dressing room. Was I supposed to go out to the car park?

The game at Reading, just before Christmas, was the only time I really lost my temper as a manager. I'd lost my temper before – but I'd *used* my temper. This time I used physical force. I grabbed a staff member, put his head on a table, and tried to pull his tie off. But he was a Reading staff member, not one of ours.

It was the first half, a tight game. Maybe the pressure was building on me – I don't know. Steve Coppell was managing Reading, and he had a couple of lads working with him, Wally Downes and Kevin Dillon. I looked across at their dugout, and Kevin Dillon was looking back across, calling me a wanker.

I go, 'What – me?'

He goes, 'Yeah – yeah. You're always on at the fucking referee.'

I said nothing back. I never got involved with opposition managers or staff – never.

We got to half-time, and I'm walking back to the tunnel beside Kevin Dillon, and I say, 'Are you calling me a wanker?'

And he goes, 'Well, you're always on at the referee.'

I said, 'I never said fuck all to the referee. Who the fuck are you calling a wanker?'

But I went to our dressing room, and thought no more of it.

The second half, and we're robbed – again – in injury time. Stephen Hunt got a shot in, and the linesman on the far side reckoned it was over the line. It wasn't, but the goal was given. It was another big, big loss for us. When it was 1–1, Kenwyne had gone through and was near to winning it for us, in injury time. So, instead of winning, we'd lost.

At the end of the game, walking down the stairs, I saw Wally Downes shaking all my players' hands.

'Unlucky, lads.'

You generally don't see staff shaking the other team's hands. I said nothing. It had been a big win for Reading; there was a lot of celebrating. I went into our dressing room. I wasn't annoyed with the players, more the decision. I spoke to the players and staff.

'Okay, we're all upset. But, whatever we do, we're Sunderland. We show a bit of class. We accept the decision – we move on and get ready for next week.'

The players were getting themselves organised, and I was waiting for my staff, to go in for a drink with Steve Coppell and the Reading lads. I didn't want to, but I kept thinking, 'We're Sunderland – we'll do things properly.'

The staff were taking ages, so I said, 'I'll go on, lads. Follow me in.'

I walked into Steve's office. Wally Downes was there, and their director of football, Nick Hammond. Kevin Dillon was sitting down.

I go, 'Well done, lads – well done.'

Wally was right in front of me, and I said, 'Wally, do you always shake players' hands after you've just beaten them?'

And he goes, 'Yeah, Roy – yeah, yeah.'

And, as I was talking to Wally, Kevin Dillon stood up, and goes, 'Don't you come in here and—'

I grabbed him, got his head on the table, pulled his tie up.

'I'm fuckin' warning you—'

Nick Hammond grabbed me.

'What are you doing?!'

'You fuckin'—'

'Get out of our office!'

I went, 'Fuck yis, anyway.'

Dillon said, 'What are you having a go at me for? I'm a Sunderland man.'

I went, 'Fuck you.'

And I walked out.

My staff hadn't come in yet.

I wasn't going back to Sunderland that night with the players. I was going home to Manchester, so I had a car waiting for me, to bring me to Heathrow.

My phone went off about ten minutes later. It was one of my staff.

'Everything all right, gaffer?'

I hadn't given them a heads-up about what had happened in Steve Coppell's office. They'd followed me in – after I'd left.

'All right, lads?'

And somebody said, 'Your manager has just attacked one of our staff.'

And apparently Raimond van der Gouw, our goalkeeping coach, said, 'Well, can we still have a sandwich?'

'No, I think it's best if you leave.'

Whether I was reacting to the pressure – two unlucky defeats, our position in the bottom three – I don't know. I'd like to think I'd have had a go at Dillon even if we'd been top of the table.

We were on a bad run now. We'd lost three in a row, and then Manchester United came to the Stadium of Light on Boxing Day.

We stayed in the Ramside Hall Hotel, near Durham, the night before the game, Christmas night. We got together at about nine or ten o'clock, to give the players more time at home with their families. I put it to the players and staff that, if they wanted, they could have one or two beers. My thinking was it might help them relax before the big game against United. But it mustn't have worked. Because they beat us 4–0. Rooney was brilliant and Ronaldo was in his pomp. There were 47,000 people there. Maybe it was my ego – 'Let's have a go at them.' We were a bit open. Ronaldo's goal, a free-kick, just at half-time, killed us. That made it 3–0.

After the game Alex Ferguson came to my office for a drink. When he was leaving, he said to me, 'Give me a call about Jonny Evans.'

He could see I was down in the dumps after the game. I think he looked at me and thought, 'He needs a dig-out here.'

It was the one time he showed me – I suppose – affection: 'I'll watch your back.'

He caught me off guard – 'He actually cares, a bit.'

Niall got on to David Gill and we got Jonny, but there was a massive loan fee. So Ferguson showed me affection, but it was business, too. But – and this is important – Jonny made a huge difference to us.

From now on every home game was going to be massive. The next one was four days after the United game, against Bolton. And we won it, 3–1. It was Kieran Richardson's first full game after his injury and that was a big boost. It was our second win in fourteen games. We were out of the bottom three for the start of the new year. Obviously, the time to be out of the bottom three is at the end of the season, but it was a psychological thing; there's always weight attached to the bottom three at the turn of the year.

Our first game of 2008 was at Blackburn. We got a penalty early in the second half. Yorkie was our penalty taker but Dean Whitehead took it instead. He missed; Brad Friedel saved it. Then Blackburn got a dodgy penalty and scored. We lost 1–0. I was fuming afterwards, and I had a go at Yorkie for not taking the penalty. I hammered him, gave him a right bollocking.

'You fuckin' bottled it.'

That might have been a bit harsh, but he should have taken the penalty. He took his bollocking well.

We'd dropped back into the bottom three because Wigan, who'd been below us, drew with Liverpool.

The transfer window was open again and we'd got Jonny Evans back on loan. Phil Bardsley came in, also from United. We brought in Rade Prica, from Aalborg, and Andy Reid, from Charlton. Of the four, three worked out well for us – and they were the three lads I knew. Rade had been strongly recommended by the scouts but he didn't do too much.

Ideally, if you're interested in a player you try to watch him, possibly ten times, in different circumstances – home, away, derby matches. The manager can't watch him that often, so he's relying on his scouts, and videos. We needed a striker, and the scouts were recommending Rade. If you don't know a player too well, you try to sort out a loan deal. But Rade cost us one or two million. I watched a few video clips of him, and it wasn't as if I was delighted with what I saw. Staff and scouts push – 'He's the answer.' I took the gamble. But he wasn't the answer.

I rang Mark Hughes about Robbie Savage. Robbie wasn't in the Blackburn team, and I asked Mark if we could try to do a deal, a permanent or loan deal.

Sparky said, 'Yeah, yeah. He's just lost his way here, but he could still do a job for you.'

Robbie's legs were going a bit, but I thought he might come up to us, with his long hair, and give us a lift, the way Yorkie had – a big personality in the dressing room.

Sparky gave me permission to give him a call. So I got Robbie's mobile number and rang him. It went to his voicemail: 'Hi, it's Robbie – whazzup!' – like the Budweiser ad.

I never called him back.

I thought, 'I can't be fuckin' signing that.'

We got knocked straight out of the FA Cup, 3–0 by Wigan – again. It proved to me once more that squad rotation doesn't work if you don't have enough top players in your squad. I'd made the same mistake in the League Cup, against Luton. A good run in the Cup could only have helped to build momentum and confidence. But we didn't get it.

We beat Portsmouth at home, 2–0. Kieran Richardson scored both goals.

We hung our hat on the home matches. We couldn't keep the ball well enough away from home. A different environment, having to travel, the fans behind the home team – they'll push their team the extra yard. The home team being used to the surroundings, so many teams like ourselves, fighting for home results – winning away from home is always very hard in the Premiership. Chelsea, United, City – 'It's going to be hard to win here.' Going to Norwich was less obvious, but the travel, from Sunderland, was difficult. There was once, we went to Birmingham and the dressing-room door was locked. We were waiting for ages. Or, we'd arrive too early – encouraged by the home club. We'd be sitting there for hours, waiting for the match. We didn't play those games at Sunderland. I always wanted the visiting team to speak highly of us.

Home win, away loss, home win, away loss – that was the pattern. We went to Tottenham, and lost. Birmingham came to us – we won. Our new lad, Prica, scored. But he never really kicked a ball after that. We jumped to a mid-table position, because we weren't drawing matches. We went to Liverpool, and they beat us 3–0. Kieran Richardson was injured again. His hamstring – we'd rushed him back because we were desperate to have him in the team. He was an important player and, as an ex-United player, he was keen to play at Liverpool. A silly mistake.

Wigan came to us, and we beat them – at last – 2–0. There were 46,000 people there. Dickson Etuhu scored our first, a header. I'd brought Dickson in from Norwich. We wanted him for his physical presence; he was a midfielder, good at set plays, defending and attacking. He'd been away at the African Cup of Nations with Nigeria. And then Daryl Murphy scored another, from an Andy Reid pass.

The win against Wigan was a good, tough, ugly result. But then we went and got beaten by Portsmouth. Kanu came on as a sub and I think some of our lads were being dead nice to him. They weren't tackling him, or aggressive enough. We gave away a soft penalty. Defoe scored it. It was our tenth away defeat in a row. So much for having a go. We should have been more defensive.

We went to Derby, and drew 0–0. That was a poor result. Derby were at the bottom of the table and we needed the three points. Michael Chopra had a goal disallowed. The decision was a disgrace; he was two or three yards onside.

But referees do have the toughest job in the game. They must enjoy it!

I'd made a lot of changes since the start of the season. I hadn't planned on making so many. But, although some of the players I'd brought in weren't working out, it was progress. We were still adjusting to the demands of the Premiership. You have to experiment a bit as you go; you don't have a choice. We needed better, and bigger; we needed experience. The key is in knowing where to make the change, and when to leave something the way it is. That's management. It's cruel for those left out or moved, but it's the nature of the game.

I put Liam Miller on the transfer list. He was late too often. I was sick of the excuses and I told him I'd had enough of it. His agent rang to tell me that Liam lived on a busy junction and it was very hard to get out.

I brought in Bill Beswick, the sports psychologist, just to mix it up a little bit – a different voice for the players. He came in a couple of days a week. He was there if any of the players or staff wanted to talk to him. Bill's office was across from mine, and I noticed immediately that a lot of the staff were going to see him. I hadn't anticipated that. So straightaway I thought, 'I'll have to get rid of them – they're talking about me.'

No – the lesson was that I had to focus on my staff, to make sure that they were okay. The staff need to feel wanted.

The sports psychology is useful, but in moderation. The lad who went to the World Cup with the England team, Dr Steve Peters, has written a book called *The Chimp Paradox*, about the chimp in your head. The chimp is running the show. I tried to read it – I'm open-minded – but my chimp wouldn't let me.

Everton came to the Stadium of Light. We were poor, and they beat us, 1–0. We had Chelsea the week after – the same result.

The disappointments are remembered more than the highs. They're what spur you on, because they hurt. I enjoyed the victories, but took them with a pinch of salt. Especially in the Premiership, you're always going, 'God, look who we've got next week.'

Then it changed.

The stats were telling us we were going down.

But we went to Villa Park, and won – our first away win. West Ham came to us – we beat them. Andy Reid's goal, a volley in the ninety-fifth minute, made it 2–1. In front of 46,000 people – it was unbelievable. It was the sixth goal we'd scored in stoppage time.

We went away to Spain for three or four days just after that win and got a bit of sun on our backs. Imagine if we'd gone after being beaten? The weather up in the North East is bleak. On a good day the wind is sixty miles an hour. Away for a few days we could mix training up a bit, the lads could get the sun, they could sit out in the evenings. At this stage of the season you're looking around at the other teams struggling – you're playing with your minds, recharging the batteries. It's the same training – same boots, same balls, same bibs, same kit man – but you're changing the scenery. The justification comes if you come back and get a few results.

We came back, went to Fulham and beat them, 3–1. It was a comfortable victory. We played well.

As a manager I was enjoying the chats with other managers after the games. Not so much enjoying what was being said, but picking up on their vibes and listening out for a little snippet of wisdom. I'd be thinking, 'What makes this club work?', or 'What are the staff like?' So I went up to see Roy Hodgson, the Fulham manager, and his assistant, Ray Lewington. It was like the scene in Steve Cotterill's office at Burnley the year before, but without the humour. Steve had turned his disappointment into a joke, but this was different. They were all going, 'We're fucked, we're fucked.'

It was embarrassing. I had my Diet Coke and one of those little sausages, and we left. I remember thinking, 'My goodness, they *are* fucked.'

But they stayed up. Roy got the Liverpool job, and now he's managing England.

We'd got nine points from three games. We'd identified these games as ones to bring up our points average. Chops and Kenwyne scored two each in those three games, and they came at the right time. Those couple of weeks, late March into early April, kept us up.

Manchester City came and beat us. They fluked it in the last minute. I got stick after the Newcastle game, away; they beat us 2–0. I think it was the only time that season when the fans got on my back a little bit. I'd played three in midfield, although it wasn't with a sitting midfielder. It was more an attacking formation. I played Andy Reid off the front, but I didn't play two out-and-out strikers. I know what derbies mean to the fans, and I think they felt the formation was negative. It wasn't, but every time you lose a football match you've got your tactics wrong. And we were a goal down after four minutes – a Michael Owen header. There were mind games going on before the match. The police got us there three hours before kick-off – players get bored, testosterone levels are high; it's too long to wait. Jonny and Phil Bardsley were injured, so didn't play. They were a big loss.

The next game was the other derby, Middlesbrough, at home. It was a brilliant game. We went behind after four minutes, Danny Higginbotham equalised two minutes later, Chops put us ahead just before half-time; Craig made some great saves, but they equalised; I put Daryl Murphy on as a sub and he scored the winner in the last minute – another late goal – a header from Grant Leadbitter's corner. This time our attitude – 'Let's go for it' – got us the result. That win kept us up. We were staying in the Premiership, with two games to spare. That win summed up our season, in a sense – it was hard going, we scraped through, the lads stuck at it, we got a late goal. We survived.

I wanted to beat Bolton in the next game, and help get them

relegated. I was thinking ahead to the next season. I didn't want to be playing Bolton again. I thought they had the strengths to cause us more problems than some of the other clubs around us. They beat us, and stayed up.

Arsenal came to us for the last game of the season. We'd a bucket of chances but they beat us.

Overall, it had been stressful and tough going; there'd been a bit of violence, and wheeling and dealing, but we achieved what we'd set out to do. In the two years, we'd got promoted and we'd stayed up.

Job done.

I wanted to leave my mark at Sunderland, but I don't think I quite did. I did okay but it wasn't good enough for me. We were promoted, and we averaged a point per game in the Premiership, which – on paper – a lot of managers would take. But I wanted more. We – I – could have done better.

Right Win for Sunderland against Newcastle, 25 October 2008. I think it was my happiest day at Sunderland. (Nigel French/EMPICS Sport)

Below Djibril Cissé shaking my hand after scoring against Blackburn, 15 November 2008. (Matthew Lewis/Getty)

Appointed Ipswich manager, 22 April 2009. Nine times out of ten, when a manager is out of work, he'll agree terms. (Jamie McDonald/Getty)

Right I was down there in the blue training kit and I was looking at it, going 'Fuckin' hell'. (Jeremy Durkin/Rex)

Below Ipswich squad on 7th Parachute Regiment training, July 2009. I don't think it created the bond or the spirit I was hoping it would. (Ipswich Town FC)

I got dog's abuse from some of the City fans. 'Do I need this?' Then Lee Dixon would be getting loads of stick from the United fans and I'd say, 'Ah, you have to deal with it.' (Carl Recine Livepic / Action)

Top left Ipswich against Nottingham Forest, 3 January 2011. That was me out the door – my last game in charge. (Jamie Mcdonald / Getty)

Left In the studio with Adrian Chiles (right) and Lee Dixon (left). ITV took a chance, throwing me in. (ITV / Rex)

Watching my first game as assistant manager
of Ireland with Martin O'Neill – a friendly
against Latvia, 15 November 2013. I played
the cool character but I had a real buzz about
myself. (Ian Walton/Getty)

Playing in the UNICEF charity match at Old
Trafford in 2012. (Dave J. Hogan/Getty)

Above Ireland v. Turkey match, 25 May 2014. We'll get it right, lads. (Jed Leicester Livepic / Action)

Left At a Villa training session with Paul Lambert, after being appointed assistant manager, July 2014. I liked the prospect of working with him. (Neville Williams / Aston Villa FC / Getty)

NINE

I have my days when I still analyse those results. But that's the manager's life.

We'd survived and I should have been thinking about surviving the next season, just a bit better. That was my big mistake: I decided we'd make it into the top eight. It was mad. We'd just finished three points, and three places, above the bottom three. Our next challenge should have been to finish six or seven places off the bottom. But I thought, because we'd survived, we'd be a lot better and a lot wiser – and we'd shoot up the table.

It takes four or five years to establish yourself in the Premiership. Teams that have a brilliant first season often drop in the second. Don't overextend yourself. Let your players and fans know: staying up for the next couple of years is the achievement; we're creating something.

We'd survived, but I ended up thinking about the games we'd let go. I started adding points to our total. 'Well, they'll be a gimme next year. We'll get those points and we'll be in the top half of the table.' I forgot about the games we'd nicked in the last minute, and mightn't win next year. No – we'd beat the same teams again and get closer to the teams we hadn't beaten.

I wasn't shouting it from the rooftops. But I was thinking it.

And it was fuckin' madness. I should have been reminding myself that, a couple of years earlier, we'd been heading to League One.

We'd buy players. There was a new owner coming in, to take us to a new level. The jargon's there – 'a new level'; we'd seen it happen at other clubs. More money would get me better players.

I got Pascal Chimbonda, Teemu Tainio, and Steed Malbranque – all from Spurs. I brought in El Hadji Diouf, from Bolton; Djibril Cissé, on loan from Marseille; David Healy, from Fulham; Anton Ferdinand, from West Ham; and George McCartney – we signed him back from West Ham.

When I started at Sunderland the recruitment of players had been frantic, because we'd only a few days. And, really, every one of them had done well. But the group of players I brought in at the start of the '08–'09 season didn't work out. I'd brought in David Meyler earlier, and he did well, and Cissé was decent, but he was on loan. None of the others gave us real value for money.

For a club like Sunderland you need certain characters. Players I'd brought in previously – Danny Higginbotham, Paul McShane – mightn't have had the talents of the new recruits. But they had better attitudes. I wouldn't go as far as to say that the new players had bad attitudes, but they just weren't right for Sunderland. They didn't plug into what we were about, the training, the area, the conditions, the demands.

George Graham made the point: if you're signing a player he has to see it as a step up. Or else he'll feel that he's doing you a favour. The lads from Spurs, in particular, left me with the impression that they thought they were doing me a favour. Previously, I'd been signing players who saw coming to Sunderland as a challenge. But the new signings – they weren't a disaster, but they weren't the hungriest group of players. And maybe that had an effect on the group we already had.

In their defence, I brought too many in, too soon. Previously,

I'd already known most of the players I'd brought in. Now, with the new lads, I expected much more, and that was unfair on them, and unrealistic. I thought, 'Well, you're better than what I've got, so we'll be finishing in the top ten.'

What had been good enough last year wasn't going to be good enough this year. Instead of eight or nine new players, I should have concentrated on bringing in two or three really good-quality players – two or three good characters. But the problem there was, the *real* quality players still weren't available to Sunderland.

We tried to buy Jonny Evans. We offered United twelve million for him, and David Gill, their chief executive, was laughing at me.

'You're wasting your time.'

He'd got fed up with Niall increasing the offer – eight, nine, ten, up to twelve. We weren't going to get Jonny. He'd have been worth every penny.

But bringing in so many players – it was too much. I can see that now, and I'm annoyed with myself for seeing it now. We already had some decent players, so it should have been about more quality, not quantity.

I'd always have doubts about the players I'm signing. If I was signing Messi today, I'd be going, 'I hope he settles into the area. I hope he likes Sunderland and the dark nights.' Because you just don't know – there's never a guarantee. You might sign a player and think, 'He's the deal', but there's always a chance that he can get injured. Every club has signed a striker who hasn't delivered the goals.

Pre-season, we were playing in a mini-tournament in Portugal and we conceded a goal in a match, in Faro. I was disappointed. It was a free-kick from thirty yards. I questioned why Craig Gordon had needed a wall.

The next day, I challenged a few players to beat me from thirty yards. I put the gloves on and I said that if they could get the ball past me I'd give them a thousand pounds each but, if they missed, they'd have to give me a hundred. Eight or nine players lined up, and I knew that Craig and the other goalkeepers were pissed off with it. They didn't even look at my goalkeeping skills. They just did their stretches. I tipped a few on to the bar, on to the post, and I kept a clean sheet. I won eight hundred quid off the players – I could have lost eight grand. I was trying to generate a bit of banter, but I'd embarrassed, and maybe belittled, the goalkeepers. I hadn't meant to. But I didn't think the keeper should be beaten from twenty-five or thirty yards. I think I lost Craig for a few weeks, and maybe longer, because of that.

We lost the first game to Liverpool – always a tough one. Then we'd a brilliant win at Tottenham. Kieran Richardson and Cissé scored for us.

We were going for a walk the morning of the game, in London. It was about eleven o'clock. We were all waiting – no sign of Chimbonda.

He turned up a quarter of an hour late.

I told him, 'You're a fuckin' joke. Late for a walk.'

He was all, 'What's up, man', very relaxed about it, not apologetic. It seemed his time was more important than ours. He was new to the club and he was sending messages, the wrong ones, straightaway. It was eleven o'clock; it wasn't six in the morning. If he'd been a bit apologetic, my response would have been different.

I'd had him in the team for the afternoon, but I dropped him. He wasn't even on the bench. We won, 2–1. After the match, everyone's buzzing in the dressing room, and Chimbonda's right in the middle of them, jumping around. And I'm looking at him, going, 'You fucker, you can't even let me enjoy the win.'

Instead of sitting there, going, 'I can't believe I was late. One of our first games – I could've cost the team', he was jumping around with everybody. That irritated me as much as the fact that he'd been late earlier. It was a sign of things to come.

Manchester City beat us 3–0, at home – a bad result. We drew away to Wigan. But we should have won. We had great chances. Four games, four points. We'd lost our first two home matches, and done well away from home. It was almost the opposite of the season before.

But then we beat Middlesbrough at home – always a big win. Seven points, from five. Then we lost at Villa. They scored from a free-kick. Two players in our wall – they didn't jump out of the way, but they didn't stand their ground either. Diouf and Chimbonda.

Michael Chopra came to see me and told me he had issues with gambling. He told me how much he'd lost – and I knew it would have been a lot more than the amount he mentioned. I made a phone call for him to Sporting Chance, and I spoke to Peter Kay, who'd founded the clinic with Tony Adams. Peter had been up to the club before, to talk to the players about the pitfalls – alcohol, gambling, drugs. And we made an arrangement, between Chops, Peter and myself, that Chops would go down to the clinic in Hampshire for a week or so. He was an important player for us, so his absence would have been noticed. Maybe our attitude was wrong, or naïve; we'd send him away for a week and he'd be fixed.

We'd had to start the season without Kenwyne Jones. He got injured in June, in a friendly in Trinidad, against England. He picked up a bad knee injury in an unnecessary collision with bloody David James. So we started the season without our main striker, because of an injury he picked up in a poxy friendly – not at the end of the season, but halfway through the summer. For politics. The FA thought that Jack Warner, the FIFA vice-president, would give them his vote in their World Cup bid if they agreed to the game. We lost Kenwyne and Warner didn't even give the FA the vote. He rang me the next season to tell me that Kenwyne was in the Trinidad squad. Kenwyne was still injured, nowhere near ready to play. Warner didn't know, and he didn't care. He told me how important he was, and that he objected to my tone. That was when I called him a clown. And more than a clown.

Dwight Yorke was probably my best signing. He was a big character, and good on the training pitch. At the end of our first season in the Premiership his contract was up. He'd got us promoted and he'd helped keep us up. But I released him.

I said, 'Yorkie – you know— There's no deal for you.'

So he went. But towards the end of the summer it looked like we weren't going to get many deals done. So I phoned and asked him if he fancied another year. We agreed that he wouldn't be playing any more internationals; he was thirty-five at this stage. He came back, having been told that he wasn't needed any more. But he got over that. I think he knew what I'd been thinking, that I was looking for younger players, with a bit more legs and energy.

But he decided to play again for Trinidad. We disagreed about that, but it wasn't heated – no swearing or not speaking to each other.

I said, 'I can't believe you're going back playing. You're thirty-four or five.'

He explained that there was some kind of financial incentive involved. That didn't please me either. I just felt he wasn't concentrating. He took his eye off the ball once or twice, and I left him on the bench, with one or two other experienced players. We played Northampton at home, in the League Cup. We were 2–0 down – this was one of the times when I was going mad. But we scored two goals in injury time and, eventually, we won on penalties.

I didn't play Yorkie that night, and he stood at the end of the tunnel during the penalties. Normally, the players on the bench group together while the penalties are being taken, but Yorkie took no interest in it. That irritated me. I left him out for one or two games. His attitude disappointed me a little bit. My plan had been to bring him back. But I just felt he could have given us a bit more, when we were under the cosh. I suppose Yorkie's argument would be that he'd been bombed out; he was out of the first-team plans. I'd made him train with the reserves for a week or two. He probably felt he deserved a bit better. Maybe I should have pulled him aside and said, 'Yorkie, come on – pull your finger out.'

What you quickly learn as a manager is you need the players more than they need you.

You make your own luck. But you still need a few breaks.

Into October, we're beating Arsenal, 1–0, at the Stadium of Light. We're into injury time, and they equalise. Fàbregas scores with a header, from a corner.

It was a turning point in my career. We'd had a mixed start. If we'd beaten them, it would have been brilliant – the injection we needed, a big win against a big team. We went to Fulham. Kieran Richardson scored from a free-kick, but the referee disallowed it. He said it was because somebody was pushing in the wall. It was Chimbonda. He shouldn't have been in the fuckin' wall. It was our free-kick. Kieran had another free-kick that hit the woodwork three times. It came off the bar, hit the post, rolled across and hit the other post. If we'd won those two games, we would have been fifth or sixth in the league.

I have my days when I still analyse those results. But that's the manager's life.

★

Ellis Short, the man who was going to take over the club, had arrived. He came in on a horse. He hadn't come on board when we bought the new players; he'd been in the process of becoming the major shareholder.

I was in the last year of my contract. There'd been talks in the background between Niall and Michael Kennedy, but nothing had fallen into place yet. Part of me was thinking, with the new man there, 'We'll see how it goes.'

Ellis Short was more hands-on. There were more phone calls than previously. I got used to that. But I don't think he knew much about football. He'd drop me the odd text – *You're playing the Gunners, man, you've gotta beat them.* And he rang me a few times at the training ground. He'd ask me about players, and why certain players weren't playing. He asked me about dropping Chimbonda, and how I was going to handle it. This was new. I'd had casual chats with Niall, about, say, when a player was coming back from injury, and players we were after – normal football chat. But I'd been left to run the team. Previously, with the consortium, meetings had been quite informal. They were clever with it, but I never felt they were questioning me. But Ellis Short's calls – I resented them a bit.

I was naïve, too. I'd say things like, 'We should finish eighth.' In reality, a great target would have been fourteenth. Maybe a key to success in the Premiership is to drop your expectations. Survival is the first goal. It's one of the things that soured the relationship between myself and the new owner. I told him, 'Yeah, yeah, we're going places.' Then, when we picked up a few injuries and results weren't going our way, he can't have been pleased.

After we beat Newcastle in our next game, we had twelve points from nine games. And it was the first time we'd beaten Newcastle at home in thirty-odd years. It was electric – the tension. Cissé scored, and Kieran. The level of player we had now had gone up since I'd come to the club. We played really well. I think it was my happiest day at Sunderland.

So the loss at Stoke, midweek, was frustrating. It would have been a real sign of progress, grinding out a result, even a point, at Stoke. Could we come down from the high of Newcastle? No, we couldn't.

Chelsea hammered us 5–0, but Chelsea could do that to anybody. The killer was Portsmouth, at home. We battered them. Their winner was a penalty, in injury time. Who gave away the penalty? Diouf – on as a sub. He just booted the lad up in the air. It was an unbelievable foul.

In the dressing room after, I said, 'Dioufy, what were you doing?'

He said, 'Well, I was just trying to tackle him.'

I think he'd been angry when I put him on, frustrated that he hadn't started the game.

It was a sticky patch we were going through, but not that sticky. We were still averaging a point a game. But there were rumours circulating at the time that I was going to leave, that I'd lost my rag with everybody and had had enough. It was nonsense. In Sunderland and Newcastle there's a big rumour every few months. And I was facing that one. I'd missed one or two days' training. But I'd do that sometimes. I'd step back, to give people a break from me. I'd be elsewhere, meeting people, or at matches. It was a step back from the training ground, not from work. I don't think it's a good idea for the manager to be visible every day. But the story this time was that I hadn't been to training at all and I wouldn't be going to our next game, at Blackburn.

We stayed in the Hilton Hotel, in Manchester, the night before the Blackburn game. I'd missed the meal, and when I got there I think it was Yorkie who said, 'Oh, we heard you'd resigned.'

We turned it into a bit of banter.

The next day, at Blackburn, we were 1–0 down. Our two strikers, Cissé and Kenwyne Jones, are giving us nothing. It was like we were playing with nine men. I ripped into them at half-time. I probably went overboard; it was a gamble. I thought they'd either respond to it – 'We'll show you' – or they'd sulk.

We went out in the second half and Kenwyne scored inside a minute. Then Cissé scored. He ran over to the dugout and shook my hand. It was nice; I enjoyed it. I thought, 'Fair play to yeh.' What I liked about Cissé, he took his bollocking. He didn't sulk. He just went and scored the winning goal.

Things were rosy again in the garden.

But we lost, at home, to West Ham, and again, to Bolton, 4–1. The pressure was on. Home form is vital. We'd lost at home to Portsmouth, we'd lost at home to West Ham, we'd lost at home to Bolton. I think the fans wouldn't have minded losing the away games. But we were doing okay in the away games, and struggling at home. It wasn't acceptable. The vast majority of the fans are seeing you at home.

I'd hoped that we could get Bolton relegated at the end of the previous season. But they'd beaten us, and stayed up. I always thought they were a team that could cause us difficulties. I'd gone to see them play at Middlesbrough the week before. I went to the game with Tony Loughlan and Ricky Sbragia. I was driving. We were chatting about management, and I asked Tony if he'd ever be interested in becoming a manager.

And Tony said, 'Nah, nah – I'd prefer to be out on the grass.'

So I went, 'What about you, Ricky?'

'No, no—!'

It was a proper overreaction.

Myself and Tony both went, 'Relax – it was just a question.'

But Ricky went, 'It's not for me – it's not for me, gaffer.'

I said, 'All right, Ricky, it was only a fuckin' question.'

Bolton beat Middlesbrough 3–1 that day. They were strong and physical. A week later, on 29 November, they beat us 4–1. The stats were ridiculous; we had so much possession. They had four shots on target. We were 1–0 ahead; Cissé scored again. But, on the back of two or three defeats, we were nervous playing at home.

Craig Gordon was carrying an injury and I'd asked him to play. He said, 'Yeah', he'd have a go, but he got injured again in the game. He played on. I feel bad about that; I shouldn't have played Craig. I know, we sometimes have to ask players who are injured to play. But this was too much of a risk. He was very unlucky. Prior to signing him, when he played at Hearts he never missed a game. His record was brilliant. He came to us and had a string of injuries, bad ones for a goalkeeper, broken wrists and ankles.

There was a lot of booing after the game, a lot of disappointment. They were booing me this time, and the team. It was a 'we're fuckin' fed up' type of booing.

I stayed in Sunderland that night and the players came in to training the next day. It wasn't a punishment. We'd planned to bring them in on Sunday, and we were going to give them the Monday off. We'd bring them in the day after a match, to check on them – any injuries or knocks from the game, precautionary stuff, standard procedure. If I was doing it again, I'd give them the day after the game off and bring them in the day after that. Their minds are elsewhere, especially after being beaten – everyone's down. Especially on a Sunday.

I was still angry that morning. Not that we'd lost but at the way we'd lost. It wasn't that we'd downed tools; we hadn't. In terms of the stats, we'd had more than decent possession, and we'd made twice as many passes as Bolton. But, I know – try explaining that to supporters when they've just watched you lose 4–1. But we'd been nervous. Individual mistakes – giving daft goals away.

But there was no argument, and no outbursts. I was disappointed that we were struggling. But I'd been in the game for almost twenty years, and I still knew that things weren't so bad.

I drove home to my family after training on Sunday afternoon. I pulled over on the way back. I was knackered, and I had a snooze in the car, on the side of the A19. I don't remember ever having done that before.

There'd been no phone calls from the owner, or from Niall, after the game. There'd been no panic. But I spoke to Niall on Monday. He was in Portugal, playing golf. I can't remember if he phoned me or I phoned him. We rarely spoke after a game. Niall mentioned that the players should be coming into training with smiles on their faces. I got the impression he'd been speaking to one or two players who'd been left out.

I said, 'I don't expect to see people with smiles on their faces when we get beaten. If you want that, you should have employed Roy Chubby Brown.'

We were there to win matches and, if we lost, I expected people to be upset. The conversation wasn't too intense or awkward, but it was the first time Niall had talked about a team matter in the two and a bit years that I'd been at the club. So it was a bit strange. But he was the chairman and entitled to say anything like that.

Later, Niall said that he hadn't used those words; he'd said that he wanted me to come back with new energy and a smile on *my* face – something like that.

I stayed at home on Tuesday and headed back up to Sunderland on Wednesday. Our reserves were playing United that night, and I was going up a touch earlier. I'd be staying in Sunderland for the rest of the week. We had a match against United on Saturday.

While I was driving, the owner rang me.

He said, 'I hear you're coming in one day a week.'

I said, 'One day a week? Who were you talking to?'

'Well, that's what I heard.'

I went, 'It's nonsense. How could I come in one day a week? I'm on the way up now anyway. We've got a game on Saturday.'

He said he was disappointed with the Bolton result. His tone wasn't good.

'Your location – where you live. You need to move up with your family.'

I was in the third year of a three-year contract. The arrangement – the flat in Durham, my family in Manchester – had suited everybody, until now.

I said, 'We've had a bit of success. Why should I move up now?'

He said, 'I think it's important that you live in the area.'

I'm not sure if I said something like, 'Why don't you move up?' He lived in London. But I did say, 'I'm not moving. I'm in the last six or seven months of my contract anyway.'

It might have been a different conversation if we'd been talking face-to-face. Then I might have said, 'Well, if I sign a new contract, I'll move up. I can understand that.'

But I said, 'It's not affected results previously.'

The conversation didn't end well. It was a case of 'No one tells me where I should live'; and the accusation that I was only coming in one day a week hung there.

There is always hearsay about managers at football clubs – there are always rumours. 'He comes in at seven in the morning' – 'he's sleeping with a girl from the office' – 'he's a big drinker'. They're always there – 'he's a loner' – 'he's too friendly with the players'. I'd lived through my career with those rumours. 'Brian Clough is rarely in' – it didn't bother me. 'Jack Charlton lets them go for a drink', and we loved him for it. If Ellis Short actually thought that I was trying to run the team on a day a week he should have arranged to see me. I thought he was talking down to me; he spoke to me like I was something on the bottom of his shoe. I felt I'd been doing reasonably well, so far. So I thought, 'I'm not putting up with this.'

I drove home.

I phoned Michael Kennedy in the car.

'Listen, Michael, I'm not having all of this.'

Michael spoke to Niall. Niall wasn't sure why the conversation between myself and Ellis Short had ended so badly. Apparently Ellis Short was surprised that I was so upset.

And, before I knew it – it was over.

Tony Loughlan got in touch with me on Thursday morning. He'd been told that Ricky would be taking the team for Saturday's game against United, and that I wouldn't be going back.

Michael had been talking to Niall.

Niall texted me, saying he'd sort the contracts out.

It must have been difficult for Niall.

Peter Walker, the chief executive, had left the club a few months earlier. I'd only met the new man, Steve Walton, once, with Niall.

There was an agreement within twenty-four hours that I would leave. There'd be a severance payment, and we'd move on. Statements were issued. It was over.

I was very disappointed, but not really shocked – although it was very sudden.

Later, Ellis Short said he'd been very taken aback at my reaction to his phone call. That might be true, but he never picked up the phone to me, to see if there'd been a misunderstanding or to arrange for us to speak again properly. Later he said that he wasn't trying to question my commitment or insist on moving my family to Sunderland. I don't think he was sorry to see me go, and I didn't want to work for him.

You lose a few matches, and suddenly everybody questions where you live.

The media reports said I'd left, I'd walked, I'd resigned. But I didn't resign. We agreed, mutually, that we'd part ways. There was a statement from Sunderland, saying that everything had been agreed amicably. But then I had to wait ages before I was paid.

I collected my bits and pieces from the flat in Durham but I didn't go back to the club. Tony collected my things from my office for me. Ricky took the job till the end of the season, and I was left wondering why he'd reacted that way when I'd asked him if he fancied management, the week before.

I didn't resign or walk out. I said I couldn't work with Ellis Short. An agreement was reached. I wasn't answerable to Ellis Short. I was answerable to the chairman or the chief executive. 'Walking out' is an unfair expression. Sometimes a manager's position is just impossible.

My career at Sunderland ended after a difficult three or four weeks. Not two or three months, like I've seen other managers get. We were still on a point a game. If you kept that up for ten years, you'd still be in the Premiership.

But it was over.

It still saddens me. I still think I should be the manager of Sunderland. I really liked the club, and I liked the people.

I can be critical of myself about many things. I know I could be more tolerant of people. I know my recruitment could have been a lot better – and, ultimately, that will make or break you. But the idea that I wasn't a hard worker, or that I only turned up now and again – it was nonsense. I knew when to go in and when to dip out, to recharge the batteries or give people a break from me.

We'd some games coming up, and I knew there were a couple of good results around the corner.

Not long before, there'd been talk of a contract extension. Now, I was gone. A bad spell is always coming. But I think I'd earned the right to get through that spell. Again – it was weeks, not months.

But Ellis Short was new – and I wasn't his manager. He owed me nothing. He wasn't there when we were promoted. I'd done nothing for him yet. I should have read that script a little bit better.

It's probably true that the working relationship was never going to work, and not because he was some big, bad Texan and I was some grumpy Northsider from Cork. I don't like being spoken down to.

Steve Bruce rang me the following summer, when he was offered the Sunderland job.

I said, 'Go for it.'

I said the same thing to Martin O'Neill.

A few days after I left Sunderland, Yorkie texted me: *All the best.* I texted him back: *Go fuck yourself.*

I saw him a few years ago. We both played in a charity match. We said hello to each other, but there was no real conversation. And it's sad, because I had great days with Yorkie. I could have handled things differently.

TEN

Maybe I'm just making loads and loads of excuses.

The penny only dropped when I left Ipswich: the owner, the chief executive and the manager had never met together while I was there. Marcus Evans, Simon Clegg and myself were never in the same room. There was the occasional video link-up to the owner, but the three of us never met. I'd meet the owner, Marcus, but Simon, the chief executive, wouldn't be there. I'd meet with Simon, but the owner wouldn't be there. Or they met when I wasn't there. I never once said, 'Can the three of us get together, to see about getting some players in?' There was never that trust – never.

You need to see people's eyes.

Michael Kennedy gave me a call. Niall had been at some sort of club owners' meeting, and he'd bumped into Marcus Evans, the owner of Ipswich Town. Whatever was said between them, Niall phoned Michael, and Michael called me. Would I go and meet Marcus Evans in London?

I got the train, then a car to his house in The Boltons, in Chelsea. He lived a few doors away from Ellis Short.

This was in April. It was five or six months since I'd stopped working at Sunderland. After the initial shock, I hadn't been missing the buzz of management. I wasn't pining. Once I knew it was over, it was over. It might seem like a cold attitude, but I always remember the club chairman talking to Brian Clough in *The Damned United*: 'First there's the chairman, then there's the directors, then there's the fans and the players, and then, bottom of the pile, there's the fuckin' manager.'

The manager is important, but not that important. I always knew I'd be gone one day. But, at the same time, I felt I hadn't finished the job at Sunderland because of the way things had ended. You always want to prove people wrong.

We're almost brainwashed into thinking that the longer we're out of work the harder it is to get back in. I was a bit anxious about it. The list of good ex-managers who've been forgotten about is frightening. But I felt I'd done enough at Sunderland to give me a chance.

I should have been more patient.

I met Marcus Evans. It was just the two of us. We talked about the club, how he'd bought it, how it'd been struggling, and would I be interested in managing it? It was an interview, I think. The job wasn't just there if I wanted it. He wasn't offering me anything. A nice guy – I liked him. I thought I'd be able to work for Marcus. I told him we'd see how it went, and I went back up home.

In the meantime, there were one or two conversations. A lawyer representing Marcus Evans spoke to Michael about potential terms. Then I was asked if I'd go back down to London, for another chat. Marcus was happy with how the first one had gone and just wanted to confirm his impressions. So I went back – I'm guessing it was a week or two later.

Ipswich already had a manager at this time, Jim Magilton. I was being touted for a job that was already occupied. But I didn't feel too bad about that. It's not good, but it's standard practice. I thought it was all right to chat about the job. I hadn't agreed to take it.

I didn't feel too sorry for Jim Magilton. I felt he'd let me down with a player when I was managing Sunderland. He was supposed to take Tommy Miller off me. We'd agreed a deal. The transfer deadline came – I can't remember which one it was. But Ipswich pulled out of the deal.

I rang Jim Magilton.

I said, 'What's happening? I've turned down other deals for Tommy because you said he was going to you.'

He was proper aggressive; he didn't give a fuck. It was all 'Fuck you', and me back to him, 'Fuck you, you're a fuckin' joke.' But it started at his end.

So, part of my thinking was, 'Fuck'm.'

It's the business. I found out later that another manager spoke to Marcus Evans while I was still the Ipswich manager. Today, I don't think I'd do it. If a club offered me the job while the manager was still in place, I'd probably say, 'No. But you know where I am.' But it's like any other business; the club has to plan ahead. I was speaking to Ipswich while the manager was still there. But they'd approached me, and it was the first approach I'd had since Sunderland. Barcelona hadn't been ringing me.

After the first meeting with Marcus Evans, I asked Tony Loughlan to go and watch an Ipswich game. They were playing in Bristol on a bank holiday Monday. I wanted to have some idea about them, in case I was offered the job. Tony went down to Bristol, bought a ticket like a normal punter, and watched them. He thought they were very average.

I'd got the impression, after the second meeting with Marcus Evans, that the job could happen, as long as we could agree terms.

Nine times out of ten, when a manager is out of work he'll agree terms.

A few days later, I was down there in the blue training kit, and I was looking at it, going, 'Fuckin' hell.'

I didn't feel the excitement I'd felt going up to Sunderland. I'm not sure why not, but I didn't. I feel bad even admitting that. Tony Loughlan was with me again, but it didn't have that innocence – 'Oh, it's exciting.' Maybe, after the Sunderland experience, I was a bit wary. There seemed to be a bit of everything about it that wasn't quite right – the set-up, my mindset, the location. But if things had gone better, I probably wouldn't be thinking that.

Tony's job description was never 'assistant'; he was always 'first-team coach'. But he was working alongside me. But you're working with twenty-odd players, so you need two coaches, at least – more voices, more support. At the time, I just had Tony. I didn't bring other people in quickly enough – straightaway. Chris Kiwomya was there, and Bryan Klug, and Steve McCall was the chief scout. They'd all played for Ipswich. It had the feel of a family club that didn't need breaking up. But that was exactly what it needed.

You need to bring in three or four people with you. Make your mark. And, if you want to be cynical about it, if the manager's having a hard time, the club will stick with him longer, because it costs a lot more money to get rid of four or five people.

'We'll give him another few weeks; he might get that result.'

But I was the same at Sunderland on my first day. It was just me and Tony. But my eyes weren't lying to me; some of the staff at Ipswich weren't up to it. There were two members of the medical staff that I disliked straightaway – what they were doing, the way they worked. I didn't like the way they allowed players to behave in front of them. I didn't think they were professional or authoritative enough. But I kept them. To be fair to the owner, he'd told me that if I wanted to make changes I should do it quickly. But I thought I'd wait till the summer, wait till pre-season. But maybe I'm just making loads and loads of excuses. That's management – deal with all that.

Eventually, into the season, in November, I brought in Ian McParland – or Charlie as he's known. I met Charlie when I was doing my Pro Licence. He had managed at Notts County, and he'd coached at Forest. I liked Charlie, but he could argue. He made me look like a saint. Tony and some of the other lads were fairly quiet, but Charlie made up for them, and me. Eventually, I brought in Antonio Gómez, the fitness coach, from Sunderland. All these men are survivors.

I hadn't been to the training ground before I took the job. There were stories later that, when I took over, fans weren't allowed in, and that I'd changed the locks. Our first session was open to the fans. But nobody came. My first day – you'd have thought a couple of school kids would have been dragged in by a dad or granddad. But there wasn't one person watching. I didn't mind, but it seemed to say something. That warmth wasn't there.

Then there was the blue training kit. I don't like fuckin' blue. City were blue, Rangers were blue. My biggest rivals were blue. Is that childish? That first day, myself and Tony went back to my office for a cup of tea. It was a cabin, like a school prefab. I'm not knocking that, but I just thought it all needed freshening up, a lick of paint. There were money difficulties at the club – I appreciate that. But myself and Tony sat down and looked at one another.

'I'm not sure about this one.'

I couldn't feel it – the chemistry. Me and the club. I get annoyed now, thinking that. I should have been able to accept it: I was there to do a job.

The biggest problem was, we won our first two games – the last two games of the '08–'09 season. I started on the Wednesday or Thursday, and we'd a game in Cardiff on the Saturday – 29 April. We were awful, but we won 3–0. Cardiff missed a penalty to go 1–0 up. They could have beaten us 10–0. I wish they had. Then I'd have thought, 'This is a rebuilding job, this.'

We had Giovani dos Santos on loan, from Spurs – he played for Mexico in the World Cup in Brazil. What he was doing at Ipswich I do not know. He was brilliant. He got us up the pitch, and scored one of the goals. We won – 'The Messiah has arrived.'

The last game of the season was at home, to Coventry. Marcus Evans told me during the week that they'd already covered my contract with season ticket sales for the next season. It was a dead rubber game – there was nothing at stake – but there were 20,000 people there. We won again, and we deserved to. I was thinking, 'We don't have to do too much here. I'll focus on the dressing rooms – get them decorated.'

When I went up to Sunderland they'd been relegated and they'd just lost their first five games of the season. The transfer deadline was in three days. I had to do things quickly – get people in who I knew and trusted. This time I started at the end of the season, the club was mid-table, and I won my first two games. So the urgency wasn't there; I wasn't walking into a crisis. If we'd lost the two games, I think I'd have been saying, 'Listen, I'm going to be busy all summer.'

When the players came back pre-season, they found great dressing rooms. But I hadn't done enough with the team or the staff.

I dropped my standards. After Sunderland I thought that maybe I should step back a bit. 'I shouldn't be so intense.' But at Ipswich I fell into that trap of thinking, 'This'll do us.' The staff – 'They'll do us.' I should have been saying, 'They definitely won't do us.'

I should have brought in more people, from the start. 'This is us – things are changing.'

When I left Sunderland, it was my gig. When I left United, it was my gig. I fought my own little wars. At Ipswich, I fought other people's battles. I went with other people's standards. That was my biggest crime.

The club's new chief executive, Simon Clegg, was an ex-Para. And we had the idea that we'd have one or two days with the forces, in Colchester, pre-season. It was my idea, but Simon had the contacts.

I was trying something a bit different; I thought it would break the monotony of pre-season training. Colchester is just down the road from Ipswich, so the players wouldn't be on a bus for six hours.

We decided to surprise the players. We told them to be ready to go away for one or two nights. Typical footballers, I think some of them thought they were on their way to some five-star hotel.

We got to Colchester and experienced the training regime of the 7th Parachute Regiment Royal Horse Artillery. The plan was, we'd stay in tents that night, out in some woods – after a series of marches.

The intense part was in the evening. The Paras are trained to live off the land, so we saw them slaughtering a pig – we had to watch. It wasn't nice. They cooked it, and we ate it. But the lads were cold – you're out of your environment and you just want to sleep.

I asked one of the officers to organise something for the morning, to get the lads up and out quickly. So, at five or six in the morning, they woke us with stun grenades, thrown to the sides of the tents. That woke us up. Every time I saw a face sticking out of a tent, the expression told me, 'If you think we're getting promoted on this, you're in fuckin' trouble.'

They were running around and climbing things – and it wasn't like the local park. The staff joined in. I had an accident on one of the bars. I went to grab it, fell back and banged my head. I got no sympathy.

Marches, and breaks, and setting up the tents. I don't think anyone was keen to share a tent with me, so I ended up with one of the Paras. I slept with my Celtic top on! There was no sitting around the fire, the banjo out, and a sing-song. Anyway, it wasn't the place to start singing rebel songs.

It was hard. It was enjoyable but the hotel might have been better. A lot of the lads ended up with blisters, from the army boots. We'd a friendly against Real Valladolid the following Friday, and one or two had to miss it because of the blisters. So the timing hadn't been great – although we won.

There was good banter, but the lads were shattered. I don't think it created the bond or the spirit that I was hoping it would. Actually, you get that by winning football matches. And it wasn't as if I'd been there a few years and had a feel for the group of players. I was guessing at what they might enjoy, and I think I guessed wrong. The medical staff weren't happy. But I thought, 'Fuck yis, you'd better get used to living off the land anyway.'

Our first game of the new season was away to Coventry. We lost, 2–1. Giovani dos Santos had gone back to Spurs by then. Our keeper, Richard Wright, had been very good for my first two games at the end of the last season, but he cost us one of the goals – and a few more to come. It's so important to get off to a good start, and we'd played quite well. But we gave away two soft goals. Jon Walters scored for us.

Teams can recover from a bad start, but a sluggish start often tells you what sort of season you're going to have. I really went overboard on the players after West Brom beat us, 2–0 – the fourth game of the season. It was over the top. West Brom had just been relegated, so they were going to be strong. I was playing a lot of young players. I was ranting and raving.

'You're all losers!'

It really wasn't my style. We'd lost to a better team and, normally, I'd have accepted that. And it wasn't just because we were losing. We'd done that at Sunderland, too. But things had taken off so quickly at Sunderland. I think I lacked a bit of patience with myself at Ipswich. I suppose I thought I could relive the Sunderland experience. But I couldn't get that momentum. I didn't feel I was bedding in. It was 31 October before we won a . match, our fifteenth game of the season.

Shane Supple was a goalkeeper, and he'd been involved in the first team. He was a really nice lad. He came to see me one morning in my office and told me he was retiring. He was only twenty-two.

The first thing I'd always suggest in a situation like that is for the player to have a break, and come back in a week or so. The player might be a bit low, or he might have had an injury, or it's a family issue. I'd had my moments when I'd felt I'd had enough. But I could just tell by Shane's eyes that he'd made his mind up. He was cool about it; he wasn't upset.

I remember saying to him, 'You're not changing your mind, are you?'

He went, 'No, no. I've thought about it.'

He didn't love the game any more. And he said he didn't want to work with people who didn't care if they won or lost. I think it was the whole industry that he disliked.

I admired him for it. People often end up in jobs that they don't want, in places where they don't want to be. And I think, too, that the pull of Ireland was there; he wanted to go home to Dublin.

I gave him the option of coming back but I knew I was wasting my time. I think he was going back to Ireland to become a Garda – a policeman – so I thought to myself, 'I'd better keep onside with Shane.'

So, that was one of our goalkeepers gone.

Of the fourteen games before we beat Derby on 31 October, eight were draws. They were all bad draws, but the 3–3 draw at Doncaster, in mid-September, was a disaster. We were winning – we're 3–2 up going into injury time. And Quinton Fortune, ex-United, cuts in. I played with Quinton, and I never saw him use his right foot. But he hits it with his right, and scores – top corner. We'd been 1–0 up, and 2–1 up, and 3–2 up.

Ten days later, we drew 3–3 with Sheffield United. The same story – they scored in injury time.

Six goals, two points. At that stage of the season, the four points we dropped would have sent us up ten places in the table.

Twenty draws in one season – it's still mind-boggling. And we had been winning so many of those games. I should have used the substitutions better – 'Get an extra defender on.' But I thought, 'It's only Doncaster', and they equalised. We'd have been better off losing ten of those draws, and winning ten. We'd have had ten more points.

Those ten days between Doncaster and Sheffield, we were nearly there. But we never really had the exhilaration of two wins in a row – a run of results. We didn't get the momentum, or the self-belief that comes with it.

Newcastle came to Portman Road. They hammered us, 4–0. It shouldn't have hurt so much. They had Andy Carroll; they'd Nolan, they'd Nicky Butt. A blind man would have got Newcastle promoted that year. But I was ex-Sunderland, the Newcastle fans travelled in numbers, there was the tribute to Bobby Robson, it was on TV.

But Newcastle weren't coming to town every day. You wouldn't have looked at us and said, 'They're not even trying.' There wasn't chaos. We didn't play particularly well when we beat Derby. We played Watford one night. We had twenty-six chances, but we drew 1–1. They scored in injury time – another bad draw. We were nearly a decent team.

The family had moved down with me, and we rented a house. I liked it; I liked the sea air. But we moved house three times in the first year. It was unsettling, but we were trying to find the right village, and villages can be funny old places. We couldn't find a Catholic school, like St Bede's in Manchester, for the kids. The school we eventually found was different; it was more convention-ally English, very middle class – cricket and rugby, tea and scones.

We went to a charity function for the school a few months after the kids had started there. It was a tuxedo job, and I ended up sitting beside a man I didn't know. I wondered how the con-versation was going to flow.

He said, 'What do you think of this new coalition government?'

I thought, 'For fuck's sake—' I nearly went 'Is there a new coalition government? Did you watch Barcelona last night?'

I thought the New Coalition was a team playing in the Suffolk League. I think I missed St Bede's more than the kids did.

And the blue kit!

It always felt a bit wrong.

Simon Clegg, the new chief executive, came on board the same day I started. Chemistry again – it wasn't there. He'd been the chief executive of the British Olympic Association, but he wasn't a footballing man. But I think it had more to do with the differences in our backgrounds. As well as being an ex-Para, he was public-school educated. I was from Mayfield, in Cork. But I had to grow up. I couldn't expect to be working with Irish people.

But the conversation has to flow.

I'd say, 'I'm interested in that player.'

He'd say, 'Well, what do I do?'

He'd never been involved in football before. I think he was all about being answerable to Marcus, not helping the manager. Everything was hard work.

Most Championship clubs lose money. Simon suggested a restructuring of the player and staff bonuses. Even as a player I'd always thought that you should only really get a bonus if you'd earned it. The idea was that the bonuses would be delivered with promotion or on reaching the play-offs. Normally a player would get a bonus for a win or a draw. The average player at Ipswich would have been on eight or nine grand a week, so holding the bonuses – three or four hundred quid a game – till the end of the season was a big incentive; one big sum, instead of small amounts.

The players were okay with the bonus restructuring; they were already sitting on eight or nine grand a week. But the staff were also affected, and they wouldn't have been on the same kind of money. The bonuses were a bigger thing for them.

I now realise that the staff bonuses are vital for morale. I didn't comprehend that at the time, but people need incentives. It's human nature – everyone loves a bonus. When a club has a win at the weekend, the training ground is a much happier place the following week. And a big reason for that is because the staff are all getting their bonuses. But that was gone, a bit. And we could tell quite early in the season that we weren't going to be promoted – so there'd be no bonuses. I should have left the staff alone – a couple of hundred quid a win. That money was a night out with their wives, or a treat for their families. Success – and the bonuses – affected the families, made them part of the club.

But I was taking something away, and they were obviously going to think less of me. It was stupid. I must have lost some of them, before the season had even started.

Some of the players – they were very quiet. We didn't have a Dwight Yorke; we didn't have the characters. I needed some new players. I'd talk to the owner over the phone, give him a ballpark figure. Tamás Priskin was at Watford, and available. The scouts were keen, and I watched him once, pre-season. He scored, played well – but it was a friendly. His contract was up in a year, and I thought he might be worth a punt. I think I mentioned a figure of £400,000 to the owner. I rang Malky Mackay, who was managing Watford.

'Listen, Malky, I'm just giving you a heads-up. We're interested in a player.'

I never spoke to other managers about a fee for a player; I never got involved.

Malky goes, 'Roy, I appreciate the call.'

I said, 'I'm leaving it to the chief executive.'

I couldn't believe it when I heard what we paid for him. I think it was £1,750,000. Watford couldn't believe their luck. That was our lack of communication, the fact that the three of us never spoke together. Priskin wasn't worth that money, but nobody had got back to me, to get my opinion.

I brought in two of the lads from Sunderland, Carlos Edwards and Grant Leadbitter. They were good lads, but we paid too much for them. I thought about two million for the two of them would have been decent. But we paid just less than four.

I phoned Steve Bruce, who was managing Sunderland.

I said, 'I can't believe how much you're getting for Grant and Carlos.'

Brucie went, 'Ah, now, Roy – they've agreed a deal.'

It had nothing to do with him. He was never going to say,

'No, no, you're paying too much.' The deal had been between Simon and Niall.

I liked the look of Jordan Rhodes. He scored at Brentford for us, pre-season, and he scored at home to Colchester. A couple of clubs rang me about him. Notts County and Huddersfield – it wasn't Liverpool and Arsenal. I'd brought a few lads in, and I'd been told that some lads would have to go out. I still get criticised for selling Jordan, and I have to accept that. But it was also a club decision. We sold him to Huddersfield, down a division, for £350,000, and he started scoring loads of goals. I think I was the one who suggested a sell-on clause, and thank God we had it, because they sold him to Blackburn for eight million. The mistake myself and the staff made with Jordan was, we discussed what he couldn't do, instead of what he could do.

I knew Lee Martin, a bit, from my playing days at United, but he didn't work out. He was a decent player, but the Championship is about good, strong characters. I don't think Lee had that quality for the Championship. Priskin, too – technically, he wasn't bad, but I don't think he worked hard enough.

My recruitment wasn't good enough. I've no excuses.

Damien Delaney came in and did okay. I was a bit hard on him sometimes, probably because I knew him and he was from Cork. But I went over the top. I was the same with another lad, Colin Healy. He was from Cork, too, and I told him he was moving his feet like a League of Ireland player. It was wrong. Colin was new to the club; I should have been bending over backwards for him. At Ipswich, I sometimes said the wrong things. Maybe I was trying too hard.

When you're a manager, people say you should never worry about the players liking you; it's about them respecting you. But we all want to be liked. You don't want the people you work with disliking you. Maybe, after the Paras experience and bringing a few lads in and letting the wrong lads go, I was trying to right a few wrongs.

We were playing away to Cardiff on 29 November, a Sunday. We'd beaten Derby and, since then, we'd had two more draws. I saw that there was a rugby match on in Cardiff the day before our game. Wales were playing Australia. And I like the rugby, so I thought, 'Well, I fancy going. How can I justify going down to Cardiff a day earlier?'

I decided I'd bring everybody. I rented a box at the Millennium Stadium, and we had a great day. I paid for it. Staff, players – we all walked up to the stadium together. It was brilliant. There's always a friendly atmosphere at rugby matches, so we weren't having to tell the players to watch their backs. It wasn't a football match we were going to, and it wasn't Ireland against England. The food wasn't ideal for the day before a match day – mashed potatoes, sausages – but we got stuck into it. They should have been having pasta. But I just thought, we'd been doing that for three months and we hadn't been getting the results. We just had a really nice day.

Maybe if we'd lost the day after I'd have blamed all the mash and sausages. But we went out and we won. Did we win because of the rugby? Probably not. But the players appreciated it. I don't think they saw it as me trying to ingratiate myself, or to win hearts and minds. There'd been photographs for the local paper and the match programme at the end of the Paras experience, and I remember thinking, 'Maybe there shouldn't be.' But at the rugby there were no photographs, no fuss, no media stuff. It brings back good memories; they were a good group of lads.

We won, but I didn't think of it as a turning point. I still knew it was going to be one of those seasons. When you don't win for the first fourteen matches, it's not all down to bad luck. There were just too many draws; we couldn't finish the job off. But the signs were better after the Cardiff match. We started to win a few games. In December, we won two, drew two and lost one.

The two draws were both 0–0, one after the other. Away to Bristol City, at home to Peterborough. At Bristol, I played Pablo Couñago, a player I didn't particularly like or get on with. He was a striker, very talented. He had a chance with about five minutes to go. We had a shot, the keeper parried it to Pablo. He was ten or eleven yards out. He took three touches, and the keeper blocked it. He could have hit it first time. There are games that sum up your spell at a club, and that was the game.

I remember people saying to me about Pablo, 'He's really no good to you away from home, and he doesn't always fancy it at home.' That wasn't a good start, because half of your games are going to be away from home.

I had a dig at him after the match.

'Fuckin' hell, Pablo, you've got to do that first time.'

He was, 'Oh', this and that.

Missing a chance like that is a reflection of the attitude to training. The first day, pre-season, Pablo walked off the training pitch, feeling his groin, or something. It wasn't from a tackle, because the players had just been running and stretching. After we'd finished, I spoke to him. He'd been at home in Spain for the last six or seven weeks, and he landed back in England at half eleven the night before. I didn't think that was great.

The next day – the second day of pre-season – I was in my office, and I saw Pablo chatting to some of the players in the car park, at about ten past nine. He was due to have treatment, and the injured lads would have been in at about half eight or nine. So I called him in – I knocked on the window.

I said, 'What are you doing? It's ten past nine.'

And he went, 'Oh yeah, but we just kind of do what we want.'

I said, 'Well, them days are over.'

My days with Pablo were numbered – but he stayed at the club for another year because we couldn't move him on. No club was interested in taking him – and I was happy to tell him that. I just found him dead lazy.

But he did get an important goal for me. We beat Coventry at home, 3–2, and Pablo scored the winner in injury time. But that, really, was the only time he produced. I'm not a big fan of judging players from DVDs, but I watched a few Ipswich matches on DVD before I took the job. There was one, Pablo came on as a sub. He walked on to the pitch – he was so lackadaisical. He looked like he was going down a coal pit for ten hours. Ipswich got a penalty, and he missed it. I thought, 'That's what you get for walking on. You're supposed to run on to the pitch, like it means something.'

I didn't like the attitude of two or three of the players, including Pablo, early on, which didn't help the flow of my message. I don't mind disagreements. I don't have a problem with a player having a bad time, or playing badly. But the attitude to training, or the impression that the player is just there to pick up his wages – that's what would get to me. Ben Thatcher, one of the senior players, seemed to have issues with me. I heard that Ben was commuting a good distance; he was coming to work from London.

I questioned him on that.

He was, like, 'Ah, yeah, I stay the odd night.'

I could have accepted it if he and a few others had been coming in and training like madmen. I might have given them Mondays off, or some arrangement like that. Management is give and take. But I was looking and thinking, 'You're not really giving much.'

Ben came in three or four hours late one morning. There'd been a crash on the M25, or the M1, or something like that.

He was in my office. No apology.

It wasn't as if they were important players to me; they weren't. But it still created an atmosphere. The training ground is quite small, so there was a tension, even passing one of them in the corridor. You're thinking, 'You, yeh fucker', and they're thinking the same thing.

To the argument 'If the player isn't good enough, get rid of him,' the reply is often, 'Where?'

'I want to move on.'

'Well, I'd love to move you on, but there've been no calls for you.'

I liked Connor Wickham. He didn't score loads of goals, but he was only sixteen or seventeen. He got kicked out of his digs one night. We'd a game; I think we were up at Scunthorpe. And I got a call. Connor had been evicted because he'd left his phone charger plugged in all night, without the phone connected to it. I had to meet the Academy manager, Sammy Morgan, a couple of days later. We discussed phone chargers for a few hours.

I had a go at him once or twice. Sometimes I didn't like his attitude to training. But he was a nice kid, although he was six foot three – a big, strong boy. He shook your hand properly. I'd shake hands with all the players as they went out to the pitch – 'Good luck, good luck' – the usual. Sometimes I'd wonder what they were putting in my hand. But Connor would grab my hand, and I knew he'd have a go for me. He played in the toughest position, if you're learning your trade in the Championship. He was a striker, and most of the centre-halves are big, experienced men and they're going to leave their mark on you. But Connor would take it all day, and he'd be knocking lads over. He did well for me in some important games, and I like to see him scoring at Sunderland, where he is now.

The crowds, always around 20,000, were good, for a team that was lingering near the bottom. There were 25,000 there when we beat QPR, 3–0. And the fans were decent to me. I could see the frustration, and understand it. But what helped, strangely, was the draws. It's hard to hammer your team when they're drawing all the time, not losing. We recovered quite well in the second part of the season. We won more games. We beat QPR, away, and Sheffield Wednesday, away. We beat Barnsley, we beat Reading. We won more games. We drew away to Newcastle.

The last game of the season, we lost 3–0 to Sheffield United, at Portman Road. There's the tradition the players go back out on to the pitch and say goodbye and thanks to the fans. They often have their kids with them. Jon Walters was our captain, and he was organising it.

I made another mistake: I wouldn't go out with them. We'd been beaten – we'd had a player sent off, which didn't help. And we'd had a bad season. But I should have gone out. I should have stood with the players. If I'd been a player and the manager had said, 'Ah, I'm too embarrassed to go out', I think I'd have thought, 'You cunt.'

I'm not that type of person – it's not my form. But sometimes my actions are not what I would want. I should have gone, 'I'll go out with you, lads.' I'd always been okay at facing the music.

I should have looked at the table at the end of the season – we finished fifteenth out of twenty-four – and said, 'That's not too bad.' We were fourteen points from a play-off place, and nine from relegation.

I should have kept my head. I should have looked at the bigger picture.

I don't think I'm a bad manager, but at Ipswich I managed badly. But all the people I've admired – they've all had difficult spells. So I probably learnt more at Ipswich than I did at Sunderland.

★

In the second season, '10–'11, it was all about playing the younger players and getting the wages down. My job description had changed. It had been about promotion. Now it was about working within a much smaller budget.

During the summer I'd had the dreaded conversation with the owner, where I was sitting in my office discussing tactics with him. We had a tactics board with us. I should have known my days were numbered.

'Well, why can't he play there?'

'Because he's this and he's not that.'

He said, 'Let's go with the young players.'

I said, 'I don't mind going with the young players but the Championship will eat them up.'

The Championship isn't a league for young players. You need a mix of young players and experienced men. Every manager who's been at Ipswich since – Paul Jewell, Mick McCarthy – they've gone for experienced players. The average age of a promoted team is twenty-eight or twenty-nine.

Kevin Kilbane came down for talks, and Shaun Derry – his contract was up at QPR.

Shaun said, 'Roy, I'd love to be able to play for you.'

I said, 'Shaun, I think I'll only be able to give you a year, and the money wouldn't be great.'

He said, 'No, I'd like to come and play for you.'

This was at the end of the first season, and it would have been a great start to the new season, to have a good, experienced pro in the dressing room. But the club never offered him a deal.

I was on holiday with my family a week later, on safari in South Africa. I was looking at some elephants when I got a call from Shaun's agent.

'Your club's not been in touch and offered a deal.'

I was embarrassed – I couldn't believe it.

I rang Simon.

'What's happened with Shaun? He wants to sign. It's only a one-year deal.'

He said, 'No, we're not going ahead with it.'

The warning signs were there.

Lee Carsley came, but the club wouldn't offer him a contract. Kevin Kilbane, the same. These were good, experienced players, and good guys.

Kevin told me, 'Roy, your club's not even got back to me.'

I rang Simon, and he rang Kevin to apologise. This was a man who'd played more than a hundred times for his country, and they couldn't even ring him to tell him they weren't going to offer him a deal.

They would all have been free transfers.

So, I gave eight players from the academy their debut. Seven of them weren't good enough. I got in one or two loan players.

We stayed local, pre-season. Our thinking was, we'd play weaker teams, win a few games, build up confidence, with a few harder games thrown in. So we played Histon, Great Yarmouth and Hadleigh United – and West Ham and PSV Eindhoven.

Charlie McParland had left, for family reasons; he'd been commuting from Nottingham. And I asked Gary Ablett to come in, as first-team coach. I'd played against Gary, and I'd met him when I was doing my Pro Licence. I liked him. He'd played at big clubs, Liverpool and Everton. He'd managed at Stockport, and he'd managed the younger players at Liverpool. He had the personality to go with the qualifications.

Gary arrived in time for the trip to PSV. We lost 1–0 – PSV were very good. I gave the lads a night out in Amsterdam. Two of them were late for the bus the next morning.

I'd warned them, 'Lads, act like men tonight. If you're having a few pints, make sure you can get up.'

But, of course, there were two stragglers. I fined them.

A club fine could be a few grand. But my fines would be smaller, three or four hundred quid, cash. And I explained to the players that the money was going into a kitty, for, say, the Christmas do or go-karting trips for the players or staff, or a few quid for the groundsmen. The lads were happy enough to pay the fines when they knew where the money was going.

The policy, staying local, except for the short trip to Holland, worked a treat. I went to watch our reserves play a Tottenham XI, at home. Pablo Couñago came on for ten minutes and he was fuckin' awful. He should have passed the ball to a striker who was in a good position with about five minutes to go.

I went down to the dressing room after the game and had a go at him.

I said, 'You should have fuckin' passed it.'

And he went, 'Well, how are we going to win anything with you as the manager?'

I nearly physically attacked him – but I didn't.

Gary hadn't felt well when we were in Holland, playing PSV.

I remember myself and the other staff getting into him.

'Are you homesick for Liverpool, Gary? Are you missing all the burnt-out cars and shell suits?'

It was all friendly banter.

And Gary was, 'Oh, I don't feel too well.'

He didn't come into work a few days. He got ill very, very quickly. He was staying in a hotel not far from where I lived, and we got the club doctor in to see him. Within a day or two, he was in the cancer ward, in the hospital in Cambridge. He had non-Hodgkin lymphoma, a form of blood cancer. He was fighting for his life. He never worked again.

Because he'd come in pre-season and there were still people on holiday, Gary's contract hadn't been finalised and signed, and although we'd agreed the package, the club wasn't legally bound to do anything.

I rang the LMA – the League Managers' Association – and said, 'You'll have to come and help one of my staff.'

But Gary wasn't a member. But, still, they were brilliant. They made sure he got all his entitlements, and the club had to honour the deal.

I had a meeting with the staff, to explain how ill Gary was. I was very emotional. I remember thinking, 'I'm not really ready for this.' But who is? I don't think I handled it very well, but I'm not sure that an older man would necessarily have handled it better.

Gary was in the process of writing a book – it's very good – and he told me he was convinced that the pressures of football had taken their toll on him. He'd had a hard time at Stockport – financial problems, transfer embargoes. The stresses and strains had damaged him.

I'd drive down to Cambridge after training to see Gary. Eventually, he was moved up to Christie's Hospital, in Manchester, so he could be nearer his family in Liverpool. I'd take my staff up to see him, or I'd see him at his house. He'd been planning to start giving talks, on his career and the pressures of the game. That was going to be his project, because getting back on the training pitch was going to be very difficult. But he never got the opportunity.

He died sixteen months after he'd been diagnosed. I was on holiday in Mauritius when I heard the news. I'd gone from Ipswich by then.

It was shocking.

★

We had a great start, three wins, against Middlesbrough, Palace and Bristol City, and two draws – Burnley and Portsmouth. We were third. I was delighted. We were taking off. We had a settled team. We were playing one up front, and hitting teams on the counter-attack. It had worked really well against Middlesbrough. A week later, mid-September, we were second, after we beat Cardiff City. But we'd lost three players.

I had a bust-up with Jon Walters.

He wanted to leave. We were four or five games into the season. He'd heard that Stoke were interested in him. Tony Pulis again – he hadn't been in touch with me about the player.

I said, 'Jon, I haven't had a call from anybody.'

I couldn't blame Jon for wanting to leave. He'd been a good player for us and he had a chance to go to the Premiership. But he did it the wrong way.

He came back a few days later.

'They're definitely after me.'

I said, 'I've heard nothing. If there's a bid, I'll tell you. I've nothing to hide from you. You can ring the owner. I don't do the business deals.'

'I'm not having this.'

There was effing and blinding, a bit of shoving.

'Why don't you fuckin' believe me?'

I didn't begrudge him the move, although I was losing one of my better players – and maybe my job. I got carried away, and Jon got carried away. I dropped him for the next game, against Burnley. We were 1–0 up, but they scored in injury time. At the press conference after the game I said that Jon would never play for the club again. That was a big no-no. His value was down already.

He was sold to Stoke a week later. It could have gone better, but I played my part. We've shook hands since.

I came in one morning.

'Where's Jon Stead?'

'Oh, he's gone for talks – to Blackpool.'

Nobody had told me about it.

A week later, he was talking to Bristol City.

I rang Simon.

He said, 'Oh, I wasn't sure if I should tell you.'

So, Jon Walters, Jon Stead and Alex Bruce had left. Jon Walters, in particular, was a big loss. We'd a couple of injuries to important players – Gareth McAuley and David Norris. The players I'd wanted, Kilbane, Derry and Carsley, would have been vital to us now.

We got a keeper, Asmir Begović, on loan from Portsmouth, but only for six games. I hadn't really seen him play but, just by the way he walked into the building, I liked him; he lifted the training ground. We were unbeaten in the six games he played, but Portsmouth called him back; I think David James was injured. Asmir's at Stoke now, and he played for Bosnia and Herzegovina in the Brazil World Cup.

They let me bring in Márton Fülöp, another keeper, from Sunderland. I wanted to bring him in on loan.

I said, 'A loan deal – a loan deal all day.'

But the owner rang and told me that they'd done a permanent deal – I think it was for £750,000.

I said, 'You know why they did a permanent deal. They obviously wanted him out the door.'

I brought in Mark Kennedy, from Cardiff, but he was injured most of the time. Jason Scotland came in, from Wigan, but he didn't pull up any trees. And he only arrived after Jon Walters and Jon Stead had left. He hadn't been part of any plan for the season.

I was looking for players on loan. I tried to call in a few favours from a few old team-mates, but I wasn't getting it back. I did get

Andros Townsend and Jake Livermore, from Tottenham. But, in 2010, they were very young, and having Tottenham tendencies in a place like Ipswich is never good. They were young lads, coming in with other young lads – all of them on small wages. We got Jack Colback from Sunderland, but then Steve Bruce needed him back for a Cup tie. Sunderland were playing Notts County.

I said, 'You're bringing him back – for Notts County?'

He said, 'Ah, yeah – we need him.'

Notts County beat them.

In mid-November, we lost six on the spin – Derby, Barnsley, Hull, Norwich, Swansea, Preston. We were down to eighteenth. We beat Leicester, 3–0, and had two games postponed because the pitches were frozen. We drew at Coventry on New Year's Day. Then, two days later, we lost to Forest, 1–0, at home. We weren't bad, we played well – but we lost. An og – Damien Delaney, a player who I was maybe quite hard on.

That was me out the door.

We were struggling. We were third from the bottom of the table. But the call still surprised me. I didn't see it coming.

I was sitting at home the next afternoon, and the owner rang me.

I'd lost my job.

I rang Charlie McParland – he'd come back to the club after Gary became ill.

I told him the news, and he went, 'Oh, I knew we'd be gone today.'

I said, 'I didn't.'

I was really hurt by it, not far from distraught. But you hide it. I was hurt for my family – my pride. I always felt that I'd left United on my terms. It had been my decision. I could have stayed; I was still under contract.

When the manager said, 'I think we've come to the end', I could have said, 'No, I don't think we have.'

I was shown the door, but I opened it and walked through.

With Sunderland, I fell out with the owner; I thought leaving was right. But I was getting the sack this time. That hurt. And I felt I hadn't really made a good go of it.

I did the school run. I picked the kids up. I went home to tell my wife.

She was holding an envelope.

'That was put under the door while you were up at the school.'

Someone had dropped it off from the club: the termination of my contract.

I didn't mind the phone call. But the letter – I thought, 'You fuckers.'

I didn't mind the owner ringing me. Even today, I'd have time for him. In his industry, I'm sure he has to do it all the time. I was another sacking.

Within forty-eight hours, my conversation with my family was, 'Let's get out of here.'

We'd bought a house, and we'd renovated it. But I wanted to get back up to Manchester. Our house there had been up for sale but, luckily, we still had it. We moved back up one or two months later.

When we got back – back in the house, kids back in St Bede's, their old school – I felt like I'd been in a coma for the last eighteen months. I wished it had never happened – but it had.

Your pride is hurt.

'It didn't work out – it could have worked out.'

One story sums up my time at Ipswich. I had to go to my first shareholders' meeting, after four or five months in the job. Marcus Evans was the major shareholder, but there were others. So I went – shirt and tie. We'd had a poor start to the season, but I was told not to worry about the meeting; it would be very straightforward.

The media man told me, 'Don't worry, Roy. There might be a bit of Q & A. They're quite low key around here. They might just ask you about the programmes or the pies.'

They'd gone through the financial aspects of the club, and there were thanks to Marcus Evans for his backing, and they noted that the academy was doing well.

'Any questions from the floor? Pass the mic down—'

The first question was, 'My name is such and such. I think Roy Keane should resign immediately from his position as manager of this football club.'

I felt like saying, 'Can you give me till tomorrow, pal?'

I'd only been in the door two minutes.

My biggest failing has been recruitment. Whether the problem was with my relationship with the scouts, or whether I brought in the wrong characters – ultimately, your signings will make or break you. I sold Jordan Rhodes, a goalscorer. Did I take the wrong advice? I wondered sometimes, 'Are they listening to me?'

I should have followed my own gut feeling.

Ideally, now, I'd like to watch players a bit more. I'd focus on what a player is good at, instead of talking constantly about what he can't do.

I also have to remember that Ipswich hadn't done much before I arrived and they haven't done too much since. I didn't take Barcelona to the bottom of La Liga. I took over at Ipswich, and we went back a bit. Self-pity kicks in too easily.

I was only gone a week when Ipswich played Arsenal in the first leg of the League Cup semi-final. I'd said that too many young lads would get eaten up in the Championship. But the young lads had done very well in the League Cup. We beat Exeter, away, after extra-time; Crewe, away; Millwall, away; Northampton, at home; West Brom. Roberto Di Matteo got the sack within two weeks of that game, after a 3–0 defeat at Manchester City. Then we were drawn against Arsenal – two legs – in the semi-final.

Ipswich beat Arsenal in the first leg. It was the first time they'd been in a Cup semi-final in thirty-odd years.

I'd trust myself a bit more now. At Ipswich, I'd be talking to a member of my staff, and I'd have to remind myself that I'd played more games at the highest level, I'd managed at a higher level – and I was taking advice from people who couldn't match that experience. That's not to say they're not worth listening to – I don't mean that. But don't underestimate yourself.

The talk is constantly about players – the players you want.

'I think he's brilliant.'

'I think he's great.'

'I think he's good.'

'I think he's bad.'

'He might be available.'

'He mightn't.'

'I think he's a great lad.'

'I think he's a cunt.'

We were at a reserve match, and I said, 'What do you think of the boy Iverson?'

And two of the staff said, straightaway, 'Nah.'

It had pissed me right off.

I came in the next day, and I pulled the two of them.

'Lads, the next time I mention a player, don't fuckin' dismiss him without considering it first.'

You get the experience by making mistakes, so – again – I have to go easy on myself. Ancelotti, van Gaal – they learnt from experience.

I would try and enjoy it a bit more. I'd try and be myself, a bit more. I think the pressure of being the boss made me play up the role. There is a role, of course. I'd played it when I was a player. But I had more control of it. I was out on the pitch; it was easier. As manager, you want the players to play for you. Ancelotti can manage Real Madrid and be a good guy. If I come up short, I can at least say, 'Well, I was myself.'

At Ipswich, I acted a bit. It was a sleepy town, and I was, 'I'll fuckin' rock this place. I'll bring them to the army. We'll eat fuckin' pigs all night.' It backfired, a bit. I made the point about Ellis Short talking to me like I was something on the bottom of his shoe. I think I spoke like that to some people at Ipswich.

Paul Jewell came in after me, and immediately said, 'Oh, I'll have to fix this mess.'

It wasn't a mess. We were well organised, we trained properly.

He brought in people like Jimmy Bullard, from Hull; he was on about twenty or thirty grand a week. It happens – there's trust in the new manager. For a while.

ELEVEN

I was a reluctant pundit. That attitude helped the quality of my commentary, I think. I tried to talk as I played – very simply. I sometimes saw Adrian looking at me, letting me know, 'We need more.'

And I was, 'You're not getting more. I've said my bit.'

I don't think I've ever used the word 'unemployed' to describe myself. I don't want the label, and it's one of the reasons I started doing things that I wasn't so sure about – PR events, signings, charity matches. They could be a fill-in, and bring in a few bob. They'd fill my soul, a little bit. I didn't want to sit around, waiting for the calls to start coming in. There's an element of shame in doing nothing. I know – it's often not a choice. But, for me, it was.

When I left Sunderland I thought I'd achieved enough to get another job. After Ipswich, I thought, 'I've not done enough to carry me into another job. Get ready for the worst.'

People say, 'When one door shuts, another one opens', but that's not always the case in football. One door shuts, they all shut. I never thought for a minute that my phone was going to be red-hot. I was eventually offered an international job, and I spoke to a Turkish club. But they didn't feel like the right opportunities. I also spoke to a Premiership club and a Championship club, and I didn't hear anything back.

I heard a college professor in his fifties tell a group of students not to worry about what they were going to do with their lives – 'I don't know what I want to do yet.' I liked that; it gave me hope.

I ended up in Nigeria, doing a gig for Guinness, in September 2011.

Guinness VIP got in touch, through Michael Kennedy. A big lump sum was offered. I'd be away for three or four days, and I'd be going with Marcel Desailly.

I asked myself, 'Do I want to go down this route?' and I thought, 'Well, I've got nothing else on and I've never been to Nigeria.'

I was being warned, 'The money's good but there are a lot of kidnappings over there.'

When my wife and kids heard about that, they were keen for me to go. There'd be nobody paying the ransom.

I thought, 'I'll try it – I'll see if I can enjoy it, or appreciate it.'

I went to London, to a hotel at Heathrow, and met the middle man – there's always an agent involved; I can't remember his name. He introduced me to Marcel. I hadn't met him before, although I'd played against him. We had a good chat, a bit of banter. I liked him.

We flew out to Lagos the following day. It was a nightmare getting through security at the airport – proper chaos. You look at a movie scene set in an African airport, and you say, 'It can't be that bad.' But it was. We had security lads looking after us, and they got us through.

The gig was called 'Guinness VIP'. We were on a stage, but it was intimate – a hundred people, maybe a touch more, sitting around us. You could turn, and engage with people. And there was a live internet link-up.

The first question was about what we'd both been doing since we'd retired from football.

I wasn't that long out of the game, so they passed me the mic and I told them that I'd been doing a bit of travelling, and that I'd tried my hand at management. But the only face they saw up there was Roy Keane: Manchester United. They weren't seeing Sunderland or Ipswich. When we'd been called up on stage, they'd listed off our honours. Mine aren't too bad. But next to Marcel's – World Cup, Champions League with Milan – they weren't that hot. So, I'm telling them all about the travel I'd been doing with my family – Australia, Vegas.

It's all fairly quiet – a muted response.

Then they go to Marcel.

'What have you been doing?'

Fuckin' hell – I thought it was the Pope I was listening to.

'Oh, I've been building schools, I've been working on projects in Africa, for the kids – because I am one of you.'

The roof came off.

It carried on for about another hour. The night was over, and we were walking off the stage.

I'd only known Marcel twenty-four hours, but I knew him well enough to say, 'You, yeh fucker – thanks for that.'

'What?'

'I'm on about Vegas and Sydney and fuckin' Bondi Beach, with my Speedos on. And you're building schools with your bare hands.'

He says, 'Roy – you've got to play the game.'

He was laughing his head off.

The next morning, we were going north, to Ibadan. There was a helicopter for us.

Marcel said, 'I'm not getting on. Flying's not for me – not in a helicopter.'

THE SECOND HALF

So, a minibus was organised. I'm a team player, so I got in. Three or four hours in the minibus and Marcel never said a word. It was all emails and the internet.

We get to the hotel about three hours after the helicopter.

We do the gig.

The first question: what have we been doing since we finished playing football?

So, I say, 'I've been doing a bit of charity work', and I mention the Irish Guide Dogs – I get that one off my chest straightaway.

I get the look from Marcel – 'That's better.'

We were flying back to Lagos the next morning. Down to the hotel reception, back outside, and Marcel got into the helicopter. We were back in Lagos in half an hour.

We landed in Heathrow. I was due to get a connecting flight to Manchester. But the screening machine at security started making noises as my bag went through. There was some sort of explosive residue on the handle of my bag. It must have been on the hands of one of the security lads who'd been carrying my bag in Nigeria. They were ex-SAS. Wherever we went, they'd been with us. They'd followed us everywhere.

I mentioned my connecting flight.

The Heathrow lads looked at me: that is the least of your worries.

'It's important that we trace it.'

'But I've been to Nigeria.'

'Oh, well. We'll put the bag through again. But if it comes up again, you're going nowhere.'

It was fine the second time through, and off I went.

Then I did a signing session with some other ex-players, at the NEC Arena, in Birmingham. People came to get our autographs.

I was sitting at a long table with other players. I remember looking at people like Denis Law, and thinking, 'You shouldn't be here – you're better than this.' Then I was looking at others, and thinking, 'I can see why you're here', because it was a good earner; the money wasn't bad. And a lot of these men played their football before the big money came in.

But people were paying for the autographs in front of us, a fiver a signature, or something. I don't think I've ever been as embarrassed in my life. I could almost hear them: 'I'll pay for his, but I'll not pay for his.'

It wasn't for me. I was cringing. I couldn't wait to get out. I'd have paid double the money to escape.

I played a few charity celebrity games. I was surprised that there was an appearance fee – for a charity gig. I passed my fees on. We played one at Old Trafford, for UNICEF. The Rest of the World v. some pop bands. And I played one up at Celtic – ex-players v. somebody.

But I felt awful.

'Is this what it's come to?'

I just didn't want to end up playing football with fuckin' JLS. That was never my master plan. You get your boots on, and you're overweight. You get injured; you embarrass yourself.

'What am I doing?'

I didn't like what I was becoming.

I don't begrudge other men their decisions. If they want to go and play in a Legends match in India, for fifty grand, I can understand that completely. But I didn't want to do it.

But I'll try things. I'd rather regret the things I did than the things I didn't do.

I did newspaper columns for a while – for the *Sun*. Again, I was being told, 'It's easy money.' I gave it a go, but I ran out of steam. And I hated it. Every Friday or Saturday, I'd be down the phone to a journalist, giving my verdict on everything. There has to come a point when you honestly say, 'I've no opinion on that.'

But that's not what makes newspaper columns. I said that once in an interview. I was asked about something to do with Manchester United, and I said, 'I've no opinion on that.' I think the headline was: 'Shock: Keane Has No Opinion on Something.'

I knew something would come up; something would fall into place. Every time I'd doubted in the past – when I was playing for Cobh; 'I'll never make it' – something happened. Forest came looking for me, then I went to United. I know: that can stop – things falling into place. But when I've had my doubts, they've been a motivation.

I never felt low. I think there's a difference between 'low' and 'down'. I sometimes felt down, but always thought that something would happen. I have a few quid in the bank; there's financial security, and I know that keeps a lot of the anxiety away. But falling back on security – doing nothing – I didn't want that. It's not necessarily about the money; it's the mind.

I'd done one match before, when I was still a player. It was one of the United–Arsenal games, and I was injured, so I was the guest, on Sky. I didn't enjoy it. It didn't seem right – I was still a player; I couldn't really say anything.

But now it was different. I was out of a job, and the League Managers' Association like to get you out there, to keep you visible – 'visibility' is the word they use. It had been four or five months since Ipswich. It was the first time I'd felt a bit unemployed. I didn't like it. The other times – after retiring from football, after Sunderland – I'd felt that I was between jobs.

I was sitting in my kitchen. My wife was out and the kids were at school. The phone rang. It was Michael. ITV wanted to know if I fancied doing the Champions League final. It was United against Barcelona, at Wembley, and I didn't have a ticket.

I thought to myself, 'Well, I could do with going to the game.'

It wasn't out of the blue. ITV had been in touch before. But it was their deadline day – the Wednesday before the final. I had to let Michael know in the next fifteen minutes.

Usually, when Michael rang with some request or job offer, I'd nearly always say, 'Let me think about it.'

He'd laugh, and go, 'You're not going to do it – I'll just tell them.'

But I'd read my horoscope that day. It had said something like, 'You can't keep saying no to people.'

So, I said, 'I'll do it.'

I wanted a ticket.

As United's captain and as a manager I'd been used to talking in front of a camera. But the last time I'd analysed a match, it had been United's game against Middlesbrough, for MUTV, which had played its part in getting me out the door.

The other guests were Gareth Southgate – he was the regular – and Harry Redknapp. Harry had managed Tottenham in the Champions League that year. Adrian Chiles was the presenter. Andy Townsend was there, too – I knew Andy. I was quite relaxed about it, considering it was the Champions League final, and I was new to it. But I'd played against Barcelona, and I'd played for United; I'd played at Wembley. So I was comfortable. And the other people – Gareth, Adrian, the ITV people – gave me a helping hand. And Harry's personality helped. It was all very relaxed – especially when you remember what a big event it was for ITV.

My main point was that I thought United, playing 4–4–2, would be overrun in midfield by Barcelona. Giggs and Carrick were in the middle of the park. They were good players, but they wouldn't be great at getting the ball back for you, when you didn't have it. I kept what I said simple. And I called it right; they got very little possession. But it didn't need an expert to predict that.

ITV took a chance, throwing me in. But I like to think they were confident enough that I'd know what I was talking about. I mightn't have the TV head on, but I'd have the football head on.

A couple of months later, into the new season, 2011–12, I was asked if I'd do a few more games. I played it by ear, match by match. I trusted ITV, but I didn't want to sign a contract. I was out of work for more than two years, so I just continued to do it.

I got used to it. I got used to the travel, the studios, talking at the pitch sides, and working with other people – the other pundits and production people.

I enjoyed the travel. I liked going to Munich. I liked Madrid – and Barcelona. I could have a wander if there were no English teams playing, because I wouldn't have to deal with the fans. We were in Athens, to cover United's game against Olympiakos, and a group of us went to have a look at the Acropolis. When I was a player I wouldn't have done that.

I enjoyed the trips to London, on the train. I enjoyed walking around London. My day in London was a bit of a treat for myself. Getting to and from the stadiums could be a problem, because of the traffic. I started getting a motorbike to the games, which I really enjoyed. I'd be couriered on the back of the bike from the station or the hotel, to Wembley or Stamford Bridge. I enjoyed the routine – getting to the games, getting home. I liked ITV – the people I was working with.

The travelling wasn't always great. We did City's away game against Villarreal. I got dog's abuse from some of the City fans, and I was thinking, 'Do I need this?' But then, we'd be covering a United game and Lee Dixon would be getting loads of stick from the United fans, and I'd say, 'Ah, you have to deal with it.'

I liked when United or City were playing at home, because they were two minutes from my house. The pay was the same for working at the Etihad as it was for going to Munich. A game in Munich was three days away. A game in Manchester was less than one.

A few occasions, I didn't enjoy it. I just wasn't in the mood for it, or the game I was watching – no goals, no action – wasn't worth all the travel. I'd be away, and be missing a family occasion, a birthday or something, and I'd think, 'This isn't for me.'

I'd tell the producer, Tony Pastor – or, later, Mark Demuth – I was finished with it; I'd had enough. I'd stop doing it for a while. Then I'd be watching a game, and I'd think, 'Maybe I could have added to that.'

A couple of weeks later, they'd get in touch: 'Are you sure you don't want to do this game?'

I'd go, 'Oh, go on then.'

I'd go back, and the lads would go, 'We thought you'd retired.'

And I'd go, 'I'm only doing it for a few more games, lads.'

My jobs as a manager had ended badly – they always do. This time, I was dictating the terms, a bit. It even gave me something to complain about, if that makes sense.

The ex-players who've fallen on hard times are the ones who ended up with nothing to do. Football had been good to me, so – although I'll always argue for a good deal – it wasn't about making money; it was about getting out of the house.

There'd be homework to do before a match. I'd have to look at the opposition – whoever was playing against an English team. I'd be sent DVDs and information on the players. You learnt you didn't want too much information because you were only on air for short spells, before the game, at half-time, and after. I was learning the tricks of the trade.

It was work, but I don't like the label 'pundit'. I don't like being labelled, generally. Although I never minded being called a footballer – because I loved being a footballer.

It wasn't like going down a pit for ten hours, but I do think the TV work serves a purpose. It creates argument – even if it's about different styles of punditry. There's a skill to it. It's a balancing act. You want to point out something that someone who hasn't played mightn't have spotted, but you don't want to talk down to people. You want to educate them, a little bit – and entertain them. If I'm eating something in a restaurant, I don't necessarily want to know everything that's going on in the kitchen – but a glimpse is interesting.

The balance is important. The more I speak, the more rubbish I talk. So I kept it short. The hours that they get to speak on Sky or RTE would kill me. I'd end up overanalysing everything.

I was learning the boundaries, the way TV worked. I had to remind myself that the reason for a player's movement, or a pass wasn't obvious to everybody.

'That's why he's ran in there.'

Adrian would go, 'Well, I don't know that.'

And I'd go, 'Well, he's ran in there, to move *him*,' or, 'It's the pace of the pass.'

I tried not to state the obvious, and I also tried not to be too clever. I'm guessing that I had the job because, 'He says it as it is', and because of my playing experience, and, possibly, because I brought a bit of unpredictability. People could say, 'Oh, he's right,' or 'Oh, he's a prick.'

And getting behind the clichés. Last year's one was 'parking the bus'. It was a new phrase, but it's been a tactic for years. Liverpool did it in the eighties. The new phrase was a gimmick, like the arrows on the screen. All that TV time needs filling. Brian Clough said, 'That's the problem with football – there's too much tactics.' My job was to keep it simple.

★

The problem for me was that the TV work felt like failure. Because I failed at management, at Ipswich. I'm referring only to myself – not to the lads who've wanted to work in the media. I was a reluctant pundit. That attitude helped the quality of my commentary, I think. I tried to talk as I played – very simply. I sometimes saw Adrian looking at me, letting me know, 'We need more.'

And I was, 'You're not getting more. I've said my bit.'

At some stage, I would like a life with a bit of anonymity. And I had to accept that the longer I did the TV work the less likely that was to happen. I'd be asked, 'What's happening at United?', and I'd feel another slice of me gone; I'd just sold something.

It wouldn't mean growing a beard and moving to Timbuktu, but it would be nice to go for a while without being asked, 'What do you think of van Gaal?', or 'What do you think of David Moyes?' You can feel a bit trapped by football – although there are worse places to be trapped.

There came a point when I asked myself, 'Is this really, really what I want to do?', and the answer was 'No.'

For the Champions League final between Real and Atlético, in May 2014 there wasn't too much homework because I'd seen quite a bit of both teams during the season. I'd been sent DVDs, and the latest injury news. I kept an eye on articles in the newspapers, for snippets that might have been useful.

If it was a team I didn't know as well – say, Schalke – I'd have to do more preparation. In 2012–13, I was covering a game with Paris Saint-Germain, and thought, 'I'm not up to date here', so I had to do a bit more homework. I'd watch at least one full game – preferably live, if possible. If it was, say, Chelsea or United, the familiarity was relaxing. I'd have a feel for the grounds; I'd played there. I'd seen the teams regularly.

Because it was the final we were on air forty-five minutes before the kick-off. I didn't like being on air too long. I understand why it's done – it's the final, there are the commercials. But it was particularly difficult before a match. It was different at half-time or after the match, when there'd be something to get into. But before the game—

'What do you think might happen?'

'Who do you think is the danger man? Bale – or Ronaldo?'

'Where can they win the game?'

We had to give our expert opinion, but I was more comfortable talking about something that we'd actually seen, not something that we might see. Although, I liked gambling a bit, putting my neck out: 'Well, this is how I think it'll pan out.'

I didn't enjoy the Champions League final. I felt distracted. I felt I shouldn't have been there. I should have been with the Irish squad, in Dublin. We were playing a friendly, against Turkey, the day after. I'd got a job in football six months before; I was Martin O'Neill's assistant, and I'd only really started. I should have been in Dublin.

At the end of the game, Real were lifting the trophy. Steven Gerrard was in the studio, the guest.

'Steven Gerrard, you know what it's like to lift this trophy—'

'Yeah, it's great.'

Xabi Alonso, the Real player, had been suspended for the game, and Adrian asked me what that felt like, because I'd been suspended for the final, in 1999.

'And, Roy. What do you think Alonso's thinking? – because you didn't play in a Champions League final.'

He'd asked the question several times. We spoke about it after the semi-final, when Alonso had picked up his second yellow card.

We spoke about it again before the final. Now I was being asked the question again. I just thought, 'Not again.'

I felt like saying, 'Adrian – fuck you.'

I didn't say it, obviously, although it was after ten o'clock, after the watershed, so I might have got away with it.

I don't like it when companies become too comfortable with me. I don't like feeling owned – it tightens the chest. If I'm to be an employee, I want it to be for a club or a football organisation, not in media.

After the game, the producer, Mark – a good lad – said, 'Everything all right?'

And I said, 'No, Mark – I'm finished with TV. Forget about the World Cup. I'm not going.'

He said, 'Are you sure now?'

I said, 'Yeah – my heart's not in it.'

When I'd worked on the FA Cup final the week before, I hadn't felt comfortable. I was a pundit. But I was also Ireland's assistant manager now, and there were Irish lads playing in the game, for Hull. I'd be coaching them a few days later. I could see myself working in TV again sometime in the future, but not while I was in a football job, working with a team. I just thought, 'No – it's not for me.'

It had been on my mind, and I was happy when I made the decision. It was like when I rang Gordon Strachan, to tell him that I wouldn't be playing again. It was a weight off the shoulders. It meant I wouldn't be going to the World Cup, but I couldn't see myself over there anyway. I'd done two or three years and the decision felt great. I know that punditry is a huge part of the football life, but I didn't want to do it any more. I just felt it was sucking my spirit.

There was once, we were at Juventus, in Turin – they were

playing Chelsea. We were standing just at the corner flag. Adrian was next to me.

He goes, 'This is great, isn't it?'

He's a proper football fan.

I went, 'I used to play in these games, Adrian.'

I wasn't being cocky.

He looked at me, and said, 'Yeah – I can see where you're coming from.'

It's about justification, and what you stand for. When I was at United, I was getting paid good money, but I could go, 'Yeah, but I'm giving it back to you.'

I didn't feel that way with this work.

'It's an easy gig.'

I don't like easy gigs.

When I heard, 'I liked your commentary last night', I knew: I was only talking bullshit, like the rest of them. Hopefully, my bullshit was a bit better.

I wanted to do something that excited me. TV work didn't excite me.

What I really enjoyed was the company. If we were covering an away game, we'd travel the day before and go for something to eat and a few drinks. I liked Adrian Chiles and Lee Dixon, and Gareth Southgate, when he was doing it, and Martin O'Neill. It was like a little team. Sometimes Andy Townsend joined us, or Clive Tyldesley, the commentator. There'd be plenty of football banter. And the people we don't see on the screen – the sound technicians, producers – I'd get on well with them too.

I was on a circuit. I'd travel to different cities and stadiums around Europe. I'd bump into the same people, doing what I did. I met and travelled with Jan Mølby. He works for Danish TV, but he lives in England. I enjoyed his company – it was good crack.

Jan played for Liverpool, and some United fans saw us together. One of them said, 'Why the fuck are you talking to him?'

I felt like saying, 'I'll speak to who I fuckin' want to. He played for Liverpool in the eighties!'

I liked meeting people – old players. Jan, Ray Houghton, Patrick Vieira, Kevin Kilbane.

I bumped into Peter Schmeichel in a hotel in London. I was having my porridge, and he said, 'Do you mind if I join you?'

We'd had a fight once, and now we were having breakfast and a bit of banter together. It was nice. We never mentioned the fight.

The fight was that time – a different environment. Patrick Vieira and myself fought in the tunnel, and now I liked meeting Patrick. I got sent off for stamping on Gareth Southgate. I get on well with Gareth now – we keep in touch. I liked meeting Ian Wright, even though we'd been on opposing sides. I kicked Robert Pires, and he laughs about it now.

I ended up thinking, 'What good guys these are.'

I wouldn't have allowed myself to see that as a player. I think the TV job brought me out of my shell, a bit.

I met Peter Reid.

I used to kick fuck out of Peter Reid – in a respectful way. I remember booting him when he was at City. I don't remember him kicking me – but he must have.

Peter did one of the England international matches, and we stayed in the same hotel in Oslo. We went out for a walk and had lunch together. He was a player I'd admired when I was a kid, when he was in that Everton team, with Adrian Heath and Kevin Sheedy. And there I was having lunch with him, in Oslo. We were sitting there, and one of us said, 'This is cool.'

And it was cool.

TWELVE

I love the game of football. I got distracted, I think – I lost track of why I love the game.

I thought Martin O'Neill was a clear favourite for the Ireland job. I'd met him on a few occasions. We'd done some TV work together. We'd done a couple of Champions League matches, away from home, and I just liked his company. And I'm hoping he might have liked mine a little bit. So when I thought, 'He's got a chance of getting the job', I also thought, 'Maybe, just maybe, he might keep me in mind.'

I thought the job would suit Martin, in terms of his character and his experience, even his age. I thought the challenge was perfect for him. And before you know it, he rang me and said, 'D'you fancy coming up for a chat?'

And I thought, 'All right – interesting.'

I'd a real enthusiasm about me then, because, after my time at United and especially at Ipswich, I'd lost a bit of love for the game – which I hate saying. Because, for me, football is still the best game on the planet.

Was I expecting it? Probably not. Was I shocked? Not shocked either. In football you just never know what's around the corner. And I thought the Irish job, being Martin's assistant, was probably perfect for me. I just thought, to work with Martin, to go back with Ireland after all the turmoil, the rollercoaster – and that rollercoaster started when I was fourteen or fifteen. Resentment is too strong a word but, from a very early age, I often wondered, 'Jesus, is this what the game is all about?'

So when Martin asked me, 'D'you fancy coming on board?' I just thought, 'Brilliant.'

I really did.

I played the cool character but I had a real buzz about myself. It gave me a bit of joy, and I'd lost that – I'd lost that in football, definitely. There are never good endings in football; I was no different from lots of other ex-players. I was doing the TV work, still going to watch matches, and enjoying them, but I had no purpose in my life. The Ireland job, and the possibility of working under Martin – I thought it would be great. And the fact that I wouldn't be the manager – that appealed to me as much as anything. I could be hands-on with the players. I wouldn't have to go to FAI meetings – and I mean that in a nice way. I thought to myself, 'I can be under the radar a little bit.'

I could get back to giving something to the players. When you're a manager you have to step back, and maybe I'd stepped back a bit too much.

I was very comfortable with the prospect of being Martin's assistant. It might have been different if it had been someone else, someone who hadn't done as much in the game. But this was Martin O'Neill. And, particularly when I was a player, I'd never minded taking orders. I didn't need to be the number one. I'd enjoyed it, picking my staff – and there's more money; there are definitely pluses to being the boss. But if I'd been asked during the years when I was out of the game, would I have been happy to work as somebody else's assistant, two or three names would have sprung to mind and Martin's would have been up there, at the top of the list.

When Steve McClaren got the manager's job at Nottingham Forest, in 2011 – Steve doesn't know this but, at the back of my mind, I thought, 'I wouldn't mind working with Steve.'

I'd known Steve at United, and he's a good coach. There were other people I'd come across and, almost subconsciously, I'd be going, 'Well, I think I'd like to work with him one day – maybe. I think I'd get on well with him.'

I think I would have liked working under David Moyes, and I might have had that opportunity if I'd signed for Everton after I left United. It's a gut feeling. I look at managers and I go, 'I like the way you come across.' Then there are others, and I go, 'Listen – that's a no go.'

People have said, 'Well, you're going to be assistant. What does that mean?' That means I'll assist. Whatever he wants me to do, I won't complicate it. If Martin says to me, 'Roy, there's a player in China that could play for us', I'll go to China. If I'm asked and it's my responsibility, I'll do it.

As for my relationship with the FAI, it's amazing how people forget that I came back and played for Ireland, in 2004. I played for two years, and got over all that awkwardness. And even then, I didn't find it that awkward. I just thought, 'I'm a player, I want to go back and play for my country.' I didn't feel I was making up for Saipan or anything that had gone wrong there. I've never regretted what I'd stood for; I just regretted that it had happened. I've never felt guilty about my part in it.

I first met Martin when I went up to Glasgow, to watch Celtic and Rangers. God knows the year, but Martin was Celtic's manager at the time. Celtic were playing at home and I got invited to the directors' lounge after the game. But our first conversation didn't get off to a good start, because the first thing Martin said to me was, 'I think you should have played in the World Cup.'

I said, '—why?'

And Martin said, 'Well – you know—'

And I said, 'You weren't there. You don't know what went on.'

He said, 'I just wanted to say that.'

And I was back at him, 'You're entitled to your opinion but, you know, there's a lot more to it than you think.'

That was our first conversation.

But a few years later, I was managing Sunderland and Martin was at Aston Villa. We played against them, twice at Villa and once at Sunderland, before I lost my job. After the games there'd be the usual get-together in his office, or mine. There'd be Martin, his assistant, John Robertson, his staff. I liked his staff; there was a warmth about them. Then myself and Martin started working together, with ITV. When we spoke about football – maybe it was down to the Cloughie thing, the fact that we'd both played under Brian Clough – we had the same ideas about the game and how it should be played. Martin might tell you different – but I enjoyed his company.

There were strange quirks, little coincidences. Martin had been up at Celtic, and I'd had a spell playing there. Martin managed Sunderland; I'd managed Sunderland. He played under Brian Clough, and so did I. Martin's really into American Football, and I like American Football. I used to watch it on Channel 4, on a Sunday night, when I was a kid. My grandmother used to go mad when I put it on. Martin's Irish, and I'm Irish. One of his daughters is called Alana and my daughter is called Alanna. Maybe that's why he gave me the job!

Over the years, I've played different roles. Sometimes I don't know what role I'm playing. I'm a family man, I'm a Cork man, a TV pundit; I'm a critic; I was a player with a skinhead. I felt like an actor sometimes. Maybe we're all like that – I don't know. I was the manager, and I'd stand off from the players but I wanted to be hands-on with them. But when I took this job, I said, 'I'm going to try to be myself, I'm going to work with the players, I'm going to enjoy myself.'

I'm not going to get into the politics, like I did sometimes as a player. Enjoy working with the team, don't get bogged down by anything else. At this moment in my life, being the number two suits me perfectly.

I love the game of football. I got distracted, I think – I lost track of why I love the game. Saipan, my argument with Ferguson – they had nothing to do with the game, in a sense. I never fell out with eleven v. eleven. Being with the Ireland squad – I'm back in the zone. Being beaten by Turkey in Lansdowne, in May, was horrible – although it was a friendly. But it was great to wake up the next morning and get out on the grass with the players.

I've not had that feeling in years.

I was working with the lads who hadn't played the night before, going, 'We'll get this right.'

That feeling was there – 'Let's make this fuckin' happen.'

Being out on the grass, for me, is getting your gear on. I hadn't put on a pair of boots in a couple of years. Puma King; apparently they're from the 1950s because they're not green, or orange – or odd. Getting the gear on, getting the balls out, getting the bibs, the cones, setting up a session. One part of the training leads to another, and to another. A warm-up, possession – five v. two, or seven v. two; six v. six, in a big area; two-touch, one-touch – all part of the warm-up. Then into a bit of crossing and finishing, and ending with a game. There might be additional rules in the game – say, one-touch finishing. If you're working with a smaller number of players, say, four v. four, you might have two-touch, with one-touch finish. A longer session might include tactical work – walking players through situations. And the shape of a session will depend on its time in the season – you won't be working on physical fitness at the end of the season – and when you last played a game, or when your next game is coming up, and the number of players you have. Then there's the manager's feel for the group, and what he thinks they need. A lot of ingredients go into a session.

In the mornings Martin discusses the session plan with myself and some other staff. He gets our thoughts and ideas, then decides on the session. That's fine, and I'm happy with it. The sessions are short, and our time with the players is short, and Martin has vast experience. But at club level, when there are a lot more training sessions, I like to get a feel for the group of players and make quick decisions myself; I like the responsibility – 'You're off tomorrow, lads; you've trained really hard.' When you're the assistant you can't make those calls, and I think, ultimately, that it might eventually frustrate me.

There's the fresh air – and getting wet, feeling cold. There's the satisfaction of a session going well, or the disappointment of it not going so well. That's the emotional side of being out on the grass. Going back for your lunch, thinking, 'I've done a bit of work.' Enjoying the food, going, 'That was a good session,' or 'That wasn't so good. He was good, he was bad, he's pissing me off.'

Drinking tea or coffee is a massive part of the job – while you talk football. Video analysis, and talk of old games and tournaments. Chatting to people who love the game as much as you do.

Qualifying for Euro 2016 is going to be tough. Germany, Poland, Scotland – and there's Georgia, too. But even that has given me an extra buzz. I haven't had that hunger for a long time.

A lot of people decide not to go into international football, because you don't get to work with the players that much – and that's fine. But I think that can actually be a hindrance, spending too much time in their company. Myself and Martin and Seamus McDonagh, the goalkeeping coach, took our first two games, friendlies against Latvia and Poland, in November, 2013. I really enjoyed it, and I think part of that was down to the fact that we were only with the players for eight or nine days. Steve Walford and Steve Guppy have been added to the staff, and that's been a huge help to us – and they add to the football stories and banter. Steve Guppy played for Martin when Martin was managing Wycombe, Leicester and Celtic, and worked as a coach for Martin at Sunderland. Steve Walford played with Martin at Norwich, then worked with him at Wycombe, Norwich, Leicester, Celtic, Villa and Sunderland.

At the end of the '13–'14 season, we had four games, against Turkey, Italy, Costa Rica and Portugal, in Dublin, London and the USA. This time, we had the players for more than two weeks.

It's very different from club football. When you're with players at a club, you start looking at what they're not good at. But when you have them for a short spell, it's 'Let's get it right for the game.'

At a club, you spend a lot of time talking about who you'd like to bring in and who you'd like to move. With an international squad, you're not thinking like that. The players you have are the players you have – and there's a plus to that. You have to look at the players positively. It's a bit like being a grandparent: you get the kids, and you give them back.

I'm working with Seamus McDonagh, and I watched Seamus playing for Ireland, at Dalymount, when I was a kid, eleven or twelve. I came up from Cork for the match, with my team, Rock-mount. It was a Wednesday night.

I was telling Seamus about it.

'Were you playing in that game, Seamus?'

'Yes, I was.'

Ireland were playing Holland. It was Ruud Gullit's first international game.

We lost 3–2.

I slagged Seamus about it.

'You threw in a few that night, Seamus.'

We'd won the trip to Dublin because we'd won a tournament, the Under-12s; it was called the Val O'Connor. We'd got to the final, and the winners would win a trip to see the Ireland team. It was my dream, to see Ireland play. We won 3–0; I got a hat trick.

I was going, 'I want to see that fuckin' match.'

But Seamus played in that game, and now I'm working with Seamus.

It's brilliant.

I bought my first ever single that day too, in Dublin – 'Karma Chameleon', by Culture Club.

Niall Quinn made the point on TV recently: Dave Langan, who played for Ireland in the seventies and eighties, would have turned up with his leg hanging off, and have said, 'I'm fit.' I think Niall was contrasting Dave's attitude to Stephen Ireland's, and how things had changed. Playing for your country used to be the pinnacle of a player's career; now it's playing in the Champions League. Maybe I got lost in that world. I need to remember that most of our players won't be playing in the Champions League. Playing for Ireland will be the pinnacle of their careers. I need to remind myself about going to Dalymount as a kid, on the bus, to see Ireland play.

I'm watching the way Martin speaks to the players, the way he handles the staff. I'm not saying that it's perfect, or that I'll try and copy it. I'm just going, 'I like that, I like that, I'm not sure about that, I like that.'

I don't have to deliver the bad news – 'You're not playing.' But I'm watching Martin do it. He has more knowledge than me, more experience to fall back on. Again, I'm not trying to copy him. I'm learning. Like I learnt when I worked for Brian Clough and Alex Ferguson.

Brian Clough gave me my chance in England. I have a thing in my makeup where there's that loyalty to people who I think have looked after me. Lads who might have given me a lift or picked me up at the airport – I might remember them for twenty or thirty years afterwards. Like Tony Loughlan and Gary Charles at Forest – one of them took me for a game of snooker. Just when you needed someone to dig you out. And Brian Clough dug me out by giving me a contract. I'd like to think I earned it. I wouldn't say a bad thing about Brian Clough. He was brilliant with me. A brilliant manager, and a brilliant man.

He met my family; he was always dead nice to them.

There was once, he took me to a charity do. He needed a player to go to the gig, and he dragged me along with him. I was very young, and single – a lot of the other lads had families. At the end of the night, he gave me fifty pounds – a fifty-pound note; I'm not sure I'd seen one before in my life. It was like one of your uncles giving you a few bob when he came to the house.

There was something underneath it; I could identify a lot with him. He was hard on me. He hit me once, and I thought, 'I know why you punched me.'

I got him – I just got him.

He kept things simple – for everybody. I think there's a warmth in that, and a cleverness. There's a genius to keeping it simple.

I worked under two great managers, and I put Brian Clough ahead of Alex Ferguson for a simple reason. What was the most important thing in my football career? Brian Clough signing me. That kick-started everything.

Different managers, both brilliant.

I think Brian Clough's warmth was genuine. I think with Alex Ferguson it was pure business – everything was business. If he was being nice, I thought, 'It's business, this.' He was driven, and ruthless. That lack of warmth was his strength. United was a much bigger club than Forest, and his coldness made him successful.

He had a different personality from Brian Clough, but his message was the same. I was never once confused by one of his team talks or his tactics, or training sessions. I never once, in all my years at United, thought, 'I don't know where you're going with that one.'

His management, and his message to the players before matches, was always fresh. I must have heard him talk before a match close to five hundred times, and I always thought, 'Yeah – that was good.'

I think that's amazing.

I know Clough's warmth was business, too. Forest were good to me, but they'd got me for fifty grand – and I was younger. I was older at United, and I could see that it was a bigger business and that the game was changing, and that Ferguson was driven. He had to be. We had massive success together. It was enjoyable, and it was great.

As a manager I'd like to take Clough's warmth and Ferguson's ruthlessness, and put them in the mix – but also add my own traits.

After the Turkey match in May, Martin had to go and face the media. I didn't. I sat in the dressing room with the players, eating chicken curry and rice, going, 'We'll get it right, lads.'

When I was a player, I shut doors on myself. Now, I don't have to.

When you're working, you're visible. People see that you're working, in a tracksuit, on the grass, and working with players.

'Maybe he's not the psycho.'

Football's a small world. Whether good or bad, people talk. Players go back to their clubs. And Martin's an intelligent man, yet he brought me on board.

'He can't be that big a head case.'

The opportunity came to go to Aston Villa, to work with Paul Lambert. At Villa, I'm the number two – and it suits me at the moment. I can keep the Ireland job; Martin and Paul, the FAI and Villa, are happy with that. My family doesn't have to move. It's back in the Premiership, with a club that I have a soft spot for. And I like the prospect of working with Paul Lambert. To be a good coach you need to get your hours in. Working alongside Paul, day-to-day, watching games at close hand, can only help me; it will make me a better, more experienced coach. And I can bring that experience, and what I'm seeing every day, to the Ireland job.

What will be will be. I think the Ipswich experience will stand me in better stead than anything else – all the lessons I learnt. The 'nearly there'. Just remember, it's hard to win football matches.

A big part of the Ireland job is going to matches, to see the Irish players. Martin will ring me, or I'll ring him.

I'll go, 'There's a game coming up next weekend, on Sunday. I'll cover it, is that okay?', and he'll go, 'Right, you go to that one.'

Everton, Stoke, Hull – where a lot of the Irish lads are playing.

It can be a bit of a gamble. I went to West Brom and Norwich last season, and Shane Long – this was before he moved to Hull – and Wes Hoolahan, the men I'd gone to see, were both on the bench. But the time is never wasted. I went to another game, at Hull. Again, most of the Irish lads were on the bench. Paul McShane, who's also with Hull, made the point: 'Well, I hope you watched the warm-up.' And I fuckin' did. I watch the players' body language and humour, the way they warm up before the game, or when they're on the bench. Then I'm looking at the team out on the pitch, and I'm thinking, 'Why aren't you in that team?'

If they're on the bench, do they get warmed up as if they want to go on? You can tell with some subs, they just don't want to go on. They should be chomping at the bit.

I try to watch the players in different surroundings. Home and away – or against a team where you think they're likely to get beaten, to see how they carry themselves, and if they keep going.

James McCarthy and Seamus Coleman have been doing really well at Everton. I saw them play, at home to Stoke. A very comfortable 4–0 victory; the two of them strolled through the game. A couple of days later, they were at United. And I thought, 'Now I'll watch them.' So I went to Old Trafford – big setting, difficult fixture – and the two of them were excellent.

I think it's important that when the squads for international matches are named all the players, whether they're in or out, will be able to say, 'Well, they have watched me.' They might be disappointed but at least they'll know we saw them play. We'll be keeping an eye on them all the time.

I'm not one for writing many notes about players. I'll have a team sheet and I might jot down a word or two. But I don't do a match report or a scouting report. I'd end up missing the match! I'm there to look at one or two of the players. I'm not examining set pieces or team shape.

I'm learning a lot more about the football clubs. And I'm finding out the clubs I really like. When I was a player, I was very robotic. I'd go in and just do my business; I didn't care what club it was. But I'm looking around now, and I'm thinking, 'What good clubs.'

The more I go back to a club, I begin to develop a routine. Getting to Everton's quite easy, and Stoke; and Wigan's a doddle. For other games, I tend to leave the house earlier; I don't want to be turning up ten minutes after kick-off. I need to be professional. I have to get a suit on. I have a role while I'm there. I'm the assistant manager of Ireland; I don't want to be turning up like I slept in a ditch. I generally travel alone, although it's nice to have a bit of company sometimes. Especially at half-time. Because when I'm on my own, I can see some people thinking, 'Ah – I've got an open invite.' Most people who come up couldn't be nicer. But sometimes people seem to think they're on a mission.

'Who are you here to watch?'

'Have a guess,' I say to myself.

'Some of the Irish lads,' I answer.

I've always been a bit wary. Always ready for the bit of abuse. But it never happens. The smart comment, or something sarcastic – never. I had abuse thrown at me when I was a player and a manager, but that was from thousands of people, the opposition fans. It's part of the game. But not from individuals; no one going, 'Hey – you wanker', or anything like that. But I'm ready for it. And I hate that about myself.

In all the years I've been in football, and whatever I've done, people have shown me massive respect. They mightn't like me, or like the way I played – opposition fans, anyway – but I never had anyone come up to me and go, 'Oh, you – you—' whatever.

I just wish I was a bit more relaxed, although I still think I have to be on my guard. In the past, when I have relaxed and let people into my space, they let me down – I've had that experience. So I think I have to keep that guard up, a little bit. But not to the extent that I have in the past.

I went to Everton last season. They were playing Norwich. The lad beside me was chatting to me, and he was talking quite cleverly about the game. I was enjoying the conversation, and I thought, 'I'll ask him who he works for', because he was talking about players and the game; he knew his stuff.

So I went, 'Who do you work for – what club are you involved in?'

'I'm Roy Hodgson's driver.'

I was laughing at myself; I'm glad I dropped my guard because I enjoyed his company. I think there's ego involved, too, when I go, 'I'll keep myself to myself.' He was a nice bloke and, being Roy's driver, he probably saw more games than I did.

Everton's another top club. The day Aiden McGeady signed for them from Spartak Moscow, I was thinking, 'Great move for you, Aiden. Another Irish lad going to Everton – brilliant.' It's good for Ireland. He's got other Irish lads around him and they've got a good manager. They can get into the Champions League in the next year or two, which can only be good for Ireland. Because the problem for Ireland is that most of the lads aren't playing at the top level.

When I was a young player, the ambition was to play for one of the big teams. You wanted to get to the very top – the trophies and the financial rewards. Today, a lot of players can become very wealthy without reaching the very top. They might play for a mid-table club, or a club in the lower half of the Premiership, or even a Championship team, and still become multi-millionaires. I don't know if that drive, that hunger, is there to get to the very top.

There's never been a time when loads of young Irish players have come through. It's always been one or two, every couple of years. I just hope they still come through. Seamus Coleman and James McCarthy, at Everton, are young, but they're not teenagers

– they've already been found. And they're the type of players we'll be hanging our hats on. Jeff Hendrick, at Derby – I like the look of him. But senior players will always play a massive role. We're always looking for players but we're not going to unearth seven or eight diamonds. And I think we can take encouragement from the fact that smaller countries did quite well in Brazil, in the World Cup. Uruguay has a population of three and a half million – smaller than Ireland's. But if we start calling ourselves a small country, we might be beaten before we start. We can look at our own football history; we've done it before. We have a nucleus of good young players.

I've never been against players who weren't born in Ireland playing for the country. If they want to come on board and they qualify, then great, as long as they've a feel for it. I think, in the past, there were one or two players who probably declared for Ireland as a career move – and I can understand that, too. They did well for the country, but I look at some of them now and I wonder if they've been back to Ireland since. So I think the attitude should be, 'Listen, if you're going to come on board, get a feel for it – have a warmth for the country. But don't just do it as a pure career move.'

But, then again, who am I to say? Love of country is a hard thing to measure. But if you see a player on the TV who played for Ireland, singing 'God Save the Queen' in a play-off final, you might just say, 'Oh, right. Maybe he's not really all that Irish.' Matty Holland would be an example. For me, Matty is as English as David Beckham. He played for Ireland and he obviously has the roots. But he played for Ipswich in a play-off final, in 2000, and he was singing 'God Save the Queen' at the top of his voice. I don't think he could have sung it any louder. Some of the other Irish lads saw him, too, so at the next couple of international matches we were going, 'Turn that rebel music up a bit.'

I think it's important that lads plug into Ireland a little bit – and the ways of the country. And I think, generally speaking, they do. They don't have a choice, I suppose. I was at an FAI dinner recently, and John Aldridge was the guest speaker. Aldo would be an example of a player born in England who gave as much to Ireland as any Irish-born player. There has to be that feeling, and a warmth for the country.

Often a manager gets the job and his first game is the next day. But our first Euro qualifier came almost a year after we were appointed. The friendly matches were important and we wanted to build a bit of momentum and get to know the players, but I was dying to get at the qualifiers – and to qualify. And justify my role. Try to win people's respect. Work with the younger players. Let them go out and enjoy it, and express themselves.

I got a call: would I go and have a chat with Dermot Desmond, Celtic's majority shareholder? I'd met him once before, in 2005, when I was signing to play for Celtic.

I met him for a cup of tea. It was in the middle of an international week, in Dublin.

At the end of the chat, he said, 'The job is yours.'

It was all pretty straightforward. There'd be one or two restrictions, about staff. They'd already picked the man who'd be my assistant, and they were insisting on him.

It didn't scare me off, although it did get me thinking. It wasn't an ideal start. Were they doubting me already?

I came back to the team hotel and spoke to Martin. I told him I'd have a think about it.

We had a game against Italy, at Craven Cottage, in London, on the following Saturday. We were busy, travelling to London from Dublin, getting the team ready. The fact that I'd spoken to Dermot Desmond had become public knowledge. It had to, because Martin had a press conference, and a few things had been leaked – as usual. It didn't worry me too much. It was a friendly match; I didn't think it was going to upset the camp, although – again – it wasn't ideal.

But I was delighted. It was a massive compliment. Over the years, when chatting with people about football and Celtic, I'd always said, 'If you're offered the Celtic job, you don't turn it down.'

So I was now in a predicament – with myself, in a sense. And my gut feeling was getting back to me – 'You're on your own with this one.'

I asked Paul Gilroy, the League Managers' Association lawyer, to speak to Celtic, to discuss terms. Money hadn't been mentioned yet. I got in touch with Celtic's chief executive, Peter Lawwell, and asked him to give me a ballpark figure, before negotiations got going.

He mentioned a figure, and he said, 'But that's it.'

So, Paul Gilroy spoke to Celtic. He told me there were a lot of clauses in the contract that he wasn't happy with. And the figures were non-negotiable.

I got my head around that. But it felt a bit too familiar. I'd been down this road before, when I'd signed for Celtic as a player. They were playing the part – 'It's Celtic' – you should almost go up there for nothing.

I felt Celtic wanted me, but they weren't showing how much they wanted me.

We played the game against Italy on Saturday. We drew, 0–0 – a good result. I had a message on my phone on Sunday from Dermot Desmond. They wanted a heads-up by tomorrow, Monday.

In the meantime, I flew back to Dublin. We had a few days off before heading to the USA, to play friendlies against Costa Rica and Portugal. I'd left my car in Dublin, so I was getting the ferry back, from Dublin to Holyhead. I was by myself, and I'd booked a cabin – a bit of privacy.

I thought about the Celtic offer. It wasn't rocking my boat. They weren't convincing me – 'Listen, you're the man for us.'

I got home to Manchester on Sunday night. I was tired. I went to Paul Gilroy's house – he lives five minutes from me. There were things I wasn't happy with in the contract. But I know, if you examined every clause too carefully you'd never sign anything.

I rang Dermot Desmond on Monday, and said, 'I'm really honoured you've offered me the job, but I want to stay with Martin.'

My decision wasn't influenced by other job offers or potential offers. I wasn't playing games; it was a straightforward decision. Had Celtic shown me enough in their negotiating – 'We'll move this, and you can move that' – a bit of give and take, I might have hesitated. But Celtic didn't give me enough of a headache. They just didn't show me that they wanted me, and I was happier staying in the Ireland job. Working with Martin has given me back a love of the game, and I'm all for showing a bit of loyalty. I'd only been in the job two minutes. We hadn't played a competitive game yet.

My wife said to me, 'I haven't seen you this happy in a long time. Why jeopardise that?'

I felt powerful saying, 'No.' I felt good. But I still wondered if I was making the right decision.

Right job, wrong time.

You need challenges and stresses, but all my life I've been chasing contentment. I was happy when I won trophies, but that kind of satisfaction doesn't last long. Contentment – a sense of relaxation – feels strange. It's almost like I'm missing a bit of chaos. Fighting myself. I'm not sure if I've relaxed in the last twenty-odd years. Maybe this is my time to start relaxing. But at the same time, I want to go to work. I want to work in football. I'll be bringing that sense of relaxation with me – for the first week!

When the Ireland job eventually comes to an end, if the question is hanging over me, 'Did I really give it everything?', I want to be able to say, 'Yes.'

When I was in America with the Ireland squad, there was some difficulty with the travel arrangements – a couple of mishaps. But my attitude was different now.

We got stuck on the train from Philadelphia to Newark. We'd been in Philadelphia for the game against Costa Rica, a 1–1 draw. We were getting off in Newark, in New Jersey – the players and the staff. We were using two doors to get out of the carriage, but the FAI official said that we should all get off through the one door.

The door shut, and myself, Martin, Seamus, Steve Guppy, three medical staff and Aiden McGeady were stuck. The train moved off.

The lads – the players – on the platform were pissing themselves laughing.

It was like a school trip.

Panic stations – people going mad and Martin was a bit annoyed.

But I was quite calm about it. I texted one of the FAI staff – *It's Saipan all over again.* But I was joking.

We went on to Penn Station, in Manhattan – about half an hour. We were lucky it wasn't Boston or Chicago. And we eventually got back to Newark, and out to the team bus. The players were sitting there, dead quiet. The two people who organised the travel were pale – white.

Everyone was quiet – very tense.

Then one of the lads put on the music. They'd gone off and

bought some speakers while we were on the train. I don't know the name of the band, but the song was 'Runaway Train', and they all started singing with it:

Runaway train, never going back –
Wrong way on a one-way track –
It was brilliant.

INDEX

Index

Index

Index

Index

Index

Index

Index

Index

Index